York County Virginia

DEEDS, ORDERS, WILLS, ETC.

1706–1708

Sherry Raleigh-Adams

HERITAGE BOOKS
2019

HERITAGE BOOKS
AN IMPRINT OF HERITAGE BOOKS, INC.

Books, CDs, and more—Worldwide

For our listing of thousands of titles see our website at
www.HeritageBooks.com

Published 2019 by
HERITAGE BOOKS, INC.
Publishing Division
5810 Ruatan Street
Berwyn Heights, Md. 20740

International Standard Book Number
Paperbound: 978-1-68034-955-9

1

York County, Virginia
Deeds, Orders, Wills, Etc.
Book No. 13
July 1706-May 1708

[The first two pages in this volume are unnumbered, but they are arbitrarily listed here as Page A and B.]

A. Will of Simon Godman. ...wages due in ship... To dau. Fra Godwin all my wages... To friend David Lawson 30 shillings. To Lawce. Jaxon 15 shillings. 8ᵗʰ day of April 1706. Wit. Edward Mann, Wm. Doger[?] Proved 24 Jul 1706.

Bond. Thomas Rogers, Joseph Chermeson and George Baskervile of co. of York to the Justices of said County, in the sum of £100. 24 June 1707. Sureties to Thomas Rogers as guardian of Robert Clark, orphan of John Clark, dec'd.

B. Bond. Elizabeth Jones, Francis Sharpe and Morris Jones of the Co. of York, to the Justices of said County, in the sum of £300. Sureties to Elizabeth Jones as Admx. of the Estate of Wm. White, dec'd., in lieu of the original Admr., Timothy Pinkethman, now dec'd. 2 July 1706. Wit. Wm. Pinkethman.

1. Will of Richard Dixon. To my son James Dixon, all my land and tenements. If he should dye without heyre...then I give all my lands in Glouster co. to my two daughters Agnes and Rebecca...and my lands in York co., I give to my two daughters Susanah and Anne. I give to my daughter Anne my brick house...called by the name of Hill House. Slaves mentioned are one negro girle comonly known by the name of Mall, in Glouster co. ...one negro woman named Hannah with her child ...one mulatto man named Will and his wife Nob. To my wife Damazinah Dixon one negro man comonly known by the name of George. To my mother Agnes Rogers 20 shillings to buy her a ring, and unto Thomas Nutting 20 shillings to buy him a ring. My wife is to keep the three younger children and their Estates untill they come to their respective ages or marriage... or until she remarries. 9 November 1705. Wit. John Hunt Senr., Thos. Nutting and John Soper. Proved 24 June 1706.

2. Deed of Gift. Sarah Jones of New Kent co, widow, to John Hilliard son of my cousin John Hilliard, late of the Parish and Co. of York, dec'd. ...one cow and one calf... and in default of Issue, then to be unto Mary Hilliard, his mother. 5 June 1706. Wit. Wm. Tunley and Mungo Somerwell.

Power of Attorney. Sarah Jones of New Kent co., to John Young of Hampton Parish, York co., her true and lawfull Attorney to acknowledge a Deed of Gift to John Hilliard. 5 June 1706. Wit. Wm. Tunley and Mungo Somerwell.

3. At a Court held by York Co. Augt. 5th 1706 per adjournment from 25th July last past. Present, Capt. Thomas Barber, Mr. Robt. Read, Capt. Lawe. Smith, Majr. Wm. Buckner, Mr. Wm. Barber, Mr. Hen. Tyler.

On reading of the orders of the 25th of July last past, John Clayton, Attorney of Robert Ranson, put in a plea in arrest of judgment in the judgment then obtained against the said Robert at the suit of James Bradford in an acion of case, which when argued, was overruled and the said judgment confirmd by the Court. From which judgment, the said Robert Ranson appeals to the next Genll. Court for tryall, giving good security.

On reading of orders of the 25th of July last past, Mr. Richd. Wharton, Attorney of John Cooper of London, merchant, put in a plea in arrest of judgment to arrest the judgment then passed against the said Cooper for the dismissal of his suit against Thomas Whitby and Mary, his wife, Extx. of Thomas Collier, dec'd. in an acion of case damage £150, which is referd to the next Court to be argued.

Major Lewis Burwell, his Deed of Sale for one mulato woman slave and her two children from Damassia Dixon, Extx. of Richd. Dixon, dec'd., together allso with the bond for performance of covenants therein contained, both bearing date under the hand and seal of the said Damasinah. Augt. 5th 1706. Wit. John Timson and Willm. Row, evidences thereto, and is orderd to be committed to record.

Nathll. Burwell, Gent., his Deed of Sale for one mulato slave Nan and her son Sam from Damasinah Dixon Extx. of Richard Dixon, dec'd. together allso with the bond for performance of the covenants therein contained, both bearing date under the hand and seal of the sd Damasinah the 5th day of Augt., was this day proved in Court by the oaths of John Timson and Willm. Row, evidences thereto, and is ordered to be committed to record.

Rebecca Pinkethman, widow and Extx. of Timothy Pinkethman, dec'd., this day presented to the Court an account of her said husbands Estate, which on her request is ordered to be committed to record.

In the suit depending to this Court between Jonathan Yates, plf. and Robert Ranson, deft. in an acion of case damage £100, the plf. this day makes his declaration and the deft. has further time to plead.

In the suit depending to this Court between Joseph Bottick, plf. against Robt. Ranson, deft. in an acion of case damage £100 , the plf. this day mended his declaration and the deft. hath further time to plead.

In the suit depending to this Court between Manvell Revelly, plf. and Robt. Ranson, deft. in an acion of case damage £60, the plf. this day mended his declaration and the deft. hath further time to plead.

In the suit depending to this Court between Samll. Miller, plf. and Robt. Ransom, deft. in an acion of case, the plf. this day mended his declaration and the deft. hath time to plead.

4. In the suit depending to this Court between Elias Corket[?], plf. and Robt. Ranson, deft. in an acion of case due for the sume of £45:18:6 due for wages on bord the ship Thomas & John whereof the said Robt. is Master and the said Robert detaind to the plf. damage £80, to which the deft. by John Clayton, his Attorney, pleaded the Act of Parliament made at a Parliament begun at Wesminster the 2d day of Augt. 1698... and from thence continued by severall Prorogaton and adjourment to the 16th day of Novr. 1699, entituled an Act for the More Effectuall Suppressing of Piracy Concerning the Desertion of Sailors in Ships Imported Beyond the Seas. The plf. replyed and said he did not desert and put himself on his country and the deft. likewise. Whereupon a jury was impanelld and sworn to try the issue, who after a full [hearing] of all evidences and pleas on both sides – departed to consult their verdict which on their return, the plf. and deft. being calld, was read viz: Wee find for the plf., £45:18, signd Henry Hayward Senr., foreman, which on mocion of the plf.'s Attorney is confirmed and orderd to be committed to record, and orderd that the plf. recover of the deft. his damage aforesaid in forme aforesaid by the inquisition found with costs alies execution.

Robt. Read Gent, his Information against Mary Hanson is referd for the Publicacion of the new Law.

Arthur Marenburgh's acion of debt to this Court depending against Rebecca Pinkethman, Extx. of Timothy Pinkethman, dec'd. is dismist for non prosecution.

John Crombie hath judgment of nihil dicit this day confirmed against Thomas Austin in an acion of case for the sume of £6 due by bill dated Feby 20th 1705, and it is ordered forthwith to be paid with costs alies execution.

John Tomer his acion of case against John Wells and Elizth., his wife, Extx. of Thomas Harwood, dec'd. is dismist for non prosecution.

John Penton hath judgmt this day granted against Peter Gibson in an acion of case for the sume of £45 due by account, and it is ordered to be paid with costs alies execution.

Wm. Tunly hath judgmt this day granted against Daniel Jaxon in an acion of case for the sume of 349 lbs. of tobaco, in ballance of all accounts between the plf. and deft., and it is ordered to be paid with costs alies execution.

Thomas Mountfort, Assignee of John Canon, his acion of debt against Robt. Shield is dismissed for non prosecution.

Thomas Mountfort, his acion of case to this Court against Robt. Shield is dismist for non prosecution.

In the suit depending to this Court between Thomas Mountfort, plf. and Charles Pain, deft., upon return of the audit ordered by the last Court, the plf. is nonsuited with costs.

The suit depending to this Court between John Hancock, plf. against Robt. Ranson, deft. in an acion of case is referd to the next Court on request of the deft.

5. In the suit depending to this Court between Francis Everett, plf. and Robt. Ranson, deft. in an acion of case due for the sume of £35:5, due for wages abord the ship Thomas & John whereof the said Robert is Master, by the said Robert detaind to the plf. damage £60, to which the deft. by John Clayton, his Attorney, pleaded the Act of Parliament made at a Parliament begun at Westminster the 2nd day of Augt 1698 and from thence continued by severall prorogations and adjournment to the 16th day of Novr 1699, entituled an Act for the More Effectyall Suppressing of Piracy Concerning the Desertion of Saylors in Ships Imported Beyond the Seas, and the plf. replyd and said he did not desert and put himself on his country, and the deft. likewise. Whereupon a jury was impannelld and sworn to try the issue, who after a full examining of all evidences and pleas on both sides departed to consult their verdict which on their return, the plf. and deft. being calld, was read Viz: Wee find for the plf. £35:5, signd Henry Hayward Senr., foreman. Which on mocion of the plf.'s Attorney is confirmed and orderd to be committed to record. Orderd that the plf. recover of the deft. his damage aforesaid in forme aforesaid by the inquisition found with costs.

The Court is adjournd till the 24th Instant.

Bond. John Adduston Rogers, John Rogers and Thomas Wooton, all of the Co. of York, to the Justices of said County, in the sume of £200. Dated this

5

8th of March 1705/6. Sureties to John Adduston Rogers as Admr. of the whole Estate of Hen Andrews dec'd. Wit. Danll. Taylor and Nich. Philips.

6. Will of Grace Nevill of Hampton, York Co. To Margaret Hudson, one dripping pan and one small chest. To Martha Davis, the daughter of Willm. Davis, one feather bed... and to Thos. Davis, his son, one pewter tankard. To Abraham Royston, one couch bed and pillow, one old rugg. Robt. Harrison to be my sole Extr. Dated this 12th day of June 1706. Wit. Alex. Miller and Willm. Spencer. Proved Sep 24, 1706.

Will of John Moreland of York Co. My body to be buried in Christian manner according to the discretion of my wife Ann Moreland, Extx., and my son Francis Moreland, Extr. To my son Mathew Moreland, one mulato girle named Kate. To my daughter Elizth. Moreland, one negro boy named Roger, and in case of mortality of my son or daughter before they come of age, then to my daughter Mary Moreland. To my son John Moreland, my tract of land I now live on containing 100 acres...and in case he should dye before he should come of age, then to my son Mathew...and in case of his death, to my son Edwd. Moreland. To wife, the use of my whole Estate unless she marries...then Estate to be divided between my wife and children, Thos. Moreland, Francis Moreland, John Moreland, Mathew Moreland, Edward Moreland, Jane Faircloth, Mary and Elizabeth Moreland. Dated this 21 day of May 1706. Wit. Mathew Jones, Edward Fuller and Thos. Lamb. Proved Sepr 24, 1706.

7. Power of Attorney. Thomas Jones, Gent, now of Virginia, but designing for England to Jno. Clayton Esq., my true and lawfull Attorney to collect debts due to myself or my wife in the colony of Virginia. Dated this 5th of Sepr. 1706. Wit. Chas. Chiswell, Reuben Welch, Jno. Nicholson, and Jos. Jno. Jackman.

8. Power of Attorney. George Giddings, late of Ipswich in the Co. of Essex in New England, merchant, to Stephens Thompson of Virginia, Gent., my my true and lawfull Attorney to collect debts due to me. 24th day of Augt. 1706. Wit. Willm. Tunley and Robt. Ryde.

Bond. Lydia Broster, Nicolas Martin and James J. Benett, all of the Co. of York, to the Justices of the said County, in the sume of 10,000 lbs. of very good sweet scented tobacco. Sureties for Lydia Broster as Admr. of the Estate of John Broster, dec'd. Dated this 24th Sepr. 1706.

9. At a Court held for York Co. Sep 24, 1706. Present: Mr. Robert Read, Mr. Henry Tyler, Major William Buckner, Capt. Lawrence Smith and Cpt. William Timson, Justices.

A Proclamation dated August 24th 1706 from the President and Councill for Entring of Publick Offices and the Examination of their particular Trust and Office was this day published in Court.

The Acts of the Last Assembly this day was published in Court.

Upon complaint of Mr. Henry Tyler, one of Her Majesty's Justices of the Peace of this County, against Barrentine Howells for severall misdemeanors and ill language by him given to the said Henry Tyler, the truth of which appearing to this Court, it is therefore ordered of the said Barrentine to be putt in the stocks for the space of 2 hours and pay costs.

Joseph Potter, his Deed of Sale bearing date November the 13th 1700 for [90?] acres of land situate in Charles Parish in this County from Samuell Singnall and Elizabeth, his wife, was this day personally acknowledged in Court by the said Samuell and also by the said Elizabeth, his said wife, who on her examination declared that she is of her own free will and not of compulsion, which is ordered to be committed to record and also the said Joseph's bond bearing even date with the said deed for performance of covenants in the said deed contained, was this day personally acknowledged in Court by the said Samuell and the said Joseph and ordered to be committed to record.

Order for a comicion of Administration of the Estate of John Broster, late of this County, was this day granted to Elizabeth, his relict (on her petition), who this day entered into bond with Nicholas Martin and James Bennet her securitys, for the administration thereof according to Law. It is ordered that the Estate of John Broster, late of this County, dec'd. be appraised at the dwelling house on the 10th of October next if the weather permitt, if not the first fine day then next following by Wm. Wise Senr., James Caltengs[?], John Drewry Senr., and John Turner or any three of them, in the best of their judgment, having first sworn before the Justice, and that a due returne thereof be made to the next Court.

Order for a Comicion of Administration of the Estate of Morgan Baptist, late of York Parish and Co., dec'd., was this day granted to Elizabeth, his relict (on her petition) entering into bond with Robert Harris and Bazill Wagstaff, her securitys, betwixt this and the next Court, it is ordered that the Estate of Morgan Baptist late of York Parish in this County be appraised at his late dwelling house on the 10th of October next if the weather permitt, if not the first fair day then next following, by John Wyth, William Allen[?], Phillip Dedman, Joseph Mountfort or any 3 of them in the best of their judgments, being first sworn before the next Justice, and that a due returne thereof be made to the next Court.

Order for a Probate of the Last Will & Testament of Grace Nevill dated the 10th day June last was this day granted unto Robert Harrison, he being therein appointed Extr., and proved by the oaths of Alexander Miller and William Spencer, evidences thereto, is ordered to be committed to record.

10. John Sergenton this day in Court acknowledged Samuell Seldon his Generall Attorney and prayd that the same might be entered on record.

Order for a Comicion of Administration of the Estate of William Aylward, formerly of Hampton Parish in this County, dec'd. was this day granted unto Joseph Walker (on his petition), he entering into bond betwixt this and the next Court with Joseph Chermison and John Mihill, who this day in trust affirmed to be his security for the administration thereof according to Law.

Stephens Thomson's Power of Attorney dated August 24th 1706 from George Gidding, late of Ipswich in the Co. of Essex in New England, merchant, was this day proved in Court by the oath of William Tunley, one of the evidences thereto, and ordered to be committed to record.

Order for a Probate of the last Will & Testament of John Moreland, late of Hampton Parish in this County, dec'd. dated May the 21st 1706 was this day granted unto Anna, his relict and Francis Moreland, his son, they being therein appointed Extrs., and proved in Court by the oaths of Mathew Jones, Edward Fuller and Thomas Lamb, evidences thereto, and is ordered to be committed to record.

William Timson, his Deed of Assignment dated this present Instant of a pattent for 50 acres of land from Arthur Lind and Mary, his wife, was this day personally acknowledged in Court by the said William, by the said Arthur, and also by the said Mary, who upon her examination declared that she did it of her own free will and not of compulsion, which is ordered to be committed to record.

Robert Read, Gent., his Letter of Attorney dated the 23d Instant for Thomas Ballard, Gent, one of the Trustees of the Portland in York Town, for the acknowledgment of the severall Portland deeds therein mencioned, was this day proved in Court by the oaths of George Baskervile, Richard Jobie, and Thomas Turner, evidences thereto, and is ordered to be committed to record.

Col. Miles Cary, his five Portland deeds bearing date May 24th 1706 from Thomas Ballard and Wm. Buckner, Gent., Trustees of the Portland in York Town, for the 5 Portland lotts in the town numbered 12, 14, 18, 19 and 20 was this day acknowledged in Court by Robert Read, Attorney of Thomas Ballard, and also by the said Wm. Buckner in proper session and is ordered to be committed to record.

Michaell MacCormack, his Deed of Sale bearing date May the 24th 1706 from Thomas Ballard and Wm. Buckner, Trustees of the Portland in York Town, for the Portland lott there known by the number 31, was this day acknowledged in Court by Robert Read, Attorney of the said Thomas Ballard, and also by the said Wm. Buckner in proper session and is ordered to be committed to record.

Wm. Tunley, his Deed of Sale bearing date June the 10th 1706 from Thomas Ballard and Wm. Buckner, Trustees of the Portland of York Town, for the Portland lott there known by the number 23, was this day acknowledged in Court by Robert Read, Attorney of the said Thomas Ballard, and also by the said Wm. Buckner in proper session and is ordered to be committed to record.

George Burton, his Deed of Sale bearing date June 10th 1706 from Thomas Ballard and Wm. Buckner, Trustees of the Portland in York Town, for the Portland lott there known by the number 43, was this day acknowledged in Court by Robert Read, Attorney of the said Thomas Ballard, and also by the said Wm. Buckner in proper session and is ordered to be committed to record.

James Bowman, his Deed of Sale bearing date June the 24th 1706 from Thomas Ballard and Wm. Buckner, Trustees of the Portland in York Town, for the Portland lott there known by the number 49, was this day acknowledged in Court by Robert Read, Attorney of the said Thomas Ballard, and also by the said Wm. Buckner in proper session and is ordered to be committed to record.

Thomas Nelson, his Deed of Sale bearing date August the 2nd 1706 from Thomas Ballard and Wm. Buckner, Trustees of the Portland in York Town, for the Portland lott there known by the number 52, was this day acknowledged in Court by Robert Read, Attorney of the said Thomas Ballard, and also by the said Wm. Buckner in proper session and is ordered to be committed to record.

John Andrews, his Deed of Sale bearing date October the 8th 1705 from Thomas Ballard and Wm. Buckner, Trustees of the Portland in York Town, for the Portland lott there known by the number 64, was this day acknowledged in Court by Robert Read, Attorney of the said Thomas Ballard, and also by the said Wm. Buckner in proper session and is ordered to be committed to record.

Miles and Emanuell Wells, their Deed of Sale bearing date June the 8th 1706 from Thomas Ballard and Wm. Buckner, Trustees of the Portland in York Town, for the Portland lott there known by the number 77, was this day in

Court acknowledged by Robert Read, Attorney of the said Thomas Ballard, and also by the said Wm. Buckner in proper session and ordered to be committed to record.

11. John Dowzings, his Deed of Sale bearing date May the 19th 1706 from Thomas Ballard and Wm. Buckner, Trustees of the Portland in York Town, for the Portland lott there known by the number 27[?], was this day acknowledged in Court by Robert Read, Attorney of the said Thomas Ballard, and also by the said Wm. Buckner in proper session and is ordered to be committed to record.

Charles Cox, his Deed of Sale bearing date May the 24th 1706 from Thomas Ballard and Wm. Buckner, Trustees of the Portland in York Town, for the Portland lott there known by the number 47, was this day acknowledged in Court by Robert Read, Attorney of the said Thomas Ballard, and also by the said Wm. Buckner in proper session and is ordered to be committed to record.

Hester Sessions, her Deed of Sale bearing date Jany. the 24th 1705 from Thomas Ballard and Wm. Buckner, Trustees of the Portland in York Town, for the Portland lott there known by the Number 29, was this day acknowledged in Court by Robert Read, Attorney of the said Thomas Ballard, and also by the said Wm. Buckner in proper session and is ordered to be committed to record.

Edward Fuller, his Deed of Sale bearing date June the 10th 1706 from Thomas Ballard and Wm. Buckner, Trustees of the Portland in York Town, for the Portland lott there known by the number 54, was this day acknowledged in Court by Robert Read, Attorney of the said Thomas Ballard, and also by the said Wm. Buckner in proper session and is ordered to be committed to record.

William Gibs bill for £2:12 due to the Court on the account of Thomas Clayton, dec'd., was this day by the Court delivered to Thomas Pinket in part of pay for a judgment past against the said Clayton's Estate at the suit of the said Pinket, there being due £1:7:8.

Thomas Pinket this day in Court comfesst judgment to call Dudley Diggs in an acion of debt for the sume of £3:11 due by protested Bills of Exchange drawn by Samuell Moor[?] March the 25th 1700 on James Conley, merchant in London, payable to the deft. and by him endorsed to the plf., and the said deft. is ordered forthwith to pay it to the plf. with 15% charge of protest which is £4:5:1 ½ with costs of suit alies execution.

In the suit depending to this Court between John Owen, plf. and Isaac Jamart, Admr. of Wm. Chalkhill, dec'd., deft. in an acion of seire facias, the plf. this day entered his reply to the deft.'s plea and the deft. prayd time to rejoine or demur to the plf.'s reply, and the Court thought not fitt to grant to the deft. delay, but on the request of the deft., the suit is postponed till tomorrow morning.

Peter Hicks, his acion of case damage £60 depending against Robert Ranson, deft. is dismist, the deft. being dead.

William Brown's acion of case damage £14 against Johnathan Yates depending is dismist, neither party appearing.

Mungo Somerville, his acion of debt depending to this Court against Isabella Broadbent, Admx. and of Joshua Broadbent, dec'd., is dismist, neither party appearing.

Mungo Somerville hath judgment by nihil dicit this day confirmed against Isabella Broadbent, Admx. of Joshua Broadbent, dec'd. in an acion of case for the sume of £1:2:6 due by note drawn on the late deft.'s by David Rox and by the land deed anopted[?] and also for the sume of £1:19:6 due of amount proved in Court and is ordered to be payd with costs alies execution.

This Court is adjourned to the hour of 9 tomorrow morning. God love the Queen.

At a Court held for York County September the 25th 1706 for adjournment from the 24th instant. Present: Robert Read, Henry Tyler, Capt. Lawrence Smith, Major Wm. Buckner, Capt. Thomas Nutting, Justices.

It is ordered by this Court that Major Wm. Buckner, Henry Tyler, Capt. Lawrence Smith and Capt. Wm. Timson appear at the next Genl. Court on the 4th day thereof on behalf of this Court to answer a summons of said Genl. Court.

It is ordered that the Estate of Richard Dixon, late of this County, dec'd. be appraised at his late dwelling house on the 7th of October next if the weather permitt, if not the first fine day then next following, by Wm. Wise Senr., Francis Callohill, John Turner and Robert Kerby or any three of them, in the best of their judgment, being first sworn before the next Justice, and that a due returne thereof be made to the next Court.

John Clayton, his Power of Attorney from Thomas Jones bearing date the 5th instant, was this day proved in Court by the oaths of John Nicholson, one of the evidences thereto, and is ordered to be committed to record.

12. In the suit of John Brown, plf. against Isaac Jamart, Admr. of Wm. Chalkhill dec'd., deft. in an acion of seire facias wherein the plf., by Stephens Thompson, his Attorney, complained against the said deft. for that the said John at a Court held for this County the 4th day of March 1704 did obtain a judgment against the said William for the sume of £200, and by the record of this Court doth appear and the execution of the said judgment still remains to be had and there having been recept issued for the summoning of the said Isaac to appear at the Court held the 24th day of May last and prayed that the said Isaac (to whom the Admr. of the said Wm.'s Estate at the time of his death was committed) might show if he had anything... to say why the said John should not have execution of the said judgement, and also for present costs. The deft. after time given him came into Court the 2d of July last past and by Robert Hyde, his Attorney, ...and for plea said that the said plf. his execution upon his said judgment menciond in the said plf's declaration is a judgment obtained by the said plf. by nihil dicit upon an acion of trespass upon the case upon a simple contract supposed to be made between the said William and the said John for sev'll good wares and merchandise alleged to be sold and deliverd by the said John to the said William upon credit amounting to £200. And this deft. saith that the said judgment by nihil dicit in the aforesaid acion is not such a judgment as execution ought to be had thereon for that there never was any legal tryall upon the said acion by a jury nor otherwise as ought to be in all acions of that nature, and this deft. further saith that for as much as the said judgment was so obtained and remained imperfect at the time of the said William's death and that there are other debts due from the said William's Estate of greater dignity in Law amounting to £86:18:5, which this deft. saith ought to be first paid before the debt sued for by the plf., that is to say one judgment of the Court obtained by Joshua Curl on the 24th day of March in the year 1704 in an acion of debt by him brought for £28:8:5. Allso there is justly due and owing to the deft. from the said William's Estate £52:12 by a bond obligatory under the hand and seal of the said will dated the 1st day of March 1704, and there is allso due from the said William's Estate to Col. Philip Lightfoot for the funerall charges of the said William by order of the Hon. Genll. Court last, £5:18, all which aforemenciond debtors ought to be first paid and satisfied before the debt or damage sued for by the plf. All which this deft. is ready to verifie, and this deft. saith that of the goods and chattles of the said William there is as yett come to his hands no more but £48:17:6, all which this deft. is ready to verify and thereon prays the Court's judgment. The plf. obtained time to reply and accordingly came yesterday into Court and by Stephens Thompson, his Attorney, replyed and said that he ought not to be precluded or barred bacause he saith that the aforesaid judgment obtained by the said John against the said William in his lifetime is a good and sufficient judgment in Law to warrant the aforesaid seire facias according to the statute in that case made and provided, and this he is ready to verifie. Wherefore he prays judgment, and the deft. prayd

time till the next Court to rejoin or demur, which the Court thought not fitt
to grant to delay the tryall but postpond it till this time at the request of the
deft., who by his Attorney rejoind and demured in these words viz: And the
said deft. comes by Robert Hyde, his Attorney, and says that the replication
of the said plf. in manner and form as he hath presented is not sufficient in
Law to maintain his seire facias and declaration thereon, for that the said
replication neither maintains the said plf.'s declaration nor answers the plea
of said deft., wherefore this deft. saith that it is a departure in the pleading of
the said plf. all which proceeding of the plf, this deft. says is insufficient in
Law and this he is ready to verifie, and therefore he prays this Court's
judgment and that the said plf. may be barred, which rejoinder and demur
being joined, argued and by the Court overruled, the plf. on the examination
and proof of his account in Court, hath judgment granted against the deft. as
Admr. aforesaid for the sum of £123:1:7, being the just ballance of the said
account, and ordered to be paid with costs when assess alies execution.

13. In the suit depending to this Court between Joshua Curl, plf. and Isaac
Jamart, Admr. of Willm. Chalkhill, dec'd., deft. in an acion of seire facias,
the plf. hath judgment granted against the deft. for the sume of £28:8:5 due
by bill dated under the deft.'s hand Novr. the 9th 1704 and proovd in Court,
and orderd to be paid with costs when assess alies execution.

Will Coman's acion of debt against Peter Wells is dismist, neither party
appearing.

Henry Hales' acion of case against Wm. Sirman is dismist, neither party
appearing.

John Morrat's acion of debt against Antony Jesper is dismist, the plf. did not
file his declaration on time.

Edward Corker arresting John Sergerton to this Court in an acion of slander
damage £500 and not filing his declaration, is nonsuited with costs.

Francis Sharp arrested John Sergerton to the Court in an acion of trespass
and declared that the said John on the 10th day of Jany. last past at the Parish
of Bruton in the County aforesaid with force and armes one guilding of the
plf. of the price of £10 , there lately found, did take ride and carry away and
other enormity then and there did against the peace to the damage of the plf.
£10, and therefore brought suit, to which the deft. pleaded not guilty in
manner and forme and the plf. joind. Whereupon a jury (viz) Jos.
Chermisson, Jon. Loyns, Thos. Burnham, John Pond, James Morris, Robt.
Crawley, Nathll. Hook, Thom Handsford, Robt. Shield, Hen. Hayward
Junr., Nathll. Crawly and John Hansford was impannelld and sworn to try
the issue, who after a full hearing of all evidences and pleas departed to

consult their verdict, and on their return, after the plf. and deft. being calld, returnd their verdict in these words. Viz: We find for the plf. 6 pence damage, signd Robt. Crawley. Which on motion of Richard Wharton, plf.'s Attorney, the same is recorded and it is orderd that the plf. recover of the deft. the damage aforesaid in manner and forme aforesaid by the inquisition found with costs alies execution.

John Roberts, being by the Sheriff summond in evidence for Francis Sharp, plf. against John Sergenton, deft. in an acion of trespass, is orderd to be paid 80 lbs. of tobaco for two days attendance at 40 lbs. per day according to act with costs.

Morris Jones, being by the Sheriff summond in evidence for Francis Sharp, plf. against Jno. Sergerton, deft. in an acion of trespass, is orderd to be paid 80 lbs. of tobaco for two days attendance at 40 lbs. per day according to act with costs.

14. John Pasture, being by the Sheriff summond in evidence for Francis Sharp, plf. against Jno. Sergerton, deft. in action of trespass is ordered to be paid 200 lbs. of tobaco for 5 days attendance at 40 lbs. per day, according to act with costs.

Richard Moore, being by the Sheriff summond in evidence for Francis Sharp, plf. against Jno. Sergerton, deft. in an acion of trespass, is orderd to be paid 240 lbs. of tobaco for 6 days attendance at 40 lbs. per day according to act with costs.

Richard Page, being by the Sheriff summond in evidence for Francis Sharp, plf. against Jno. Sergerton, deft. in an acion of trespass, is orderd to be paid 240 lbs. of tobaco for 6 days attendance at 40 lbs. per day according to act with costs.

Charles Chiswell's acion of trespass damage £10 against Humpr. Moody is dismisst, neither party appearing.

In the suit brought to this Court by Willm. Farber, plf. against Rebeca Pinkethman, Admx. of Timothy Pinkethman, dec'd., deft. in an acion of case damage £10, the deft. by Geo. Baskervile, her Attorney, hath an imparlance granted till next Court.

Willm. Broadnex, his acion of trespass on the case against Willm. Kaydie is dismisst., neither party appearing.

Wm. Taylor's acion of debt against John Newman is dismisst, neyther party appearing.

The suit brought to the Court by Stephens Tompson, Esqr., Attorney of our Sovereigne Lady, the Queen, against Wm. Sherman and Corn. Jones of the Parish of Bruton and Co. of York, in an acion of debt damage £100, is discontinued, the plf. failing further to prosecute.

Francis Callohill's acion of case against Peter Waggoner is dismisst, neyther party appearing.

Jonathan Jones' acion of case against Jon. Gibbons is dismisst, neyther party appearing.

Robt. Bee's acion of debt against Henry Flemming is dismisst, no party appearing.

In the suit brought to this Court by Thomas Mountfort, plf. against Henry Fleming, deft. in an acion of debt damage £30, the deft. hath an imparlance granted till the next Court.

John Wythe hath judgment this day granted against Damazina Dixon, Extx. of Richd. Dixon, in an acion of debt for the sume of £20:10:6, due by protested Bills of Exchange, one bearing date April 21, 1704 and the other May the 12th 1704, and is orderd to be paid with his damage of 15% charge of protest and costs of suit alies execution.

Mungo Somerwell's acion of debt against Damaziah Dixon, Extx. of Richd. Dixon, dec'd. is dismist, the plf. failing further to prosecute.

Mungo Somerwell's acion of case against Damaziah Dixon, Extx. of Richd. Dixon, dec'd. is dismissed, the plf. failing further to prosecute.

Jon. Penton's acion of case against Damazia Dixon, Extx. of Richd. Dixon, dec'd., is continued by consent of both partyes.

15. In the suit brought to this Court by John Adduston Rogers and Jane, his wife, Admrs. of Henry Andrews dec'd., plf. against Damazia Dixon, Extx. of the last Will & Testament of Richd. Dixon, dec'd., deft. in an acion of debt damage £2, the deft. hath an imparlance granted till next Court.

Thomas Woodfield's acion of debt against Damazinah Dixon, Extx. of Richard Dixon, dec'd., is dismissed, the partyes being agreed.

Henry Cary hath judgment this day granted against Damazinah Dixon, Extx. of Richd. Dixon, dec'd. in an acion of debt for the sume of £9:12 due by protested Bills of Exchange dated April the 10th 1704 and is orderd to be paid with damage of 15% charge of protest and costs of suit alies execution.

John Penton's acion of debt against Thomas Wooten is dismissed, no party appearing.

Peter Gibson's acion of case against Peter Dickeson is dismissed, no party appearing.

Edward Corker's acion of debt against Joseph Bottick is dismissed, no party appearing.

Wm. Tunley, Assignee of Isaac Sedgwick, his acion of case against John Dozwell Junr. is dismist, neyther party appearing.

Wm. Gordon this day in Court confest judgment to James Priest in an acion of debt for the sume of 350 lbs. of good sound sweet scented tobaco due by bill dated May the 24th, 1705, and is orderd forthwith to pay it unto the plf. with costs alies execution.

Andrew Young's acion of case against Peter Dickeson is dismist, no party appearing.

Nathll. Hook's acion of case against Martin Bean is dismist, no party appearing.

In the suit depending to this Court between Robt. Folda, plf. against Richd. Aldo, deft. in an acion of Ejectione firmae, John Loynes was this day on his prayer admitted deft., who pleaded not guilty and entered into the common rules, and the suit is referred till next Court for triall.

Willm. Wise's acion against Alice Gilbert is dismist, he having no cause of suit.

Willm. Davies and Elizabeth, his wife, their petition against the Estate of James Darbeshire is continued.

Robt. Ranson being dead, his plea in arrest of judgment against Persivall Shepherd is dismist.

In the suit depending to this Court between John Redwood, plf., and Isaac Jamart, Admr. of Wm. Chalkhill, deft. in an acion of case damage £120, the plf. is nonsuited with costs, not proving his declaration.

Willm. Cant, his acion of case damage £20 to this Court depending against Henry Hayles, deft., declared for the sume of 2000 lbs. of tobacco and cask convenient, the deft. pleads that the plf. his agent refused to accept a lawfull tender. Wherefore the suit is referd for proof of the said tender.

Lawrence Smyth, his attachment formerly obtained against James Withe is continued to the next Court.

16. Upon the tryall of the diference depending to this Court between Katherine Masterton, plf. and Willm Forbar, deft. in an acion of trespass wherein the plf. by Stephens Tompson, her Attorney, declares that the deft. on the 1st day of May last past in the Parish of Bruton and Co. of York, with force and armes upon her the said Katherine, an assault did make and her beat, wounded and evill treated so that of her life it was dispaired and one muzlin hood of the said Katherine of the value of 30 shillings did rend and leave and other enormityes to her did against the peace and to the damage of the said Katherine £50, to which the deft. by Richd. Wharton, his Attorney, pleaded not guilty in manner and forme and put himself on his country, and the plf. likewise. Whereupon a jury was impanelled and sworn to try the issue, who after a full hearing of all evidences and pleas, departed to consult their verdict and on their return, plf. and deft. being called, returned their verdict in these words, viz: We find for plf. 6 pence, signd Willm. Wise Senr., foreman. Which on mocion of the plf.'s Attorney is recorded and it is orderd that the plf. recover of the deft. her damage aforesaid in manner aforesaid by the inquisition found with costs alies execution.

John Jeff, being by the Sheriff summond an evidence for Katherine Masterton, plf., against Willm. Forbar, deft. in an acion of trespass, is orderd to be paid 320 lbs. of tobaco for 8 days attendance at 40 lbs. per day, according to act with costs.

Robt. Weaver, being by the Sheriff summond an evidence for Katherine Masterton, plf, against Willm. Forbar, deft. in an acion of trespass, is orderd to be paid 320 lbs. of tobaco for 8 days attendance at 40 lbs. per day, according to act with costs.

John Loynes, being summond an evidence for Katherine Masterton, plf., against Willm. Forbar, deft. in an acion of trespass is orderd to be paid 320 lbs. of tobaco for 8 days attendance at 40 lbs. per day, according to act with costs.

Wm. Brown's acion of debt depending against Joseph Bottick is dismisst, the plf. not further prosecuting.

Mary Greenfield hath judgment this day granted against Edwd. Davies in an acion of debt for the sume of 10 shillings, due by ballance of a bill dated under his hand Octr. the 19th 1705 and is orderd to be paid with costs alies execution.

Robt. Mynne hath judgment by nihil dicit this day granted against Andrew Young in an acion of case for the sume of £12 and the next Court to be confirmed on the like default.

Joseph Walker's acion of debt depending against Jon. Handsford is dismisst, the partyes being agreed.

John Sergerton hath judgment of nihil dicit this day granted against Jon. Nicholson in an acion of debt for the sume of £6:5 and the next Court to be confirmed on the like default.

In the suit depending to this Court between Thos. Whitby, plf. and Isaac Jamart , Admr. of Wm. Chalkhill, dec'd., deft. in an acion of debt, the deft. on his mocion hath an imparlance granted till the next Court.

17. The suit depending to this Court between Abraham Spranger and John Maynard, plf. against John Handsford and Willm. Huite, Extrs. of Charles Handsford, dec'd., in an acion of case is dismisst, the plfs. not proving their declaration.

In the suit depending to this Court between Thomas Green, plf. against Rebeca Pinkethman, Admx. of Timothy Pinkethman, dec'd., deft. in an acion of case, an imparlance is granted the deft. till next Court.

Charles Cox hath judgment this day granted by nihil dicit against Anthony Jesper in an acion of debt, damage £5, and the next Court to be confirmd on the like default.

John Adduston Rogers and Jane, his wife, Admrs. of Henry Andrews, dec'd., hath judgment this day granted by nihil dicit against Thos. Walker in an acion of case damage £25:8:9 and the next Court to be confirmd on the like default.

John Adduston Rogers and Jane, his wife, Admrs. of Henry Andrews, dec'd., hath judgment of nihil dicit this day granted against Peter Gibson in an acion of case damage £5 and the next Court to be confirmd on the like default.

John Adduston Rogers and Jane, his wife, Admrs. of Henry Andrews, dec'd., hath judgment of nihil dicit this day granted against Use Gibson in an acion of case damage £5 and the next Court to be confirmd on the like default.

Thomas Douglas hath judgment this day granted against Wm. Gordon in an acion of debt for the sume of £1 money and 148 lbs. tobaco due by bill dated under the deft.'s hand March the 24th 1704/5, and is orderd to be paid with costs alies execution.

Thomas Bass hath judgment by nihil dicit this day granted against John Duke in an acion of debt for the sume of £1:18:4 and the next Court to be confirmd on the like default.

Nathll. Davies' acion of case against Robt. Ranson is dismisst, the deft. being dead.

Edward Arnold's acion of case against Robt. Ranson is dismisst, the deft. being dead.

Josua Sled hath judgment by nihil dicit this day granted against John Duke in an acion of case for the sume of £1:10 and the next Court to be confirmd on the like default.

Thomas Burnham this day in Court confest judgment to Joseph Walker and Sarah, his wife, Extx. of Joseph L. Ring, dec'd. in an acion of debt for the sume of £2:10:9 due by bill dated Jany. 29th 1702/3, and is orderd forthwith to pay the plf. with costs alies execution.

John Wythe's Information against Anne Banks for fornication is dismisst, the informant, not further prosecuting.

Robt. Read, his Information against Mary Hanson for bastardizing, is dismisst, the informant not further prosecuting.

The Court is adjourned to the hower of 9 tomorrow morning.

18. At a Court held for York Co. Sepr. the 26th 1706 from adjournment of the 25th Instant. Present: Majr. Wm. Buckner, Capt. Thomas Nutting, Henry Tyler and Capt. Law. Smith.

In the suit brought to the Court by Archibald Blair, plf. against Isaac Jamart, Admr. of Wm. Chalkhill, dec'd. in an acion of seire facias, the plf. has judgment granted against the deft. for the sume of £13:5:7 ½ due by account, proovd in Court, and ordered to be paid with costs assess alies execution.

Andrew Young's petition for the Ferry of York Towne to Tindall's Point is granted, he entering into bond with John Adduston Rogers and Willm. Lee, his securities, for his performance of his duty therein according to Law.

George Holloway, being by a former order of this Court summond to give an account of which goods and chattles he had in his possession of Mark Provoo, orphan of Mark Provoo, dec'd. and confessing one cow and cow calf in his possession, is orderd to deliver them the 10th of March next to Benje. Shepherd, Guardian of the said orphan, for the said orphan's use, with costs alies execution.

Charles Chiswell's Information against Anne Mackentash for fornication is dismisst, he failing further to prosecute.

Peter Gibson's acion of trespass on the case against Thomas Whitby is continued, the deft. being sick.

Peter Gibson's acion of trespass upon the case against Elizabeth Handsford is continued till next Court by consent.

In the suit depending to this Court between James Ming, plf. and Danll. Park, Esq., deft., in an acion of case, the deft. this day demurred to the plf.'s reply and the plf. hath time to argue it.

Benj. Lillingston's acion of case against Rebeca Pinkethman, Admx. of Timothy Pinkethman, dec'd. is referd till next Court.

Benj. Lillingston's acion of case against Rebecca Pinkethman, Admx. of Timothy Pinkethman, dec'd. is referd till next Court.

Jonathan Yates' acion of case depending against Robt. Ranson is dismisst, the deft. being dead.

Joseph Botwick's, the like.

Edward Cocker's, the like.

Manvell Revell's, the like.

Frances Everitt's, the like.

Samll. Miller's, the like.

John Hancock's, the like.

Peter Hicks', the like.

John Cooper of London, merchant, his plea in arrest of judgment against Thomas Whitby and Mary, his wife, Extx. of Thomas Collyer, dec'd., is continued till next Court by consent, the said Whitby being sick.

19. In the suit depending to this Court between Wm. Barbar, late Sheriff of York Co., plf., against Nathll. Crawley, deft. in an acion of debt declared for the sume of £4:5 due by bill dated under the hand and seal of deft. and John Marshall May the 2d 1705, being for [?] bought at the outcry of Wm. Chalkhill, dec'd., to which the deft. produced by way of descompt a note dated under the hand of the said Wm. Chalkhill Novr. 30ᵗʰ 1704 and proovd in Court by the oath of Wm. Dalton, evidence thereto, for the sume of £6, and making oath that he never received more than 15 shillings 6 pence ½ satisfaction, and pleaded by John Clayton, his Attorney the Act of Assembly entituled an Act Declaring How Long Judgment Bonds Obligation and Accounts Shall be in Force for the Assignment of Bonds and Obligations, directing which proof shall be sufficient in such cases, ascertaining damage upon protested Bills of Exchange. Which was thought by the Court a good descompt against the bill sued for, and the ballance thereof, £5:4:5 ½, being more than the debt sued for, the suit is dismisst. From which judgment, the plf. appeals for tryall before the Honorable Gen'll Court, Robt. Hyde, securety.

In the suit depending to this Court between Math. Tiplady, Assignee of Wm. King, plf. and David Robertson, deft. in an acion of debt, the plf. hath judgment granted against the deft. for the sume of £14:7:6, being the ballance made appear in Court between them, and it is orderd that the said David pay the said sume to the plf. with costs alies execution [ifs with corps?] Octr. 2 1703.

Abraham Royston, mulato son of Elizabeth Chilinaid, is orderd to be brought to the next Court and to the Clerk provide an indenture to bind him to Thomas Holliday, boat wright, after the manner of an apprentice to learn the said craft or mistery and at the end or expiration of his time to have corne and cloathes according to the Law of this countrey.

Rebeca Stephens, being by virtue of a former order of this Court summond to answer the Information of John Wyth, Church warden of York Parish, for having a mulato bastard male child lately born of her body, and confessing the father to be a negro, it is therefore orderd that she be by the said John Wyth sold for five yeares for the sume of £15 current money of Virginia for the use of the said plf., according to the late Law in that case made and provided, entiteld An Act Concerning Servants and Slaves.

Wm. Wise Senr. hath judgment this day granted against Damasinah Dixon, Extx. of the last Will & Testament of Richd. Dixon, dec'd. in an acion of debt for the sume of £7:6:9 due by account proovd in Court by the plf.'s oath and is orderd forthwith to be paid with costs alies execution.

The acion of case brought to this Court by Thomas Nutting against Damazinah Dixon, Extx. of Richd. Dixon, dec'd., lyeth for want of account.

Richd. Slater, his acion of case against Damazinah Dixon, Extx. of Richard Dixon, dec'd. is dismisst per non prosecution.

Joseph Charmison, Assignee of Wm. Kaydye, hath judgment this day granted against Damazinah Dixon, Extx. of Richd. Dixon, dec'd. in an acion of debt for the sume of £9 due by bills dated under his hand May the 11th 1705, and is orderd to be paid with costs alies execution.

Nathaniell Hooke hath judgment this day granted against Damazinah Dixon, Extx. of Richard Dixon, dec'd. in an acion of case for the sum of £2:3 due by account proovd in Court and is orderd to be paid with costs alies execution.

John Ausiter's acion of case against Henry Robertson is dismist, neither party appearing.

John Shaw's acion of case to this Court against Wm. Smith is dismisst, neither party appearing.

Edwd. Corker's acion of debt to this Court against Timothy Macdonell is dismisst , the deft. being yet not found in his baliwick.

Walter Cromby's acion of case against Willm. Smith is dismist, neither party appearing.

20. Henry Hayward Junr.'s acion of case for words against Willm. Wise, Senr. is dismisst, the partyes being agreed.

Peter Gibson's acion of case for words against Edwd. Whitwick is dismist, the plf. not filing his declaration [?] plf. 4 days.

Willm. Barbar, late Sheriff of York Co., bringing suite to this Court against Willm. Dalton in an acion of debt declared for the sume of £6:7:6 due by bill and he not appearing, order is granted the plf. against Andew Young, the deft.'s security, and the next Court to be confirmed if he causeth not the deft. then personally to appeare and answer the same.

Wm. Thisfickle, his acion of trespass on the case against Wm. Smyth is dismisst, no party appearing.

John Dod's acion of case against Willm. Smith is dismisst, neither party appearing.

Wm. Greenland's acion of case against Wm. Smith is dismist, neither party appearing.

Thomas Mountfort's acion of case against Willm. Taylor is dismist, the deft. being by the Sheriff returnd.

Adam Galt, having brought suit to the Court against Mungo Somerwell in an acion of case damage £12, who not appearing, the plf. hath an attachment granted against his Estate for the said sume with costs returnable to the next Court, he being by the Sheriff on oath returnd non est Inventus.

Wm. Kaydyie, having brought suit to this Court against Mungo Somerwell in an acion of case damage £10, who not appearing, the plf. hath an attachment granted against his Estate for the said sume with costs returnable to the next Court, he being by the Sheriff on oath returnd non est Inventus.

Walter Crombie, having brought suit to this Court against Mungo Somerwell in an acion of case damage £4, who not appearing, the plf. hath an attachment granted against his Estate for the said sume with costs returnable to the next Court, he being by the Sheriff on oath returnd non est Inventus.

Thomas Mountfort's acion of case against Vernon Parkman is dismisst, the deft. not being found in this baylwick.

John Andrews arresting James Bowman in an acion of case declared for the sume of £1:18:9 due by account, and the deft. not appearing, the plf. hath order granted against Willm. Barbar, Sheriff and the next Court to be confirmed if he causeth not the deft. then personally to appeare and answer the same.

Wm. Barbar, H.S., hath an attachment granted against the Estate of James Bowman for the sume of £1:18:9 with costs returnable to the next Court, he failing to appear at this to answer the suit of Jno. Andrews.

Edw. Whitwick, his acion of case to this Court against Henry Hilton is dismisst, neyther partye appearing.

John Martin's acion of debt against Robt. Kay is dismisst, neyther party appearing.

Henry Hayward Junr. arresting Jon. Dozwell Senr. to this Court in an acion of debt declared for the sume of £13:10:1 due by protested bills with damage of 15% charge of interest and costs, the deft. not appearing, the plf. hath order granted against Wm. Barbar, Sheriff, and the next Court to be confirmd if he causeth not the deft. then personally to appeare and answer the same.

Wm. Barbar, H.S., hath an attachment granted against John Dozwell Senr. for the sum of £13:10:1 with costs returnable to the next Court, he failing to appeare at this to answer the suit of Henry Hayward Junr. in an acion of debt for the like sume.

21. John Tomer arresting John Wills and Elizabeth, his wife, Extx. of Thomas Harwood, dec'd., in an acion of case damage £10, the deft. not appearing, the plf. hath order granted against Wm. Barbar, H.S., and the next Court to be confirmd if he causeth not the deft. then personally to appeare and answer the same.

In the suit brought to this Court by Peter Gibson, plf. against John Thomas in an acion of case, the deft. on his mocion hath an imparlance granted till the next Court.

John Cromby's acion of case against Thomas Douglas is dismisst, neither party appearing.

Thomas Mountfort's acion of case against Thomas Douglas is dismisst, neither party appearing.

John Penton's acion of debt against Thomas Mountfort is dismisst, neither party appearing.

Thomas Mountfort's acion of debt against Thomas Walker is dismisst, neither party appearing.

Andrew Young's acion of trespass against Charles Cox is dismisst, neither party appearing.

Thomas Handsford arresting Isaac Sedgwick, Extr. of Willm. Sedgwick, dec'd. to this Court in an acion of case declared for the sume of £1:13 due by account and he not appearing, order is granted against Wm. Barbar, H.S., and the next Court to be confirmd if he causeth not the deft. then personally to appeare and answer the same.

Richd. Pate's acion of debt to this Court against John Sebrell is dismisst, the deft. not being found in the bailiwick.

In the suit brought to this Court by Charles Bartlet, plf. against Thomas Graham, late of Pensilvania and Nathll. Maclanen, late of Princes Anne Co. in an acion of debt damage £150, the deft. on his mocion hath oyer of this bond granted till the next Court.

Henry Hayles, his acion of case against Wm. Sherman and Mary, his wife is dismisst, the deft. being returnd not to be found.

John Bates having brought suit to this Court against Alexander Miller in an acion of debt declared for the sume of £2:10:4 ¼ due by bill and he not appearing, the plf. hath an attachment granted against the deft.'s Estate for the said sume with costs returnable to the next Court, he being by the Sheriff on oath returnd non est inventus.

John Bates arresting Thomas Pinket to this Court in an acion of debt declared for the sume of £1:8:2 due by note and he not appearing, the plf. hath order granted against Wm. Barbar, H.S., and the next Court to be confirmd if he causeth not the deft. then personally to appeare and answer the same.

Wm. Barbar, H.S., hath an attachment granted against the Estate of Thomas Pinket for the sume of £1:8:2 with costs returnable to the next Court, he failing to appeare at this to answer the suit of John Bates in an acion of debt for the like sume.

John Handsford's acion of debt to this Court against Wm. Barbar, Admr. of John Brice, is referd till next Court for the deft. to bring an account of the decedent's Estate.

Henry Hayles arresting Thomas Pinket to this Court in an acion of case declared for the sume of £1:6:1 ½ due by account and he not appearing, order is granted against Wm. Barbar, H.S., at the next Court to be confirmd if he causeth not the deft. then personally to appeare and answer the same.

Job Williams having brought suit to this Court against James [no name given] in an acion of debt declared for the sum of £2:14 due by bills and he not appearing, the plf. hath an attachment granted against the deft's Estate for the said sume with costs returnable to the next Court, he being by the Sheriff on oath returnd non est inventus.

Thomas Adkinson's acion of debt against Thomas Rose is dismisst, neither party appearing.

22. John Bates, having brought suit to this Court against Edward Foulks in an acion of case declared for the sume of £3:3 due by bill and account and

he not appearing, the plf. hath an attachment granted against the deft.'s Estate for the said sume with costs returnable to the next Court, he being by the Sheriff returnd non est inventus.

Thomas Gray's acion of case against Jon. Collingwood is dismist, neyther party appearing.

John Marshall's acion of case against Adduston Rogers is dismist, neyther party appearing.

John Marshall's acion of case against James Priest is dismist, neither party appearing.

John Marshall's acion of case against Michael Mackcormack is dismist, neither party appearing.

John Owen's acion of case against David Robinson is dismist, neither party appearing.

Andrew Young's acion of debt against Henry King is dismisst, neither party appearing.

William Tunley's acion of case against Use Gibson and Peter Gibson is at the request of the said Use referd to the next Court.

W. Dramond hath judgment this day granted against Richard Browne and Damazinah, his wife, Extx. of Richd. Dixon, dec'd. in an acion of trespass on the case for the sume of £15:2:6 due by protested Bills of Exchange by the said Testator drawne the 15t^h of Jany. 1703/4 on Micaga Perry and Comp., merchants in London, payable to Philipe and Jonas Prichard and by them endorsd to the plf., and the plf. is orderd to be paid with his damage of 15% charge of interest and costs alies execution.

John Martin's acion of debt against Richd. Browne and Damazina Dixon, his wife, Extx. of Richd. Dixon, dec'd., is continued by consent till the next Court.

John Hall hath judgment this day granted against Richd. Browne and Damazinah, his wife, Extx. of Richd. Dixon, dec'd. in an acion of case for the sume of £9:4:5 due per account proovd in Court, and is orderd to be paid with costs alies execution.

Thos. Jones' acion of case against Wm. Gordon is dismisst, neither party appearing.

In an acion of case of James Bowman with Wm. Casey, damage £2, the deft. hath an inparlance granted till the next Court.

James Bowman arresting Thomas Ellenor to this Court in an acion of case for words and not showing any cause of acion, is nonsuited with costs Ex [est Corp...?].

John Cromby's acion of case against James Bowman is at the request of the deft. referd till the next Court.

John Duke's acion of case damage £10 against Nichs. Philips is referd till the next Court at the request of the deft.

Wm. Gordon's acion of case against Randolph Plat is dismisst, neither party appearing.

Thomas Burnham arresting John Wells to this Court in an acion of trespass, damage £20, and he not appearing, order is granted against Wm. Barbar, H.S., and the next Court to be confirmd if he causeth not the deft. then personally to appear and answer the same.

Cuthbert Gray's acion of debt against Use Gibson is dismisst, neither party appearing.

Thomas Handsford hath judgment this day granted against James Morris in an acion of case for the sum of £3:4 due by account prooved in Court and is orderd to be paid with costs alies execution.

Henry Duke arresting John Cocklin in an acion of debt declared for the sume of £5 due by bill and he not appearing, order is granted against Wm. Barbar, H.S., and the next Court to be confirmd if he causeth not the deft. then personally to appear and answer the same.

In the suit of Barrentine Howell, plf. against Nathll. Huggens in an acion of trespass, damage £20, an imparlance is granted the deft. till next Court.

23. Henry Hale's acion of debt against John Moris and Henry Tiler lyeth for a fuller Court.

Stephens Thomson's acion of case against Robt. Nappier is dismisst, neither party appearing.

The sevll. suits depending to this Court between David Robertson and Willm. Freeman (Viz) the said David against the said Willm. in an acion of trespass on the case for his consenting to the owne use of goods of the said

David, 200 gallons of rum of the value of £60 and 2,000 weight of muscovado sugar of value of £100, damage of the said David £150, and the said Willm. against the said David in an acion of case for the sum of £22:1 for wages on board the Ship Elizabeth, whereof the said Davis is Master, by him detained to the damage of the said Willm. £30, are referd to Arbitrators to arbitrate and settle the matters in diference between them. On their mocion to the Court, each party at the Barr entered into reconizc. of £50 to stand to and abide the award and judgment of such arbitrators this Court should appoint. It is therefore orderd that Robt. Read, Jno. Hunt and John Martin meet at York Towne the 28th Instant, then and there to arbitrate and settle the matters in diference between the said partyes and make report of their award to the next Court.

Stephens Thomson arresting Willm. Handsford to the Court in an acion of case damage £5 and he not appearing, order is granted against Wm. Barbar, H.S., and the next Court to be confirmed if he causeth not the deft. then personally to appeare and answer the same.

Charles Chiswell's acion of case against Robt. Nappier is dismisst, neither party appearing.

Charles Cox's acion of debt to this Court against Timothy Johnson is dismisst, the Writ being not executed.

Henry Emerson bringing suit to this Court against John Ross in an acion of case damage £10 and he not appearing, the plf. hath attachment granted against the deft.'s estate for the said sume with costs returnable to the next Court, he being by the Sheriff on oath returnd non est inventus.

James Aynsworth this day by Jon. Owen, his Attorney, came to this Court and complained against John Hunt in a plea of case that the said Hunt oweth unto him the sume of £250 (for the fraight of 100 negros in the Brigantine Lark) and the sume detaineth to the damage of the Complainant of £200, which declaration the said Hunt accepted to answer without acion executed and pleaded that he did not assume in manner and forme as the plf. in his declaration set forth, and both parties agreed to refer the matter to the Court, who upon disagreeing of the partyes in their pleading, dismisst the suit.

Orderd that a Court for laying the County levy be held the first day of Novr. next.

The Court is adjorned to the 24th of Novr. next. God save the Queen.

24. York Co. debts November 5th 1706.

To Capt. Thomas Barbar as burgess 60 days attendance, one day going and one day coming, 62 at 130 per day…8,060 lbs. Tobaco

To Cash pd.[?]…645 lbs.

To Col. Thomas Ballard…8,705 lbs.

To Wm. Randolph for Laws…2,000 lbs.

To ditto for cash…4,460 lbs.

To Wm. Tunley…3,080 lbs.

To Capt. Lawrence Smith for overcharges in the Publick Levy for payes two negros last yeare and charges…442 lbs.

To ditto for 17 delinquent at 27 ¼…459 1/9 lbs.

To ditto for 3 and carting…150 lbs.

To ditto for one days attendance at Genll. Court by order of County Court…130 lbs.

To cash for the same…17 lbs.

To ditto Majr. Willm. Buckner…347 lbs.

To ditto Henry Tyler…147 lbs.

To I.D. for an inquest at Coroner with cash…347 lbs.

To Wm. Sherman, Constable for Jury and Evidences…140 lbs.

To Wm. Tunley for Book Record…108 lbs.

To I.D. for the Queen's Armes…4-- ;bs/

Tp sallary for 22984 ½…2,295.98 lbs.

To Use Gibson for Prison Mending…178 lbs.

To Cl. and Sheriff for Extraordinary Services…700 lbs.

York Co., continued is credited anno 1706.

Coll. Miles Cary for 5 lots at 180 each…900 lbs.

Wm. Tunley for lots, viz. Martins, Owens, Andrews, [?] and Nelson…1,080 lbs.

Robt. Read for James Bowman's Lot…180 lbs.

Edward Fuller for his Port Land Lott…180 lbs.

Wm. Gordon for two Lotts…360 lbs.

John Dowzing for one Lott…180 lbs.

Robert Read for one Port Land lot…180 lbs.

Miles and Emanll Wills, 1 port Land Lot…180 lbs

Willm. Tunley for Burton's Lott…180 lbs.

3415 Tillables at 16 per pole is…22,640 lbs.

At a Court held for York Co. for laying the County Levy Novr. 1st 1706. Present: Capt. Thomas Barbar, Hen. Tyler, Majr. Wm. Buckner, Capt. Lawc. Smith.

It is orderd that Wm. Barbar, H. Shf. of the said County, do collect of every tillable person of the said County 16 lbs. of tobaco for defraying the County charges this present yeare, and in case of deniall of payment, then he destraine for the same and that he give and render an account of all such persons as have not listed themselves, and the persons having credit in the present levy are orderd to take their dues proportionally in each respective Parish.

25. Will of John Hunt of Philadelphia in the Province of Pensilvania, merchant at present in Virginia. My friend, Benj. Ball...to convey my body up the Bay to Philadelphia to be interred at the discretion of my kinswoman, Elizabeth Palmer. To my mother, Elizabeth Hunt of the Island of Barbados, £200[?] . To my son, John Hunt, £1,000 and my two negro slaves named Quad[?] and Maria. To the said two negro slaves, £5 a piece. To my kinswoman, Elizabeth Palmer, £300. To my friend, John Martin, in consideration for his care of me in my sickness...£50. The residue of my Estate...to my three children, John Hunt, Elizabeth Hunt and Rebecca Hunt...when they reach the age of 18 years. Elizabeth Palmer...to have custody of my children. My friend, Nathll. Curtis of the Island of Barbados...to be my Extr. in high, and under him...my friend, the Hon. Dudley Diggs, Esq. an Extr. of the effects I have in Virginia. My friend, Richard Bennett of Maryland, Esq. to be an Extr. of the effects I have in Maryland. My friend, Anthony Palmer of Pensilvania to be an Extr. of the effects I have in Pensilvania. Dated 7th day of Octr. 1706. Wit. J.W. Thouston, Phill. Moody, Ben Ball, and Wm. Tunley.

26. At a Court held for York Co. Dec the 24th 1706. Present: Capt. Thomas Barbar, Col. Thomas Ballard, Capt. Thomas Nutting, Majr. Wm. Buckner, Capt. Lawrence Smith.

Joseph Walker, his Deed of Sale bearing date the 23rd instant from Samuell Dickenson for half his Portland Lott numbered 11 in York Town and County and also the land for the performance of the covenants therein contained, was this day in Court personally acknowledged by the said Samuell Dickenson to the said Joseph Walker and ordered to be committed to record.

On reading of the judgment of the 25th of September last past obtained by John Owen, plf. against Isaac Jamart, Admr. of William Chalkhill, dec'd. in an acion of seire facias, Robert Hyde, Attorney of the deft., this day entered his plea to accept the said judgment, which is referred till the next Court to be argued on mocion of Stephens Thomson, Attorney for the plf.

Joseph Walker, together with John Mihill and Joseph Chermisson, his securitys, this day in Court acknowledged a bond of this Instant date for the said Joseph's due administration of Wm. Aylward's Estate according to Law and orderd of this Court, which is ordered to be committed to record.

Robert Read, his deed dated the 2nd instant from Col. Thomas Ballard and Major William Buckner, Trustees of the Portland of York Town, for the two Portland Lotts 73 and 74, was this day in Court personally acknowledged in Court by the said Thomas to the said Robert Read and ordered to be comitted to record.

According to a former order of this Court, Lydia Broster, Admx. of John Broster, late of this County, dec'd., this day returned to the Court an Inventory & Appraisement of the said decedent's Estate on oath, which is ordered to be comitted to record.

According to a former order of this Court, Damazinah Brown, formerly Damazinah Dixon, Extx. of Richard Dixon, dec'd., this day returned to the Court an Inventory & Appraisement of the said Estate on oath, which is ordered to be comitted to record.

Thomas Whitby this day came into Court and acknowledged a certain pair of Indentures of Lease and Release dated under his hand and seale the 17th and 18th of November last past, for severall goods, chattels therein mentioned to Capt. Thomas Barbar and Major William Buckner to the intents and purposes therein mentioned, which is ordered to be committed to record.

William Thacker this day on his petition obtained order for a comission of admin. of the Estate of Elizabeth Philpot, late of this County, dec'd. with her noncupitive will annexed, whose date was the 14th of [?] instant and this day proved in Court by the oath of Daniell Burton and Thomas Raley, evidences thereto, and ordered to be comitted to record.

It is ordered of the Estate of Elizabeth Phillpot, late of this County, dec'd. be appraised the 2d of Jany. next if the weather permitt, if not the first fair day then next following, by Richard Kendall, Henry Gilson, Wm. Hansford and Robert Harris, or any three of them, in the best of their judgment, being first sworn before the next Justice, and due returne thereof be made to the next Court.

Major Wm. Buckner as guardian of Jane Young, orphan of Alexander Young, dec'd., this day on his petition obtained order for a comision of Admin. of the Estate of John Hilliard, dec'd, as greatest creditor, giving good and sufficient security for his due administration thereof, according to Law.

It is ordered that the Estate of John Hilliard, late of this County, dec'd., be by the Sheriff of this County sold on the first day of Jany. next at Publique Outcry for bills, with good and sufficient security for sterling money payable Feby. next come twelve months, and that the Clerk attend the outcry for taking of the said bills.

Mary Hilliard, relict of John Hilliard, dec'd., this day making humble suit for an order of this Court for a bed, a pott and a pan, a dish and a spoon and other small necessarys out of her said dec'd. husband's Estate, it is therefore ordered that the same remain in her hands till further order of this Court. And it is further ordered that she present a true and perfect inventory of the said Estate upon oath to the next Court.

The last Will & Testament of John Hunt, late of Philadelphia in the Province of Pensilvania, merchant, bearing date the 17th day of October last past on the mocion of John Clayton, was this day proved in Court by the oaths of Wm. Tunley and Phillip Moody, two of the evidences thereto, and ordered to be comitted to record.

Wm. Coman, his Power of Attorney from Robert Green and Abigale, his wife, bearing date November the [?] 1706 was this day proved in Court by the oaths of Henry Hayles, one of the evidences thereto, and ordered to be comitted to record.

John Harrison, his Deed of Sale bearing date under the hands and seals of Robert Green and Abigale, his wife the 27th of November 1706 for 200 acres of land (more or less), situate in this County, together with the bond for the performances of the covenants therein contained of the same date, was this day acknowledged in Court by Wm. Coman for and on behalf of the said Robert Green by virtue of a Power of Attorney bearing his oath for the said dated bond and also by the said Abigale in proper person, who on her examination declared that she did it of her own full will and not of compulsion, which is ordered to be comitted to record.

27. John Wythe, his Power of Attorney from Thomas Hubbard of Nansemond Co. and Martha, his wife, dated November the 25th 1706 was this day proved in Court by the oaths of James [?] and Sarah Hows, two of the evidences thereto, and ordered to be comitted to record.

John Dozwell Junr., his Deed of Sale dated the 26th of October from Thomas Hubbard of Nansemond Co. and Martha, his wife, for 50 acres of land in this County and also the bond of the same date and partys for performance in the said deed contained was this day acknowledged in Court by John Wythe, Attorney of the said Thomas and Martha, and ordered to be comitted to record.

John Ausiter of the Parish of St. Andrews in the Co. of Middlesex in the Kingdom of England, his Deed of Mortgage by way of Lease and Release bearing date under the hand and seale of Thomas Mountfort the 20th and 21st day of August last past, and also the bond of performance of covenants in the said deed contained and of the same date was this day in Court personally acknowledged by the said Mountfort and ordered to be comitted to record.

An Inventory & Appraisement of the Estate of Morgan Baptist, dec'd., was this day presented in Court by Elizabeth, his Relict (Admx. of the same) on oath and ordered to be comitted to record.

On reading of the inquisition taken by Danll. Taylor, Commissioner of Charles Parish in this County the 15th of November last past on the body of Richard Brown (who came by an untimely death) and the opinion of the jurors thereunto subscribed is that the said Richard Brown came to his death by a pipe struck into his eye accidentally by Job Jones, the said Job Jones pleaded that he was bailable, who after the examination of Thomas Woodfield and Damazinah Brown, Relict of the said dec'd., as evidences and was comitted to prison.

John Gibbons and Simon Stacy of this County this day in Court affirmed themselves bound in the penalty of £100 apiece payable to... the Queen... for the appearance of Job Jones at the first day of the next Generall Court, then and there to answer the indictment that shall be brought against him concerning the death of Richard Brown, late of this County, dec'd.

Thomas Woodfield of the Co. of Warwick and John Saunders of the Co. of York this day in Court affirmed themselves bound unto... the Queen... in the penalty of £100... for their personall appearance at the 4th day of the next Genll. Court, then and there to give their evidences on oath... concerning the death of Richard Brown, late of this County, dec'd.

It is ordered that Joshua Sledd be by the Sheriff summoned to the next Court to answer the complaint of Mary Limus, who in the meantime may be entertained by any person in the Parish soul prejudice.

On reading of a judgment obtained September the 25th last by Robert Hyde, Attorney of Joshua Curle, plf. against Isaac Jamart, Admr. of Wm. Chalkhill, dec'd., deft. in an acion of debt, the power of the said Hyde being objected against, he produced his warrant from the said Curle dated the 24th day of Feby. 1704, which is ordered to be comitted to record.

Wm. Erotten[?], Confesser of the lower precinque of Charles Parish, is discharged from his said office and Wm. Wise Junr. is appointed in his stead, and it is ordered that he be sworn in front of the next Justice for the performance of his duty therein according to Law.

33

John Dozwell Junr., Surveyor of the highways in the upper precinque of Charles Parish in this County, on petition is discharged and John Dozwell Senr. is appointed in his stead, and it is ordered that he forthwith acquire and from time to time continue the performance of his duty therein, according to Law.

Capt. Edmund Berkley of Glocester Co., his Letter of Guardianship dated under the hand and seale of Joseph Ring, Orphan of Joseph Ring, Gent, late of this Co., dec'd., Jany. the 5th, 1705, was this day proved in Court by the oath of James Bray, one of the evidences thereto, and ordered to be certifyed.

The Court is adjouned to the 9th of Jany. Next. God love the Queen.

28. To the Sheriff of York Co., Greeting. Whereas it was considered in our Court before our Justices at York aforesaid that Dudly Diggs should have execution on the within written order in the Court recovered against the Izabella [Broadbent], whereof she is convicted, the said Dudly afterwards came into the Court and by the statute in this case made and provided, chose all the goods and chattles of Joshua [Broadbent] except his oxen and beasts of the plow and his horse and armes for the militia and also the moyetie of all his lands and tenements in York Co. to be deliverd to him to be held as his freehold to him and his assigns, according to the form of the said statute untill the debt and damage therein menciond he hath thence levyed. Therefore, wee command you that all the goods and chattels of the said Joshuah except his oxen and best the plow and horse and armes for the militia and allso one moyetye of all the lands and tenements of the said Joshua in York Co. of which the said Joshua was levyed' or possessed at the time of his death in the hands of the said Izabella to be administerd without delay to the said Dudley, you shall cause to be deliverd by a reasonable price and extent the said goods and chattles to be held by him as his proper goods and chattles and allso the moyetye of the said lands and tenements to be held as his freehold by him and his assigns according to the forme of the said statute untill the debt and damage aforesaid he hath thence levied and this writt you have executed you shall certifie to the next Court. Dated Novr. 11th 1706. Thomas Ballard.

York Co., Jany. the 2nd 1706. In pursuance of the 10th in writ, I have seized one moyety of half of a certain Lot of Portland in York Towne with the appurtenances, which the said Joshua [Broadbent] died seized of... and have delivered the same to the said Dudly Diggs at a reasonable price (Viz: of £8 per annum, to be held as his freehold by him and his assignes), according to the forme of the statute in that case made and provided, untill the contents of the above judgment be fully satisfied and paid. Witness my hand the date above said. Wm. Barbar.

34

Bond. Ann Moreland, widow, and Francis Moreland of James Citty, Robert Harris and Bazill Wagstaff, all of the Co. of York, to the Justices of said County, in the sum of £500. Sureties for Ann Moreland and Francis Moreland as Extrs. of the Estate of John Moreland, dec'd., late of York Co. Dated this 28th day of Sepr. 1706. Wit. Willm. Tunley, Hester Sessions and Mary M. Wagstaf.

29. Bond. Joseph Walker, John Mihill and Joseph Chermison, all of the Co. of York, to the Justices of the said County, in the sum of £500. Dated this 24th day of December 1706. Sureties for Joseph Walker as Admr. of the Estate of Willm. Aylward, dec'd. Wit: Wm. Tunley.

30. Bond. Sarah Stannup, Robt. Crawley and Phillip Moody, to the Justices of York co., in the sume of £100. Sureties for Sarah Stannup as Admx. of the Estate of Richard Stannup. Dated the 24th of March 1706. Wit. Elizabeth Moody, J. Walker and Wm. Tunley.

December the 14th 1706. Noncupitive Will of Elizabeth Fillpot of Bruton Parish in the Co. of York. Willm. Thacker to have her son, James Merick, untill he comes of age and he should have two yeares schooling. If he dies before the age of 21, her small Estate to go to Willm. Thacker. Wit. Danll. Burton and Thomas Hayley.

31. At a Court held for York co. Jany. the 8th 1706 per adjournment from the 29th of December last past. Present: Robt. Read, Capt. Thomas Nutting, Col. Thomas Ballard, Capt. Lawc. Smith, Maj. Wm. Buckner and Capt. Wm. Timson, Justices.

Damazinah Browne, formerly Damazina Dixon, Extx. of the Last Will & Testament of Richard Dixon, late of this County, dec'd., this day made return of the account of the remainder of the said Testator's Estate according to her former oath which is orderd to be added to the inventory already on record.

Mary Whitby by her oath this day in Court prooved her accout of £1:15:0 against John Hilliard due for medicine and visits in the home of his families' sickness.

Abraham Royston, mulato son of Elizabeth Chilmaid, according to a former order of this Court, was this day bound an apprentice for the term of 7 yeares now next coming to Thomas Holliday, boatwright for the consideration mentioned in an Indenture of this present date, this day by the said Abraham and Thomas signed, seald, deliverd and acknowledgd each to other in the presence of the Court, which Indenture is orderd to be committed to record.

Wm. Davis, his bill from Robt. Philipson dated June the 28th 1705 was this day sworne to in Court by the said Davis that he never received any satisfaction for the sume, which is orderd to be certified.

Capt. Daniel Taylor, his Deed of Sale dated this present Instant from Col. Thomas Ballard and Major Willm. Buckner, Trustees of the Portland in York Towne, for the Portland Lot numbered 25 was by the said Trustees signd, seald and acknowlegd in Court and orderd to be committed to record.

Cornelius Wilson, his Deed of Sale dated this present Instant from Col. Thomas Ballard and Major Wm. Buckner, Trustees of the Portland in York Towne, for the Portland Lot numbered 44 was by the said Trustees signd, seald and acknowlegd in Court and orderd to be committed to record.

Wm. Gordon, his two Deeds of Sale dated the 24th day of June last from Col. Thomas Ballard and Major Willm. Buckner, Trustees of the Portland in York Towne, for the Portland Lots numbered 78 and 79 was by the said Trustees signd, seald and acknowlegd in Court and orderd to be committed to record.

It is orderd that Jon. Brooks, Willm. Lee and Willm. Davies or any two of them, meet at the house late of John Hilliard, dec'd. on the 13th of this present month and value in the best of their judgments the goods of the said dec'd. seized by Charles Collier for rent, being first sworn by the next Justice, and that a due return thereof be made to the next Court.

Charles Chiswell bringing his servant boy, Charles Elliot before this Court for a running away and craving an allowance for the same accordingly as the Law directs, and the boy confessing that he ran away the space of one whole week and killed his master's horse of the value of £10, which he stole at the time of his running away, the said motion is referd untill next Court for judgment.

In the suit depending on this Court between Wm. Farbar, plf. against Rebecca Pinkethman, Admx. of Timothy Pinkethman, dec'd. in an acion of case damage £10, the deft. by her Attorney pleads Plene Administravit and the suit is referd till next Court to argue the said plea.

Thomas Mountfort hath judgment of nihil dicit this day granted against Henry Fleming in an acion of debt damage £30, and the next Court to be confirmd on the like default.

The suit depending to this Court between John Adduston Rogers and Jane, his wife, Admrs. of Henry Andrews, dec'd., plfs. against Damazinah Dixon,

Extx. of Richard Dixon, dec'd. in an acion of debt damage £12 is referd for proof of the plf.'s declaration.

Damazinah Dixon, Extx. of the Last Will & Testament of Richard Dixon, dec'd., this day in Court confessed judgment to Jno. Penton in an acion of case for the sume of £7.8 due by account and is ordered forthwith to pay it to the plf. with costs alies execution.

32. The suit referd to this Court for tryall between Robt. Faldo, plf. and John Loynes, deft. in an acion of ejectione firmae, on objections this day made against the Sheriff summoning a jury to try the issue being of him to the plf., is continued till the next Court and it is orderd that the Coroner of the Parish of York in this County summon an able jury to try at the next Court.

The petition of Willm. Davis and Elizabeth, his wife, Admx. of Thomas Jefferson, dec'd., against the Estate of James Darbyshire is continued till the next Court.

In the suit depending to this Court between Wm. Cant, plf. and Henry Hales, deft. in an acion of case wherein the plf. declared for the sume of 2,000 lbs. of tobaco and cask convenient in the upper part of York Co., which the said Henry the 8th day of March last did assume to pay to the said Willm. for a certain woman servant named Elizabeth Mallory, which the said Willm. did sell and deliver to the said Henry, who denyed payment to the damage of the said Willm. £20 and therefore brought suit, to which the deft. by Richd. Whotton, his Attorney, pleaded that the plf. and his agent refused to accept a lawfull tender and put himself on his country and the plf. likewise. Whereupon a jury (viz) John Wyth, John Dozwell Senr., Thomas Walker, Simon Stacy, John Chapman, Thomas Wotten, Willm. Wise Junr., John Loynes, Wm. Davis, John Wills, Willm. Sheldon and Henry Hayward Senr. was impanelld and sworn to try the issue, who after a full hearing of all evidences and pleas departed to consult their verdict, which on their return (the plf. and deft. being called), was read (Viz) Wee find for the plf. £13:10, signd Henry Hayward, which on mocion of Stephens Thompson, Attorney of the plf., is comitted to record and it is considerd that the plf. recover of the deft. his damage aforesaid in forme aforesaid by the inquisition found with costs alies execution.

John Bates being summond an evidence for Henry Hales, deft. against Will Cant, plf. in an acion of case is orderd to be paid 160 lbs. of tobaco for 4 days attendance at 40 lbs. per day according to act with costs.

Lawc. Smith, Gent., his attachment formerly obtained against the Estate of James Wyth is continued till the next Court.

In the suit depending to the Court between Robt. Mynne, plf. against Andrew Young, deft. in an acion of case, the plf. hath time to mend his declaration, paying costs.

In the suit depending to the Court between John Sergenton, plf. and John Nicholson, deft. in an acion of debt, the plf. hath upon the deft. demurred time to mend his declaracion, paying costs, or join in demurrence.

Thomas Whitby hath judgment of nihil dicit this day granted against Isaac Jamart, Admr. of Willm. Chalkhill, dec'd., deft. in an acion of debt declared for the sume of £4 with costs and the next Court to be confirmd on the like default.

Thomas Green, his acion of case to this Court against Rebecca Pinkethman, Admx. of Timothy Pinkethman, dec'd. is dismisst, he failing further to prosecute.

Charles Cox, his acion of debt against Anthony Jesper depending to this Court is dismissed, he failing further to prosecute.

In the suit depending to this Court between Jno. Adduston Rogers and Jane, his wife, Admrs. of Henry Andrews, dec'd., plfs. and Thomas Walker deft. in an acion of case wherein the plfs. declare that the deft. on the first day of November 1705 was indebted to the said Henry the sume of £25:8:9 for severall goods, wares and merchandize sold by the said Henry to the said Thomas for which the said Thomas did assume to pay to the said Henry in his lifetime the said sume of £25:8:9, which assumsion not minding, did not pay the said sume now as yet to the plfs. as aforesaid, tho often thereunto required. Whereupon they brought suit, to which the deft. by Samll. Selden, his Attorney, pleaded non assumpsit in manner and forme. Whereupon a jury was impannelled and sworne to try the issue. (Viz) Charles Collier, J.W. Wells, Simon Stacy, Willm. Wise Junr., John Dozwell Senr., John Chapman, John Loynes, Thomas Wooton, Willm. Davis, Willm. Sheldon, Henry Hayward Senr. and John Wythe, who after a full hearing of all evidence and pleas departed to consult their verdict, which on their return, after the plf. and deft. being calld, was read (Viz) Wee find for the plf. £23:7:6, signed Henry Hayward, foreman. And on motion of the plf.'s Attorney, Stephens Thompson, is recorded and it is considered that the plfs. recover of the deft. their damage aforesaid in forme aforesaid by the inquisition found with costs alies execution.

33. John Dozwell Junr. being summoned an evidence for John Adduston Rogers, plf. against Thomas Walker, deft. in an acion of case, is orderd to be paid 40 lbs. of tobaco for one days attendance, according to act with costs.

John Adduston Rogers and Jane, his wife, Admrs. of Henry Andrews, dec'd., hath judgment this day granted against Peter Gibson in an acion of case for the sume of £1:10, being the just ballance of account between the said dec'd. and deft., and ordered to be paid with costs alies execution.

John Adduston Rogers and Jane, his wife, Admx. of Hen. Andrews, dec'd. hath judgment this day granted against Use Gibson in an acion of case for the sum of £2:7:8, being the ballance of all accounts between the dec'd. and deft., and is orderd to be paid with costs alies execution.

Thomas Bass hath judgement this day granted against John Dickeson in an acion of debt for the sume of £1:18:4 due by bill dated under the deft.'s hand May the 3d 1706 and is orderd to be paid with costs alies execution.

Joshua Sled hath judgment this day granted against John Duke in an acion of case for the sum of £1:5 due by account… and is ordered to be paid with costs alies execution.

Peter Gibson's acion of case depending against Thomas Whitby is dismisst, he failing further to prosecute.

Peter Gibson's acion of case depending against Elizabeth Hansford is dismisst, the plf. failing further to prosecute.

The suit depending to this Court between James Ming, plf. and Danll. Park, Esqr., deft. in an acion of case wherein the plf. declared for the sum of 4032 lbs. of tobacco due for surveying of 1080 acres of land in King William Co. on the 20th day of July 1702, being hired and imployd by the deft. …to the duty of a Surveyor and allso 310 lbs. of tobacco for other services thereabout due and expended for transport of horses, loss of time in going and returning and five days upon that service upon the Survey amounting to the sum of 4,342 lbs. of tobacco, which the deft. refuseth to pay and therefore the plf. brought suit. To which the deft. by Stephens Thompson, his Attorney, pleaded that the plf. his acion ought not to have because he did not agree with, hire, or imploy the said James as in his declaracion is set forth at any time within three yeares next before his comencing that acion. To which the plf. by Richd. Whitby, his Attorney, replys and sayes that he ought not to be precluded from this acion for this Jane Park, wife and Attorney of the deft. then beyond the seas, made request to the plf. on the 20th day of July 1702 to forbear to sue for the said debt till the comeing in of the then next fleet and she would then pay him, from which time and untill the plf. brought suit three yeares did not elaps. To which replyed the deft. by the said Stephens Thompson, her Attorney, demures Genll. and the plf. obtaines time to mend his replycacion, paying costs or rejoyn, which reply being amended, the said Thompson this day againe generally demures to, which demurer being argued, is found good and the suit is dismisst with costs.

From which judgment the plf. appeals to the Hon. and Genll. Court for tryall and Joseph Chermison and Richd. Wharton as securities of the said James entred into bond for the said James' due prosecution of the said appeal according to Law.

In the suit depending to this Court between Benjamin Lillingston, plf. and Rebeca Pinkethman, Admx. of Timothy Pinkethman, dec'd. in an acion of case, the deft. this day by George Baskervile, her Attorney, put in her plea in writing (Viz) Plene Administravit, and the plf. hath time till next Court to reply.

34. In the suit depending to this Court between Benje. Lillingstone, plf. and Rebeca Pinkethman, Admx. of Timothy Pinkethman, dec'd. in an acion of case, the deft. this day by George Baskervile, her Attorney, put in her plea in writing (viz) Plene Administravit, and the plf. hath time till next Court to reply.

John Cooper, his plea in arrest of judgment depending to this Court against Thomas Whitby and Mary, his wife, Extrs. of Thomas Collier, dec'd., this day being argued is overruled and dismisst with costs. From which, the said John Cooper by his Attorney, Wm. Blackburn, appealed to the Hon. and Genll. Court for tryall. And Willm. Blackburn, Attorney of the said John, together with Richd. Wharton, his securety, hath entred into bond for the due prosecucion of the said appeal according to Law.

Thomas Nutting, Gent., hath judgment this day granted against Damazinah Dixon, Extx. of the last Will & Testament of Richd. Dixon, dec'd. in an acion of case for the sume of £5:14:3 due by account proovd in Court by the plf.'s oath, and is orderd to be paid with costs alies execution.

This Court is adjourned to the 24th Instant.

At a Court held for York Co. Jany. 24 1706. Present Coll. Thomas Ballard, Capt. Lawc. Smith, Robt. Reade, Willm. Pinkethman, and Major Wm. Buckner, Justices.

Col. Miles Cary, Surveyor of this County, this day in Court took a solemn oath for his true and faithfull execution to discharge to the best of his knowledge and power his said trust, office and imployment according to a late Law entituled an Act Directing the Duty of Surveyors of Land and Ascertaining Their Fees.

James Hubbard this day made suit to the Court that Willm. Hansford might be admitted his Guardian and not showing sufficient reason, is denied.

It is orderd that Willm. Rylands be summond to the next Court to answer the complaint of Josiah Draper.

Upon the petition of James Broster, Orphan of John Broster, James Bennet is appointed his Guardian if betwixt this and the next Court he enter into bond with John Pond and Thomas Page, his securetyes for the due performance of his trust therein, according to Law.

On the petition of Wm. Wise Junr., Contable of the lower precinque of Charles Parish in this County, Edmund Curtis is appointed his head borough and it is orderd that he be sworn before the next Justices to perform his office and duty therein as the Law requires.

It is orderd that Nicholas Philips be summond to the next Court to answer the complaint of Amie Banks, who shows that she hath fullfilled her time by Indenture or other obligation and is detained contrary to all Law and justice.

Richard Oliver of the Island of Barbados, Esqr., his Deeds of Sale by way of Lease and Release dated under the hand and seal of John Martin of York Parish and Co. in Virginia the 20th and 21st of this Instant Jany. for about 470 acres of land in Warwick Co. in this Collony was this day personally acknowledged in Court by the said John Martin and orderd to be committed to record.

John Bates, his Deed of Sale bearing dated under the hand and seale of Robert Ivory, Novr. the 26th 1706 for 100 acres of land more or less situate in Bruton Parish in this Co. was this day in Court personally acknowledged by the said Robt. to the said John and orderd to be comitted to record.

35. Mrs. Mary Whaley, her Deed of Sale bearing date under the hands and seals of George Brack and Margt., his wife, of the Co. of James Citty November 25th 1706 for the Reversion of a certaine messuage [?]ment now or late in the occupation of Charles Chiswell, together with 100 acres of land thereto belonging, situate in the Co. of York and James Citty, after the private examination of the said Mary, it was personally acknowledged in Court by the said George and Margt. to the said Mary and ordered to be comitted to record.

On mocion of Stephens Thomson, Attorney of Our Sovereigne Lady the Queen, it is orderd that the Sheriff take and in his safe custody keep Diana, the wife of Joseph Dwite till she gives bond with good and sufficient security to appear at the next Court held for this County, then and there to answer on the Maj.'s behalf the complaint of Hen. Hayles.

Use Gibson, his Power of Attorney from Thomas Rose bearing date the 24th of this Instant was this day proovd in Court by the oath of Nathll. Huggens, one of the evidences thereto, and orderd to be committed to record.

The acion of debt brought against Willm. Dalton by William Barbar is dismisst, the plf. failing to prosecute.

In the suit depending to this Court between Adam Galt, plf. and Mungo Somerwell, deft. in an acion of case declared for the sum of £10 by the plf. lent to the deft., who did assume to pay the same to the plf. when thereto required, but not regarding his promise the same hath not paid, wherefore the plf. brought suit and to which the deft. pleads that he owes the plf. nothing and put himself on his country, and the plf. likewise. Whereupon a jury (viz) Willm. Davies, Edward Palmer, Thomas Wooten, John Adduston Rogers, John Bedford, Joseph Dwite, Willm. Hansford, Samll. Cooper, Thomas Whitby, Jno. Drury, Humphry Nixon and Henry Hayward Junr. was impanelld and sworn to try the issue, who after a full hearing of all evidences and pleas produced, departed to consult their verdict, which on their return, the plf. and deft. being calld, was read (viz) Wee find for the plf. £10 current money, signd Willm. Handsford, which on mocion of Richd. Wharton, the plf.'s Attorney, is admitted to record and it is considered that the plf. recover of the deft. his damage aforesaid in form aforesaid by the inquisition with costs alies execution. From which judgment, the said Mungo appeals to the Hon. and Genll. Court for tryall and accordingly entered into bond with security according to Law.

In the suit depending to this Court between Walter Cromby, plf. and Mungo Somerwell, deft. in an acion of case declared for the sume of £3... lent by the plf. to the deft., who assumed and promised to pay the same to the plf. when thereto required, but not regarding his promise hath not paid the same nor any part thereof altho by that plf. he hath been thereto required, so herefore the plf. brought suit, to which the deft. pleads the he oweth the plf. nothing and put himself on his Country and the plf. likewise. Whereupon a jury (viz) Willm. Davies, Edward Palmer, Thomas Wooten, John Adduston Rogers, John Bedford, Joseph Dwyte, Wm. Hansford, Samll. Cooper, Thomas Whitby, John Drury, Humphry Nixon and Henry Hayward Junr. were impannelld and sworne to try the issue, who after a full hearing of all evidences and pleas departed to consult their verdict. And on their return the plf. and deft. being calld, returned for verdict, Wee find for the plf. £3 current money, signd Wm. Handsford, foreman. And on mocion of the plf.'s Attorney it is admitted to record and it is orderd that the plf. recover of the deft. his damage aforesaid in forme aforesaid by the inquisition found with costs alies execution. From which judgment, the plf. appeals to the Hon. and the Generall Court for tryall and accordingly entred into bond with his security to prosecute the said appeal.

In the suit depending to this Court between Wm. Kaydie, plf. and Mungo Somerwell, deft. in an acion of case declard for the sume of £9:10… by the plf. lent to the deft., who assumed and promisst to pay the same to the plf., but not regarding his promiss, hath not paid the same nor any part thereof altho thereunto requird. Wherefore the plf. brought suit, to which the deft. pleaded non assumpsit and put himself on his Country and the plf. likewise. Whereupon a jury (viz) Wm. Davis, Edwd. Palmer, Thomas Wooten, John Adduston Rogers, John Bedford, Joseph Dwite, Wm. Handsford, Samll. Cooper, Thomas Whitby, John Drury, Humpy. Nixon and John Tomer was impanelld and sworn to try the issue, who after a full hearing of all evidences and pleas produced, and the plf.'s oath to his account of sumes lent, departed to consult their verdict and on their return, the plf. and deft. being calld, returnd for verdict, Wee find for the plf. £9:10 current mony, signd Wm. Handsford, which on moccion of Stephens Thompson, Attorney for the plf., is admitted to record and it is considerd that the plf. recover of the deft. his damage aforesaid in form aforesaid by the inquisition found with costs alies execution.

36. The acion of case of John Andrews, plf. against James Bowman, deft. is dismisst, no cause of acion appearing.

Wm. Barbar, Gent, H.S., his attachment obtaind against the Estate of James Bowman is dismisst for non prosecution.

Henry Hayward Junr. hath judgment of nihil dicit this day granted against John Dozwell, Senr. in an acion of debt for the sume of £13:13:1 ½ due by protested Bills of Exchange dated Augt. 18th 1705, together allso with his damage of 15% charge of protest and costs and the next Court to be confirmd on the like default.

Wm. Barbar, H.S., his attachment formerly obtained against John Dozwell Senr. is dismisst for non prosecution.

John Tomer hath judgment of nihil dicit this day granted against John Wills and Elizabeth, his wife, Extrs. of Thomas Harwood, dec'd. in an acion of case for his damage of £10 and the next Court to be confirmd on the like default.

Peter Gibson, his acion of case against John Thomas is dismisst, not proving his declaration.

43

Thomas Handsford, his acion of case against Isaac Sedgwick, Extr. of Willm. Sedgwick, dec'd. is dismisst, no cause of acion appearing.

Charles Bartelot hath judgment of nihil dicit this day granted against Thomas Grayham, late of Pensilvania and Nathll. Maclanan, late of Princes Anne Co. in an acion of debt for the sume of £600 of current money due by bond under the defts.' hands and seales dated April the 26th 1706, and the next Court to be confirmd on the like default.

John Bates, his attachment formerly obtaind against Alexander Miller in an acion of debt is continued till the next Court.

John Bates, his order formerly obtaind against Willm. Barbar, H.S., for the sume of £1:8:2 for the non appearance of Thomas Pinket to answer the suit of the said Bates in an acion of debt declared for the said sum being due by a protested noat under the said Pinket's hand Feby. the 7th 1705/6 is confirmed, the said Pinket now likewise failing to appeare and answer the said suit, and it is orderd that the said Wm. Barbar pay the said sume to the plf. with costs alies execution.

Wm. Barbar, Gent, H.S., his attachment formerly obtained against Thomas Pinket's Estate, is continued till the next Court.

John Handsford hath judgment this day granted against Wm. Barbar, Admr. of Jon. Brice, dec'd. in an acion of debt for the sume of £3:15 due by bill under the decedent's hand Octr. the 29th 1703 and is orderd to be paid with costs alies execution.

Henry Duke hath judgment this day granted against John Corklin in an acion of debt for the sume of £5 due by bill dated Jany. 1st 1704/5 and is orderd to be paid with costs alies execution.

The Court is adjourned to the 24th of February next.

37. At a Court held for York Co. Feb 24th 1706. Present: Capt. Thomas Barbar, Robt. Reade, Capt. Daniel Taylor, Col. Thomas Ballard, Capt. Thomas Nutting, Thomas Roberts, Capt. Lawc. Smith, Maj. Wm. Buckner and Wm. Pinkethman, Justices.

Maj. Wm. Cary of Warwick Co., his Deed of Sale bearing date this present Instant from Col. Thomas Ballard and Majr. Wm. Buckner, Trustees for the Portland of York Towne, for the Portland lot no. 48, was this day personally acknowledged in Court and admitted to record.

Capt. Lawrence Smith, his Deed of Sale bearing date the Tenth of this Instant from Col. Thomas Ballard and Major Wm. Buckner, Trustees for the Portland of York Town, for the Portland lot no. 53, was this day personally acknowledged in Court and admitted to record.

Humphry Moody, his Deed of Sale bearing date the third of this Instant from Col. Thomas Ballard and Majr. William Buckner, Trustees of the Portland of York Town, for Portland lott number 45, was this day personally acknowledged in Court and admitted to record.

William Harwood, his Deed of Sale bearing date the 22nd of this Instant from Col. Thomas Ballard and Majr. William Buckner, Trustees of the Portland of York Town, for Portland lott number 66, was this day acknowledged in Court and admitted to record.

James Shields, on his petition this day obtained order for a Lycense to keep an ordinary at his dwelling house in the city of Wmsburgh in this County for the ensueing year if he enter into bond with Richard Wharton and John Loynes, his securitys to performe his duty therein as the Law directs.

Elizabeth Somerwell, widow and relict of Mungo Somerwell, late of this County, dec'd., on her petition hath order granted for a comission of Administration of the said decedent's Estate if she enter into bond with James Slater and John Wyth, her securitys for the performance thereof according to Law.

It is ordered that the estate of Mungo Somerwell, late of this County, dec'd. be appraised at his late dwelling house on the fifth day of the next month by John Martin, Bazill Wagstaff, William Allin and Phillip Dodman or any three of them in the best of their judgments, being first sworn before the next Justice, and that a due returne thereof be made to the next Court and that the Clerk attend the appraisement.

It is orderd that the Clerk on the account of the County pay unto Michael Archer on order 400 lbs. of tobaco for the abridgment of the new Laws this day presented in Court.

Certificate according to Act of Assembly was this day granted unto Joseph Chermison for his owne right, he making oath that as yet never any land taken up for him by himself aut alies est.

Certificate according to Act of Assembly was this day granted unto Mary Ramsey for the following rights [Viz] James Ramsey, John Ramsey, David Ramsey and Mary Ramsey, she making oath that as yet never any land was ever taken up for them by her aut alies est.

John Crombie is appointed Constable for York Town instead of Mungo Sommerwell, late dec'd., and it is orderd that he be sworn before the next Justice for the performance of his duty therein according to Law.

On petition of Thomas Cox, John Gibbons is appointed his Guardian instead of Thomas Gibbons, late dec'd. if he enter into bond with good and sufficient security for performance of his duty therein according to Law betwixt this and the next Court.

An Inventory & Appraisement of the Estate of Elizabeth Philpott, late of this County, dec'd., according to a former order of this Court was this day returnd by Wm. Thacker, Admr. of the same, on oath, which is ordered to be committed to record.

Certificate according to Act of Assembly was this day granted unto Henry Gilbert for his owne right, he making oath that as yett never any land was taken up for him by himself aut alies est.

Certificate according to Act of Assembly was this day granted unto Willm. Sherman for his owne right, he making oath that as yett never any land was taken up for him by himself aut alies est.

John Saunders, Constable of the lower precinque of Hampton Parish in this County, on his petition, is discharged from his said office and Willm. Davis , carter, is appointed in his stead and it is ordered that he be sworn before the next Justice for the due performance of his office therein, according to Law.

38. Joseph Dwyte is appointed constable for the lower precinque of Bruton Parish in this County and it is orderd that he be sworne before the next Justice for the due performance of his duty therein, according to Law.

The petition of John Hunt Junr. and Thomas Woodfield in behalf of themselves and wifes, Legatees of Richard Dixon, dec'd., complaining to Damazinah Brown, formerly Dixon, Extx. of Richard Dixon, dec'd., hath not rendered to this Court a perfect inventory of the said Testator's Estate, was this day read in Court and she the said Damazinah hath time till the next Court to perfect the said inventory.

James Wallace, clerk, his test. of medicaments administerd to Richard Dixon in the time of his sickness, was this day proved in Court by his the said James' own oath and admitted to be lodged in the office.

Wm. Sherman this day in Court appointed Samuell Seldon his Generall Attorney and at his request the same is admitted to record.

Whereas by the late Law entituled an Act Prescribing the Method of Appointing Sheriffs, it is enacted that the Court of every County within this Dominion, at some convenient time between the last day of Jany. and the last day of March yearly, shall present to the Governor or Comander in Chiefe of this Dominion for the time being a list or recommendation of three such persons (being Justices) in the same County Court respectively as they shall think most fitt and able to execute the office of Sheriff of their respective County for the year then next ensueing, it is therefore ordered that the clerk returne to the Governor or Commander in Chiefe for the time being before the last day of March next a list of Capt. Wm. Timson, Wm. Barbar and Wm. Pinkethman, who are by said Court thought most fitt and able persons of this the Justices of this County to execute the said Office of Sheriff.

John Hawkins, his Deeds of Sale by way of Lease and Release both bearing date this present Instant for a tract of land lying and being in Charles Parish in this County from William Whitaker and Sarah, his wife, together also with the bond to perform the covenants therein contained, and after the private examinacion of said Sarah, was personally acknowledged in Court and ordered to be comitted to record.

Henry Hayles, his acion of debt against Thomas Pinket is dismist, the plf. failing further to prosecute.

Job Williams, his attachment formerly obtained against James Blackhurst is dismisst, the plf. failing further to prosecute.

John Bates, his acion of case against Edward Foulks is dismist, the plf. failing further to prosecute.

William Tunley hath judgment by nihil dicit this day granted against Peter Gibson and Use Gibson in an acion of case for the sume of 1,750 lbs. of tobaco and the next Court to be confirmed on the like default.

John Martin hath judgment this day granted against Richard Brown and Damazinah, his wife, Extx. of Richard Dixon, dec'd. in an acion of debt for the sume of £13 due by protested Bills of Exchange dated May the 10th 1705, and is ordered to be payd with his damage of 15% of costs charge of protest and costs of suit alies execution.

John Andrews, his acion of case against James Bowman is dismist, no cause of acion appearing.

Richard Drewry, his acion of trespass on the case against John Sergenton was dismist, the plf. failing further to prosecute.

Thomas Wotton hath judgment this day granted against Lydia Broster, Admx. of John Broster, in an acion of case for the sume of 530 lbs. of tobacco due by account proved in Court and is ordered to be payd with costs alies execution.

In the suit depending to this Court between James Bowman, plf. and Wm. Casey, deft. in an acion of case, the plf. is nonsuited with costs, not further prosecuting.

John Dukes hath judgment by nihil dicit this day granted against Nicholas Phillips in an acion of case damage £8 and the next Court to be confirmed on the like default.

Thomas Burnam, his action of trespass depending to this Court against John Wells is dismist per non prosecution.

Henry Hayles, his acion of debt to this Court depending against John Morris and Henry Tyler is dismist per non prosecution.

Stephens Thomson, his action of case damage £5 depending against William Hansford is continued by consent.

39. Henry Emerson, his attachment formerly obtained against John Ross' acion of case damage £10 is continued till the next Court.

Barentine Howells, his acion of trespass depending to this Court againt Nathaniell Huggins is dismist per non prosecution.

John Pond hath judgement this day granted against Benjamin Shepherd in an acion of debt for the sume of 600 lbs. of tobacco and two barrills of Indian Corn due by bill dated under the deft.'s hand Feby. the 27th 1705, and the deft. on his mocion hath an injunction in Chancery granted him for his relisse[?] against the said bill.

John Bates, an acion of trespass brought to this Court against Richard Jones is dismist per non prosecution.

In the suit brought to this Court by John Marrat, plf. against Anthony Jesper in an acion of debt, the deft. hath an imparlance granted till next Court.

In the suit brought to this Court by John Maratt, plf. against Timothy Johnson, deft. in an acion of case, the deft. hath an imparlance granted till the next Court.

John Marratt, his acion of debt to this Court brought against Rephon[?] Penten is dismist, the plf. failing to prosecute.

In the suit brought to this County by Joseph Chermison, plf. against Oliver Perron, deft. in an acion of case, the deft. hath an imparlance granted till the next Court and Capt. James Bray in Court assumed the said Joseph's security for his appearance and his abiding and standing to the award and judgment of the Court.

Peter Manson, his acion of debt brought to this Court against William Coman is dismist, the plf. failing further to prosecute.

Henry Lightfoot, his acion of case brought to this Court against Robert Case is dismist, the plf. failing further to prosecute.

In the suite brought to this Court by William Farbar, plf. against Timothy Johnson, deft. in an acion of debt, an imparlance is granted the deft. till the next Court.

In the suite brought to this Court by William Farbar, plf. against Timothy Johnson, deft. in an acion of case, an imparlance is granted the deft. till the next Court.

Joseph Chermison, his attachment obtained against the Estate of Oliver Perron from a Justice of the Peace of this County, is dissolved on the appearance of the said Oliver.

John Owen, his acion of case damage £110 brought to this Court against David Robertson, mariner, is dismist, the plf. not further prosecuting.

In the suite brought to this Court by John Owen, plf. against David Robertson, mariner, deft. in an acion of case damage £160, an imparlance is granted the deft. till the next Court.

James Aynsworth of the Island of Barbadoes, merchant, his acion of case to this Court brought against John Hunt is dismist, the deft. being dead.

Joseph Dunbar, his acion of case brought to this Court against Carroline Wilson is dismist, the plf. failing further to prosecute.

Thomas Harton, his acion of case brought to this Court against James Bowman is dismist, the plf. failing further to prosecute.

Thomas Harton and Elinor, his wife, their acion of trespas against James Bowman and Mary, his wife is dismist, the plfs. failing further to prosecute.

49

Thomas Mountfort arresting Use Gibson to this Court in an acion of case damage £50 and he not appearing, order is granted against Wm. Barbar, Shf., and the next Court to be confirmed if he causeth not the deft. then personally to appear and answer the same.

Thomas Mountfort arresting Edward Newman to this Court in an acion of case for £1:10 and he not appearing, order is granted against John Dozwell Senr., his security, and the next Court to be confirmed if he causeth not the deft. then personally to appear and answer the same.

Wm. Kaidye, his acion of case brought to this Court against Adam Galt is referred to the next Court at the deft.'s request.

40. Barbara Hutton being summond to this Court to answer the Informacion of John Wythe, Church Warden of York Parish, and she not appearing, it is ordered that the Sheriff take and in safe custody keep the said Barbara Hutton untill she enter into bond with good and sufficient security for her personall appearance at the next Court to answer the said Informacion.

William Tunley arresting David Robertson to this Court in an acion of case for the sume of 321 lbs. of tobacco and he not appearing, order is granted against Wm. Barbar, Sheriff, and the next Court to be confirmed if he causeth not the deft. then personally to appear and answer the same.

Wm. Bentwell, his acion of debt against Isaac Hill is dismist, no party appearing.

John Cromby arresting Ephriam Corket to this Court in an acion of case damage £3 and he not appearing, order is granted against Andrew Young, his security, and the next Court to be confirmed if he causeth not the deft. then personally to appear and answer the same.

John Keydon, his acion of case against William Rowis is dismist, no party appearing.

John Martin, his acion of debt against John Dozwell Junr. is dismist, no party appearing.

William Tunley, his acion of case to this Court against Ralph Baker is continued till the next Court by consent.

John Penton's acion of debt to this Court against Joseph Mountfort is dismisst, neither party appearing.

50

Thomas Mountfort arresting Samuell Cooper to this Court in an acion of case damage £20 and he not appearing, order is granted against William Barbar, Sheriff, and the next Court to be confirmed if he causeth not the deft. then personally to appear and answer the same.

Thomas Mountfort arresting William Roberts to this Court in an acion of case for the sume of £1:15 and he not appearing, order is granted against Use Gibson, his security, and the next Court to be confirmed if he causeth not the deft. then personally to appear and answer the same.

Andrew Young, his acion of debt to this Court against Henry Dukes is dismisst, neither party appearing.

Richard Wharton, his acion of debt damage £100 against John Redwood is continued to the next Court by consent.

Wm. Timson, his acion of debt brought to this Court against Robert Green is dismist, neither party appearing.

In the suite brought to this Court by Hester Sessions, plf. against Barintine Howells, deft. in an acion of debt, the deft. on mocion of Henry Holdcraft, his Attorney, hath an imparlance granted till the next Court.

John Pond hath judgment this day granted against John Adduston Rogers in a plea of debt for the sume of 856 lbs. of tobacco due by bill and is ordered to be payd with costs alies execution.

Silas Love, his acion of debt against John Comes is dismist per non prosecution.

Wm. Tunley acion of case against Wm. Brown is dismist per non prosecution.

Thomas Hill's acion of trespas against Mathias Henderson is dismisst per non prosecution.

Lewis Burwell's, acion of debt against Thomas Lamb is refered for the Sheriff's oath to his returne of the Writt.

Wm. Tunley's acion of case against Ralph Baker is continued by consent.

Thomas Page arresting Lydia Broster, Admx. of John Broster, dec'd. to this Court in an acion of debt and not further prosecuting, the suite is dismist.

Edward Moss, his acion of debt against Lydye Broster, Admx. of John Broster, dec'd. is by consent continued for proofe of the declaracion.

James Calthrop's acion of case against Lydia Broster, Admx. of John Broster, dec'd. is dismist per non prosecution.

Use Gibson arresting Ralph Baker to this Court in an acion of case and not further prosecuting, is nonsuited with costs.

John Gibbons being by the Sheriff returned summoned for Ralph Baker, deft. against Use Gibson, plf. in an acion of case, is ordered to be payd 80 lbs. of tobacco for 2 days attendance at Court at 40 per day according to act with costs alies execution.

John Penton arresting Michaell Cormack to this Court in an acion of debt damage £20 and he not appearing, order is granted against Thomas Mountfort, his security, and the next Court to be confirmed if he causeth not the deft. then personally to appear and answer the same.

41. Isaac Jamart, Admr. of William Chalkhill, dec'd., his plea in arrest of judgment against John Owen (to arrest the judgment by him obtained at a Court held for this County on the 25th day of September Last against the said Isaac as Admr. aforesaid) Viz. And the said deft. by Robert Hyde, his Attorney, comes and humbly moves in arrest of judgment for these following causes. First for that the said plf. hath not proved his acion for which he hath brought his suite by one wittness before himselfe and his own oath that there is no discount to be made or what discount to be allowed to the said deft., and also for that the said plf. hath not made it appear that his account was contracted before the death of the said William, which he ought to have. And for that the said plf. in his acion hath charged the said William with protested bills of exchange, which he alledgeth to be protested and so named in his account without showing any [proof?] in Court. Also if any protest of the said bills yet it could not be before this suite brought, therefore cannot maintain this acion, all which this deft. saith are sworn, for which this deft. saith that the said judgment ought to be arrested, and being this day the deft. argued and the causes found not sufficient to arrest the judgment, wherefore the said judgment is confirmed. From which judgment the said Isaac appeals to the Hon. and Genll. Court for tryall and accordingly entered into bond with security to prosecute the said appeale.

The former order for the returne of the outcry of John Hilliard's Estate is continued till the next Court.

The former order for Mary Hilliard, relict of John Hilliard, dec'd. to returne an account of the said dec'd. Estate is continued till the next Court.

The former order for the summoning of Joshua Sled to this Court to answer the complaint of Mary Lymus is continued till the next Court.

Charles Chiswell, his complaint against Charles Elliot, his servant, for running away is continued till the next Court for judgment.

William Farbar hath judgment this day granted against Rebecca Pinkethman, Admx. of Timothy Pinkethman, dec'd. in an acion of case for the sume of £3:1:3 for severall goods, wares and merchandizes... delivered by the plf. to the said dec'd. for which the said dec'd. assumed payment, and the said plf. is ordered to be payd with costs when assess alies execution.

Thomas Mountfort hath judgment this day granted against Henry Flemming in an acion of debt for the sume of £9:10:7 half peny due by ballance of the condicion of a bond bearing date under his hand and seale Jany. the 9th 1700 and is ordered to be payd with costs alies execution.

Charles Pain being by the Sheriff summoned to this Court an evidence for Henry Flemming, deft. against Thomas Mountfort in an acion of debt, is ordered to be payd 200 lbs. of tobacco for 5 days attendance at Court at 40 lbs. per day according to act with costs.

In the suite depending to this Court between John Adduston Rogers and Jane, his wife, Admrs. of Henry Andrews, dec'd., plfs. against Damazinah Dixon, Extx. of Richard Dixon, dec'd. in an acion of debt declared for the sume of £12 ...which the said Richard in his lifetime for severall goods, wares and merchandizes by him received did assume to pay to the said Henry in his lifetime, but never payd the same nor any parte thereof, to that the deft. pleaded non assumpsit in maner and forme, whereupon a jury Viz: John Mihille, Thomas Wootton, Edmund Curtis, Charles Collier, Thomas Whitby and John Dozwell was impanelled and sworne to try the issue, who after a full hearing of all evidences and pleas on boath sides, departed to consult their verdict and on their returne, plf. and deft. being called, returned for verdict, Wee find for the plf. £9:17:4, signed John Mihill, foreman. Which on request of Stephens Thomson, Attorney for the plf., is admitted to record and it is considered that the plf. recover of the deft. the damage aforesaid in maner aforesaid by the inquisition found with costs alies execution.

In the suite depending to this Court between Robert Faldo, plf. against John Loyns, deft. in an ejectione firmae, the plf. failing to prosecute is nonsuited with costs.

Robert Bee being summoned an evidence for John Loynes, deft. against Robert Faldo, plf. hath order granted to be payd 160 lbs. of tobacco for 4 days attendance at Court at 40 per day according to Act with costs.

Wm. Coman, the likewise for 5 days attendance.

Wm. Davis and Elizabeth, his wife, their petition against the Estate of James Darbyshire, dec'd. is dismist per non prosecution.

Lawrence Smith's attachment against James Wyth the like.

42. In the suite depending to this Court between Robert Mynne, plf. against Andrew Young, deft., the plf. this day mending his declaracion, the deft. obtained time till the next Court to plead.

In the suite depending to this Court between John Sergenton, plf. against John Nicholson, deft. in an acion of debt, the declaracion of the plf. being this day amended, the deft. obtained time to consider it.

In the suite depending to this Court between Thomas Whitby, plf. and Isaac Jamart, Admr. of Wm. Chalkhill, deft. in an acion of debt, the deft. this day pleaded that he had fully administered and the plf. replyed that the deft. he had not fully administered and the issue is referred till the next Court for tryall.

Benjamin Lillingston hath judgment this day granted against Rebecca Pinkethman, Admx. of Timothy Pinkethman, dec'd. in an acion of case for the sume of £9:13:1 due by account and is ordered to be payd with costs when assess alies execution.

Thomas Lee arresting John Redwood to this Court in an acion of debt damage £20 and he not appearing, order is granted against Wm. Barbar, Sheriff, and the next Court to be confirmed if he causeth not the deft. then personally to appear and answer the same.

Richard Wharton arresting Thomas Pinket to this Court in an acion of debt for the sume of £5 and he not appearing, order is granted against Wm. Barbar, Sheriff, and the next Court to be confirmed on the like default.

Wm. Barbar, Sheriff, hath an attachment granted against the Estate of John Redwood for the sume of £20 with costs returnable to the next Court, he the said Redwood failing to appear at this Court to answer the suite of Thomas Lee for the like sume.

James Bray, Assignee of John Austin, his acion of debt against Thomas Fear Junr. is dismist, the plf. failing further to prosecute.

In the suite in Chancery brought to this Court by Joseph Walker, Admr. of William Aylward, dec'd., complainant against Wm. Davis and Eliz., his wife, Admrs. of Thomas Jefferson, dec'd., the deft. is ordered to put in his answer tomorrow.

In the suite brought to this Court by Thomas Saunders, plf. against James Morris, deft. in an acion of seire facias declared for the sume of 323 lbs. of tobacco, being the costs of the suite in an acion of trespass formerly brought by the said Morris against the said Saunders and on May the 25th 1705 dismist with costs, the said Moriss being summoned and making no defense, the plf. hath judgment renewed for the said sume and is ordered to be payd with costs alies execution.

Wm. Barbar, Sheriff, hath an attachment this day granted against Thomas Pinket's Estate for the sume of £5 with costs returnable to the next Court, he the said Pinket failing to appear at this Court to answer the suite of Richard Wharton for the like sume.

In the suite brought to this Court by Henry Hayles, plf. against Joseph Dwyte, deft. in an acion of debt, the deft. hath oyer of the bond granted till next Court and it is ordered that John Bedford his security remain.

Robert Hyde, his acion of trespass on the case against Mungo Somerwell is dismist, the deft. being dead.

John Morris' acion of case against Michaell Cormack is continued by consent till the next Court.

Benjamin Shepherd's acion of case against John Sargan is dismist per non prosecution.

Benjamin Shepherd arresting Daniell Taylor to this Court in an acion of case for the sume of £11:5 due by account and he not appearing, order is granted against William Barbar, Sheriff, and the next Court to be confirmed if he causeth not the deft. then personally to appear and answer the same.

Thomas Ballard, his acion of debt to this Court against Wm. Buckner, Admr. of John Hilliard, dec'd. is refered till the Sheriff returne an accunt of the said dec'd. Estate.

43. Thomas Ballard arresting John Dozwell Senr. to this Court in an acion of debt in the sume of £24:10:9 in damage costs and charges of prostest and

he not appearing, order is granted against Wm. Barbar, Sheriff, and the next Court to be confirmed if he causeth not the deft. then personally to appear and answer the same.

The Court is adjourned till the hour of Nine tomorrow morning. God Love the Queen.

At a Court held for York Co., Feby. the 25th, 1706 per adjournment from the 24th instant. Present: Coll. Thomas Ballard, Capt. Thomas Barbar, Henry Tyler, Majr. Wm. Buckner, Capt. Lawrence Smith, Wm. Pinkethman, Justices.

Josiah Draper, his complaint against William Rylands is dismist per non prosecution.

The former order for James Bennet to give bond of security for James Broster's Estate is continued till the next Court.

Anna Banks, her complaint this day being [?], she is found free and by this Court discharged from her master, Nicholas Phillips and it is ordered that he the said Nicholas pay unto her Corn and Cloths according to Law.

Henry Hayles on the 16th of September 1706 complained… that he had in the month of June last or thereabouts been robbed of goods of the value of £30 and obtained… order… for the Sheriff of this County or his Deputy to search for the same and upon discovery of any of the said goods or suspicious persons to take them into custody… which people came into the hands of George Baskerville… who upon search found two certain pieces of ribband in the custody of Joseph Dwite and carried the same ribband, which the said Joseph before the William Pinkethman, before whom the said Henry made oath as parte of the goods stolen. Whereupon the said Joseph was comitted to the Sheriff untill he should give bond to answer the said complaint, who accordingly the last Court appeared and on mocion of Stephens Thomson, Attorney for the Queen, Dionitia, wife of the said Joseph was ordered to be summoned to this Court to answer the said complaint and accordingly this day appeared and after a full examinacion of the said Joseph and Dionitia and hearing the full mater, no further evidence appearing, they are discharged.

Henry Hayward Junr. hath judgment by nihil dicit this day confirmed against John Dozwell Senr. in an acion of debt for the sume of £13:13:1 half peny due by protested Bills of Exchange bearing date August the 18th 1705 and is ordered to be payd with his damage of 15% costs charges of protest and costs alies execution.

In the suite depending to this Court between John Tomer, plf. against John Wells and Elizabeth, his wife, Extrs. of Thomas Harwood, dec'd, the deft. this day put in his plea and the plf. hath time till the next Court to reply.

The suite depending to this Court between Charles Bartelot, plf. against David Graham, deft. in an acion of debt is continued till the next Court by consent for the setting of the accounts.

John Bates, his attachment formerly obtained against Alexander Miller is continued till the next Court.

William Barbar, Sheriff, his attachment formerly obtained against Thomas Pinket is continued till the next Court.

Thomas Whitby and Mary, his wife, Extrs. of Thomas Collier, dec'd. arresting Damazinah Brown, formerly Damazinah Dixon, Extx. of Richard Dixon, dec'd. in an acion of debt for the sume of £2:10 damage and 15% costs and she the said Damazinah not appearing, order is granted against Wm. Barbar, Sheriff, and the next Court to be confirmed if he causeth not the deft. then personally to appear and answer the same.

Wm. Tunley, his acion of trespass against John Andrews is refered till the next Court.

Barintine Howells' acion of debt against Henry Fleming is referred till the next Court.

44. William Sanders' acion of debt to this Court against Thomas Walker is dismist per non prosecution.

Edward Palmer having brought suite to this Court against Elizabeth Goodwin in an acion of case and she not appearing, the plf. hath an attachment granted against the deft.'s Estate for the sume of £1:5 with costs returnable to the next Court, she being by the Sheriff on oath returned non est inventus.

Richard Wharton, his acion of debt against Robert Shields is dismist, the plf. failing further to prosecute.

Nathaniell Hook and Rebecca, his wife, their acion of case against Anna Watkins is dismist, per non prosecution.

Isaac Sedgwick, Extr. of William Sedgwick arresting Thomas Walker to this Court in an acion of debt for the sume of 595 lbs. of tobacco and he not appearing, order is granted against Wm. Barbar, Sheriff, and the next Court to be confirmed if he causeth not the deft. then personally to appear and answer the same.

Wm. Barbar, Sheriff, hath an attachment this day granted against the Estate of Thomas Walker for the sume of 595 lbs. of tobacco and costs returnable to the next Court, he the said Thomas failing to appear at this Court to answer the suite of Isaac Sedgwick, Extr. of Wm. Sedgwick in an acion of debt for the like sume.

Nicholas Phillips' acion of debt against Wm. Platt is returned retracted[?].

Wm. Sheldon's acion of debt against Edward Woodhouse is returned retracted[?].

Thomas Bass' acion of case against Thomas Mountfort is dismist per non prosecution.

John Eaton's acion of debt against Edward Davis is dismist per non prosecution.

William Sherman arresting John Cozby to this Court in an acion of debt for the sume of £6 and he not appearing, order is granted against Wm. Barbar, Sheriff, and the next Court to be confirmed on the like default.

Wm. Sherman having brought suite to this Court against Anthony Jesper in an acion of debt for the sume of £5:11:6 and he not appearing, the plf. hath an attachment granted against the deft.'s Estate for the said sume with costs returnable to the next Court, he being by the Sheriff on oath returned non est inventus.

Wm. Sherman having brought suite in this Court against Anthony Jesper in an acion of debt for the sume of £3:5s and he not appearing, the plf. hath an attachment granted against the deft.'s Estate for the said sume with costs returnable to the next Court, he being by the Sheriff on oath returned non est inventus.

Wm. Sherman having brought suite to this Court an acion of case against Anthony Jesper for the sume of £6:17:2 and he not appearing, the plf. hath an attachment granted against the deft.'s Estate for the said sume with costs returnable to the next Court, he having by the Sheriff (on oath) returned non est inventus.

Wm. Bird, Esqr., his acion of debt against Thomas Mountfort is dismist, the partys being agreed.

On hearing of the diference between Joseph Walker, Admr. of Wm. Aylward, dec'd., Complainant and Willm. Davis and Elizth., his wife, Admrs. of Thomas Jefferson, dec'd., Respondent in Chancery (by consent), it is decreed that the goods of Wm. Aylward, dec'd. in the custody of the said respts. on the 4th day of March next if the weather permitt, if not the first faire day then next following, be appraised by Wm. Lee, Charles Collyer, Thomas Whitby and Robert Peters in the best of their judgments, being first sworne before the next Justices, and that the Sheriff deliver the same to the complt. if he will accept them and pay to the respts. the sume of £20[?], if not the said goods to redeliver to the respts. and that a due return thereof be made to the next Court.

Willm. Whitaker, his acion of case brought to this Court against Joseph Walker, Admr. of Wm. Aylward, dec'd. is referd to the next Court at the request of the deft.

45. Tillett[?] Johnson, his acion of case against Willm. Kaydee is dismist, neyther party appearing.

Wm. Chesley, his accon of debt against Nathll. Norris is dismist per non prosecution.

John Bates, Assignee of John Prewit, having brought suit to this Court against Anthony Jesper in an acion of debt for the sume of £2:10 and he not appearing, the plf. hath an attachment granted against the deft.'s Estate for the said sume with costs returnable to the next Court, he being by the Sheriff on oath returned non est inventus.

In the suit brought by the Court by George Walker, plf. against Oliver Perron, deft. in an acion of debt, the deft. by John Clayton, his Attorney, hath oyer granted of the bill sued for till the next Court.

John Andrews' Deed of Sale bearing date this present instant from Coll. Thomas Ballard and Majr. Wm. Buckner, Trustees of the Portland in York Towne, for his Portland deed there known by the number 65, was this day personally acknowledged in Court by the said Trustees to the said Andrews and ordered to be committed to record.

It is ordered by this Court that Coll. Miles Cary, Surveyor of this County, survey the [plat?] of York Town the 10th of March next.

This Court is adjourned till the 24th of March next.

Bond. Elizabeth Baptist, widow, Robert Harris and Bazill Wagstaf, all of the Co. of York, to the Justices of said County, in the sume of £500.

Sureties for Elizabeth Baptist as Admx. of the Estate of Morgan Baptist, dec'd. Dated this 24th day of Sepr. 1706. Wit. Robt. Read and J.W. Martin.

46. At a Court held for James City Co. the 6th day of November 1706.

In the acion of debt between Charles Chiswell, plf. and John Holloway, deft. for £100, one of a certain bill obligatory bearing date the 21st day of March 1703, it is more fully set forth in the declaracion the deft.'s Attorney desineing to withdraw his plea put in last Court, judgment by default is granted the plf. against the said deft. for the aforesaid sume of £100, and ordered that he pay the same to the plf. with costs alies execution.

47. Inventory & Appraisement of the Estate of Richard Dixon, dec'd., late of Charles Parish in York Co. Among other items, 3 negros named Sampear, Kitt and Peter Senr., an Indian man named Charles, 1 negro woman named Betty, 3 negro boys named Rinter, Peter and Billy, an old negro woman named Hagar. Total value of estate, £369:16:4 ½. Appraised by John Tomer, Wm. Wise Senr., Francis Callohill, and Robert Kerby and presented by Damazinah Brown, Extx. on December the 24th 1706.

48. Part of Richard Dixon's Estate that was left unproved being now appraised by John Tomer, Wm. Wise Senr. Francis Callohill and Robert Kerby. Total value £16:10:0 ½. Presented by Damazinah Browne, formerly Damazinah Dixon, Extx. of Richd. Dixon, dec'd. according to her former oath and is according to order recorded.

This is to authorize you, Robt. Hyde, to be my Attorney at Law in all Courts of Judicature in this Dominion of Virginia and this shall be your warrant and allso to oblige me to pay you 20 shillings for your fee as witness my hand this 24th day of February 1704. Joshua Curl.

49. Inventory & Appraisement of the Estate of Morgan Baptist, dec'd. Among other items, 1 negro man, 2 negro women and 1 negro boy. Total value of estate, £202:13:9. Appraised by Phil. Dedman, Willm. Allin and Joseph Mountfort and presented by Elizabeth Baptist on December the 24th 1706.

Inventory & Appraisement of the Estate of John Broster, dec'd dated this 30th day of Octr. 1706. Total Value of estate, £34:11:10. Appraised by Wm. Wise, Senr., John Tomer and John Drewry and presented by Lidia Broster on December the 24th 1706.

50. Inventory & Appraisement of the Estate of Elizabeth Philpot, dec'd. Total value of estate £16:19:9. Appraised by Richard Kendall, Robt.

Harrison, Hen. Gilbert and Wm. Hansford and presented by Willm. Thacker on December the 24th 1706.

51. This Indenture made this 8th day of January 1706, witness that Abraham Royston, mulatto son of Elizabeth Chilmaid, late of York Co., dec'd., by and with the consent and advice of the worshipfull Justices of the County aforesaid, hath and by these presents according to an order of the said Justices bearing date Sepr. the 26th last past, doth put himself an apprentice with Thomas Holliday of the County aforesaid, boatwright to learn the said mistery or occupacion of boat wrighting with him, said Thomas after a manner of an apprentice to dwell and serve for and during the span and terme of 7 yeares now next comeing. During all which time the said Abraham his said Master faithfull shall serve, his secrets keep, his comands lawfully everywhere in the said calling gladly do. Hurt to his said master he shall not do, nor suffer to be done of others, and in all things as a good and faithfull apprentice he shall behave himself. And the said Thomas for his part doth covenant and agree the said Abraham the said mistery to learn, teach and instruct after the best way and means as he may or can. And allso to find and provide the said Abraham meet competent and sufficient diet, washing, and lodging and all other necessaryes meet and convenient for an apprentice of this collony during the said terme and at the expiracion thereof to give unto the said Abraham corn and clothe, according as is prescribed by the Law of this County for the conformacion of which each and both parties to these presents have set their hands and seales this day and year first above written. Wit. Wm. Randolph.

Bond. Willm. Buckner and Willm. Barbar, both of the Co. of York, to the Justices of said County, in the sum of £100. Dated this 24th day of December 1706. Sureties to Willm. Buckner as Admr. of the Estate of John Hilliard, dec'd. Wit. John Martin and Wm. Tunley.

52. Bond. John Gibbons, John Dozwell Senr. and Thomas Walker, all of the Co. of York, to the Justices of said County, in the sume of £50. Dated the 24th of Feby. 1706. Sureties for John Gibbons as Guardian of John Cox, orphan of Thomas Cox, dec'd. Wit. Elizabeth Moody and Wm. Tunley.

January the 13th 1706/7. We the subscribers, in obedience to an order of York Court bearing date January the 8th, did meet at the house of John Hilliard, dec'd. and there did value to the best of our Judgment, 2 heyfers at £3 and one broak mare at £3:10. John Brooks, Wm. Lee and Willm. Davis.

Bond. Elizabeth Sommerwell, James Sclater and Jno. Wythe, all of the Co. of York, to the Justices of the said County, in the sume of £1,000. Dated the 24th day of February 1706. Sureties for Elizabeth Sommerwell as Admx. of the Estate of Mungo Sommerwell, dec'd. Wit. Thomas Nelson and Thomas Whitby for Elizabeth Sommerwell, and John Cromby and Wm. Tunley for John Wythe.

53. Inventory & Appraisement of the Estate of Wm. Aylward. Among other items, one Indian woman valued at £25. Total value of Estate, about £30. Appraised by Robt. Peters, Wm. Lee, Thomas Whitby and Charles Collier on March the 4th 1706/7.

54. Mary Whaley, widdow, now in the Collony of Virginia, but bound on a voyage for England, to Henry Cary and Edward Jackling, Gentm., my true and lawfull Attorneys to collect debts due to me from persons in Virginia. And if Henry Cary Senr. dies, Henry Cary Junr. to be my Attorney. Dated the 24th day of May 1707. Wit. Michll. Archer and Christr. Jackson.

55. Will of Thomas Pinchback. To my wife Luce Pinchback, the plantacion that I now live on and all of my personall estate. My wife to be my Extx. Dated the 29th of April 1707. Wit. Willm. Pinkethman, Willm. Campbell and Charles Barker. Recorded May 24th 1707.

Bond. Willm. Thacker, Charles Cox and Joseph Chermison, all of the Co. of York, to the Justices of said County, in the sume of £100 . Dated the 24th of Feby. 1706. Sureties for Willm. Thacker as Admr. of the Estate of Elizabeth Philpot, late of this County, dec'd., with her noncupitive will annext. Wit. Wm. Randolph.

56. Deposition taken by Robert Beddingfield, Knight Lord Mayor of the Citty of London and the Alderman of the same citie. Robert Bullock of London, merchant, has testified that on or about the month of Octr. 1673, he did sell to Major John Seasbrook, dec'd, who was father of John Seasbrook in Virginia, planter, and to Edmond Chessman, brother in Law of the said late major John Seasbrook... a certain Mill calld Warwick River Mill situate at the head of Warwick River in Warwick Co. in Virginia. He further testifies that he did not at any time since sell the same to David Condon and Thomas Mountfort or either of them. Dated in London the 6th day of February 1706. Wit. John Marshall, Thomas Bagwell, Thomas Bagwell, Junr. and Benjamin French.

57. At a Court held for York Co. March the 24th 1706. Present: Major Willm. Buckner, Hen. Tyler, Capt. Daniel Taylor and Capt. Lawc. Smith, Justices.

Joseph Dwyte was this day in Court sworn Constable of the lower precinque of Bruton Parish in this County.

It is orderd that the Sheriff summone 24 freeholders of this County to the next Court to serve as a Grand Jury to enquire into the Breach of the Penall Laws and present offenders and that the said Sheriff give them notice that they will be discharged when the Court adjourns, but if their presentments are not then finished, they shall make them to the next Court as the Law directs.

Orderd that the Creditors of John Hillyard's Estate produce their claimes to the next Court and that the Sheriff give notice thereof.

Certificate according to Act of Assembly was this day granted unto Thomas Barbar of his rights to 50 acres of land, he making oath in Court that as yett never any land was taken up by himself aut alies est.

Certificate according to Act of Assembly was this day granted unto Mary Mathews of her rights to 50 acres of land, she making oath that as yett never any land was taken up for her by herself aut alies est.

Certificate according to Act of Assembly was this day granted unto Joseph Bernald of his rights to 50 acres of land, he making oath that as yett never any land was taken up for him by himself aut alies est.

Order for a commission of Administration of the Estate of Richd. Stannup, late of this County, dec'd. was this day granted unto Sarah, his Relict, if she enter into bond with Philip Moody and Robt. Crawley, her securityes, betwixt this and the next Court for her due administration thereof according to Law.

John Redwood this day on his peticion obtained order for a License to keep ordinary at his now dweling house in the Citty of Williamsburgh in this County giving bond with good and sufficient security for the same as the Law directs.

James Sclater, his Deed of Sale dated this present Instant from the Trustees of the Portland of York Town in this County for the Portland lot no. 70, was this day in Court signd, seald, deliverd and acknowlegd and orderd to be recorded.

The former order for a return of the Inventory and Appraisment of Mungo Sommerwell's Estate, dec'd. by Elizabeth, his Relict and Admx., is continued till the next Court.

The former order of Willm. Thacker to give bond with good and sufficient security for the administration of Elizabeth Philpot's Estate is continued till the next Court.

63

The former order for Damazinah Brown to perfect the Inventory of the Estate of Richd. Dixon, her dec'd. husband, is continued till the next Court.

Willm. Tunley hath this day judgment granted against Use Gibson and Peter Gibson in an acion of case for the sume of 1,750 lbs. of tobaco due by account proovd in Court and is orderd to be paid with costs alies execution.

John Cromby's acion of case depending against James Bowman is dismist per non prosecution.

58. In the suit depending to this Court between John Duke, plf. and Nicolas Phillips, deft. in an acion of case, the deft. this day put in his plea and the plf. hath time to reply.

In the suit depending to this Court between Stephens Tompson, plf. and Willm. Handsford, deft. in an acion of case damage £5, wherein the plf. declared that the deft. owed him the sum of £5 by his assumpsion for transacting, performing and negociating sevll. matters, actions and lawsuits, to which the deft. pleaded non assumpsit and both partys agreed at the Barr to refer the issue to the Court for tryall, who finding after a discompt pleaded that the deft. owed to the said plf. the sum of £3:4, for which judgment is granted the plf. and orderd that the deft. forthwith pay it to the plf. with costs alies execution.

Henry Emerson, his attachment formerly obtained against John Ross is dismisst per non prosecution.

Benjamin Shepherd, his Information in chancery against John Pond is continued till the next Court.

John Marrot hath judgment of nihil dicit this day granted against Anthony Jesper in an acion of debt for the sum of £8:6:6 and the next Court to be confirmd on the like default.

John Marrot hath judgment this day granted against Timothy Johnson in an acion of case for the sum of £3:12:11 ½ and the next Court to be confirmd on the like default.

Joseph Chermison, his acion of case depending in this Court against Oliver Peron is continued till the next Court by consent and the deft.'s security, James Bray, is discharged.

Willm. Farbar hath judgment of nihil dicit this day granted against Timothy Johnson in an acion of debt for the sum of £1:19:0 and the next Court to be confirmed on the like default.

Willm. Farbar hath judgment of nihil dicit this day granted against Timothy Johnson in an acion of case for the sum of £4:1:3 and the next Court to be confirmed on the like default.

John Owen, his acion of case damage £60 depending against David Robertson is continued till next Court by consent.

Thomas Mountfort, his acion of case damage £50 depending in this Court agaist Use Gibson is continued by consent.

Wm. Kaydyee hath judgment of nihil dicit this day granted against Adam Galt in an acion of case declared to the plf.'s damage £20 and the next Court to be confirmed on the like default.

Thomas Mountfort, his acion of case depending to this Court against Edwd. Newman is continued till the next Court by consent.

The former order for the secureing of Barbary Hutton till she should give bond with security to appeare to answer the Information of John Wyth for fornication is continued till the next Court.

Wm. Tunley hath judgment this day confirmd against Willm. Barbar, High Sheriff, for the sum of 321 lbs. of tobaco for the non appearance of David Robertson to answer the suit of the said Willm. in an acion of case for the like sum and is ordered to be paid with costs alies execution.

In the suite depending to this Court between Willm. Tunley, plf. and Ralf Baker, deft. in an acion of case declared for the sum of 727 lbs. of tobaco due by account, the deft. pleaded by Samll. Selden, his Attorney, that he oweth nothing. Whereupon a jury was impanelld and sworn to try the issue, who after a full hearing of all evidences and pleas, departed to consult their verdict and at their comeing in againe, returned their verdict in these words (Viz) Wee find for the deft., signd Joseph Walker, forman, which on mocion of the deft.'s said Attorney is admitted to record and the suit is dismist with costs.

59. John Chessman, being by the Sheriff summond in evidence for Ralph Baker, deft. against Wm. Tunley, plf. in an acion of case, is ordered to be paid 200 lbs. of tobacco for 5 days attendance at Court at 40 per day according to act with costs.

Thomas Walker being by the Sheriff summoned an evidence for Ralph Baker, deft. against Wm. Tunley, plf. in an acion of case, is ordered to be paid 40 lbs. of tobacco for one days attendance according to act with costs.

Thomas Mountfort, his acion of case damage £20 depending to this Court against Samll. Cooper is referd to the next Court at the deft.'s request.

Thomas Mountfort, his acion of case against Wm. Roberts is by consent of the plf.'s Attorney dismisst.

Richd. Wharton, his acion of debt damage £100 depending to this Court against John Redwood is continued to the next Court by consent.

Richard Wharton's acion of debt against Thomas Pinket is dismisst by consent of the plf.

Hester Session hath judgment of nihil dicit this day granted against Barantine Howells in an acion of debt for the sume of £1:5 and the next Court to be confirmd on the like default.

Lewis Burwell, Gent., his acion of debt depending to this Court against Thomas Lamb is dismist, the plf. failing further to prosecute.

Edward Moss hath judgment this day granted against Lydia Broster, Admx. of John Broster, dec'd. in an acion of debt for the sume of £3:5:8 due by bill dated under the dec'd. hand Feby. 27th 1703, sworn in Court by the plf. no satisfaction received, and is orderd to be paid with costs alies execution.

John Penton hath judgment of nihil dicit this day granted against Michall Maccormack in an acion of debt for the sume of £17:17:1 and the next Court to be confirmd on the like default.

The former order for the return of the Outcry of John Hillyard's Estate is continued till the next Court.

The former order for the return of an account of John Hilliard's Estate by Mary, his Relict, on oath is continued till the next Court.

Mary Limus, her suit depending to this Court against Josuah Sled is dismist, she showing no cause of complaint.

Charles Chiswell's complaint against Charles Elliot being continued to this Court for judgment, and the said Chiswell this day pursuing his acion of charge against the said Elliot for running away (viz) for a horse 2,500 lbs. of tobaco, for taking him up in New Kent 200 lbs. of tobaco, for taking in York Co. 200 lbs., for his absence in the first running away 8 days, also Court charges and attending three courts, and the Court finding no Law to direct an allowance for the horse, but for running away, it is therefore orderd that the said Charles Elliot serve the said Charles Chiswell after the expiracion of his time by Indenture or custome according as the Law directs. From which judgment, the complainant appeales to the Hon. and Genll. Court for tryall.

In the suit depending to this Court between Robert Mynn, plf. against Andrew Young, deft. in an acion of case, the deft. this day pleaded not guilty to the plf.'s declaration and obtain time to try at next Court.

In the suit depending to this Court between John Sergerton, plf. and John Nicholson, deft. in an acion of debt, after mending of the declaration, the deft. by Stephens Thomson, his Attorney, put in his plea and the plf. hath time granted till the next Court to reply.

In the suit depending to the Court between Thomas Whitby, plf. and Isaac Jamart, Admr. of Wm. Chalkhill, dec'd., deft. in an acion of case, the deft. this day demurd to the plf.'s reply and the plf. hath time till the next Court to join in demur or mend his replicacion.

Thomas Lee hath judgment this day granted against John Redwood in an acion of debt for the sume of £15:7:8 current mony due by bill dated under the deft.'s hand November the 24th[?] 1706, and is ordered to be paid with costs alies execution.

60. Henry Hales hath judgment this day granted against Joseph Dwite in an acion of debt for the sum of £26:5:3 due by bill obligatory dated under the deft.'s hand and seal August the 9th 1706 and is ordered to be paid with costs alies execution.

John Morris, his acion of case depending to this Court against Michaell Mackcormack is dismisst, partyes being agreed.

Benjamin Shepherd, his acion of case depending to this Court against Daniell Taylor, Gent., is continued till next Court, the deft. being sick.

Thomas Ballard, Gent., his acion of debt depending to this Court against Willm. Buckner, Gent., Admr. of John Hilliard, dec'd. lyeth for want of a Court.

Thomas Ballard, Gent., his acion of debt depending to this Court against John Dozwell Senr. is dismist, he failing further to prosecute.

In the suit depending to this Court between John Tomer, plf. and John Wells and Elizabeth, his wife, Extrs. of Thomas Harwood, dec'd. in an acion of case, the plf. this day demurd generally to the deft.'s plea and the deft. hath time to the next Court to join in demurrence or mend his plea, paying costs.

Charles Bartelot hath judgment this day granted against Thomas Graham of Philadelphia, merchant, in an acion of debt declared for the sume of £600:5 current money of Virginia due by a writing obligatory dated under the deft.'s hand and seale and under the hand and seal of Nathaniel Maclaney Aprill the 26th 1706, and is orderd to be paid with costs alies execution.

John Bates, his attachment formerly obtained against Alexander Miller is dismist, he not further prosecuting.

Wm. Barbar, his attachment formerly obtained against Thomas Pinquat is dismist per non prosecution.

Thomas Whitby and Mary, his wife, Extrs. of Thomas Collier, dec'd., hath judgment this day granted against Damazinah Brown, formerly Damazinah Dixon, Extx. of Richard Dixon, dec'd. in a plea of debt for the sume of £2:10 due by protested Bills of Exchange dated under the said Testator's hand May the 17th 1704 and is orderd to be paid with costs alies execution.

Wm. Tunley hath judgment of nil dicit this day granted against John Andrews in an acion of trespass for the sume of £50 and the next Court to be confirmd on the like default.

Barrantine Howells, his acion of debt depending to this Court against Henry Fleming is dismisst per non prosecution.

Edward Palmer, in his acion of case depending to this Court against Elizabeth Goodwin, is nonsuited, not prooving his declaracion.

Thomas Walker this day in Court confest judgment to Isaac Sedgwick, Extr. of Wm. Sedgwick, dec'd. in an acion of debt for the sum of 537 lbs. tobaco due by bill dated under his hand and seale June 16th 1704, and is orderd to pay it to the plt. with costs alies execution.

William Sherman hath judgment this day confirmed against Wm. Barbar, Sheriff, for the sume of £6 for the non appearance of John Cozby at this Court to answer the suite of the said Sherman in an acion of debt for the like sum due by bills dated under his hand Aprill 1st 1706, and is orderd to be paid with costs alies execution.

Wm. Shearman, his attachment obtain against Anto. Jesper in an acion of debt is continued till the next Court at the request of the plf.

Wm. Sherman, his attachment obtaind against Antony Jesper in an acion of debt is continued till next Court by the request of the plf.

Will Shareman, his attachment obtained against Anthony Jesper in an acion of case is continued till the next Court at the plf.'s request.

61. Joseph Walker, Admr. of Willm. Aylward, this day presented in Court an Inventory & Appraisement of the Estate of Wm. Aylward that is allready come to his hands, which is orderd to record.

John Bates, Assignee of John Prewet, his attachment formerly obtained against Antho. Jesper is dismisst, the plf. failing further to prosecute.

George Walker, his acion of debt depending to this Court against Oliver Perron is dismist, he failing further to prosecute.

Willm. Whitaker hath judgment this day granted against Joseph Walker, Admr. of Willm. Aylward, dec'd. in an acion of case for the sum of £1:19:6 due by bill dated under the dec'd. hand May the 26th, 1704 and is orderd to be paid with costs alies execution.

It is ordered that the Ordinary Keepers Rates within this County be published.

Wm. Barbar, High Sheriff, hath an attachment this day granted against the Estate of John Cosby for the sume of £6 with costs returnable to the next Court, he the said Cosby failing to appeare at this Court to answer the suit of Willm. Shareman in an acion of debt suffering judgment to be confirmd against the said Sheriff for the like sume.

Joseph Walker, his Deed of Sale dated under the hand and seal of Samll. Dickenson Febr. 17 1706 and allso his bond bearing date as aforesaid for the performance of the covenants in the said deed contained, were this day in Court acknowledged to the said Joseph by Hen. Holdcraft by virtue of a Power of Attorney bearing date under the hand and seal of the said Samll. this present date and proovd in Court by the oaths of Robt. Crawley and Francis Hooper and is orderd to be committed to record.

Jonathan Druit this day published his departure out of this Collony with no objection made to the contrary.

The Court is adjournd to the 24th of May next.

62. At a Court held for York Co. May the 24th 1707. Present: Lieut. Coll. Thomas Ballard, Hen. Tyler, Majr. Wm. Buckner, Wm. Pinkethman, Capt. Law. Smith and Capt. Daniel Taylor, Justices.

Adduston Rogers Junr., his Deed of Gift bearing date under the hand and seal of Mathew Tiplady this present Instant, for one grey mare and horse colt was this day personally acknowledged in Court and orderd to be comitted to record.

Order for a Probat of the Last Will & Testament of Thomas Pinchback, late of Bruton Parish in this County, dec'd. was this day granted unto Lucy, his Relict, she being therein appointed Extx. and prooved by the oaths of Willm. Pinkethman, Wm. Cambbell and Charles Barker, evidences thereto, and orderd to be comitted to record.

Thomas Wade bringing his negro boy, Kitt, before this Court for judgment of his age, the Court adjudgeth him of the age of 13 yeares.

A Grand Jury of 19 freeholders (viz) Wm. Davis, Ralph Hubbard, Thomas Feare Junr., Ambo. Cobb, Richd. Kendall, Robt. Jaxon, Robt. Peters, Charles Collyer, Thomas Whitby, Wm. Lee, Thomas Chessman Junr., Hen. Hayward Senr., Hen. Hayward Junr., John Tomer, John Adduston Rogers, Wm. Sheldon, John Moss, Willm. Allen and Charles [no last name] being this day impanelld and sworn to enquire into the Breach of the Penall Laws and present offenders went forth and on their return made presentment of severall of the offenders, which is orderd to be recorded.

James Bowman being by the Grand Jury presented for entertaining wicked and profane persons in his house, is orderd to be sumond to the next Court to answer the same.

John Loynes for keeping whore in his house and absenting from the Church.

Elizabeth Starnes for entertaining wicked persons in her house.

John Phips, John Pattison, Thomas Wooten and Willm. Jones for absenting from the Church.

Danll. Mackentash for absenting from the Church and as a vagrant.

John Sandover, Wm. Ryland, Danll. Hazelgrove[?], Henry Clark, James Everit, Benj. Lovell and Jno. Mackendy for absenting from the Church.

Elizabeth Thomson and Katherin Masterton for bastardizing.

Adduston Rogers, Thomas Vines and Jonathan Lark for not keeping the roads in repair in the precincts.

It is ordered that the Sheriff take an Inventory of the Estate of Cornelius Wilson, dec'd. and that it be appraised by Willm. Allen, Bazil Wagstaf, John Wythe and Charles Cox or any three of them on the 27th Instant and make return thereof to the next Court.

63. It is orderd that Capt. Willm. Timson take and receive the List of Tithables in the upper precinque of Bruton Parish in this County and make return thereof, according to Law.

It is orderd that Henry Tyler take and receive the List of Tithables in the lower precinque of Bruton Parish in this County and make return thereof, according to Law.

It is orderd that Coll. Thomas Barbar take and receive the List of Tithables in the lower precinque of York Hampton Parish in this County and make return thereof, according to Law.

It is orderd that Coll. Thomas Ballard take and receive the List of Tithables in the lower precinque of York Hampton Parish in this County and make return thereof, according to Law.

It is orderd that Capt. Danll. Taylor take and receive the List of Tithables in the lower precinque of Charles Parish in this County and make return thereof, according to Law.

It is orderd that Capt. Thomas Nutting take and receive the List of Tithables in the lower precinque of Charles Parish in this County and make return thereof, according to Law.

It is orderd that Joseph Thrift be summond to the next Court to answer the complaint of Willm. March and Elizth., his wife, late widow and Relict of Job Cocking, concerning one Jno. Bartlett and to bring the said John with him.

Willm. Bird, Esqr., his Deed of Sale bearing date under the hand and seale of James Shell May the 12th 1707 for ½ acre of land and housing in the Citty of Williamsburgh in this County No. 24, was this day personally acknowledged in Court to the said Willm. Bird, also Hanah, wife to the said James, after private examinacion acknowledged her right of dowry, and is orderd to be comitted to record.

It is orderd by this Court that Elizabeth Ditcher be by the Sheriff summond to the next Court to answer the Informacion of Peter Goodwin, Church Warden of York Parish, for bastardizing.

Willm. Barbar hath judgment this day granted against the Estate of John Hilliard, dec'd. for the sume of £2:8:4 due by account for the Outcry of the said Estate and is orderd to be paid out of the bills for the said Estate taken.

Wm. Tunley hath judgment this day granted against the Estate of Jno. Hillyard, dec'd. for the sum of 393 lbs. of tobaco due by account for attending the Outcry and administration fees, and is orderd to be paid in money at 10% out of the bills.

Majr. Wm. Buckner as Guardian of Jane Young, orphan of Alexander Young, dec'd. hath judgment this day granted against the Estate of John Hilliard, dec'd. due to the said orphan for the rent of a certain house and lot in York Towne and is orderd to be paid out of the bills taken at the Outcry of the said Estate.

In the suit depending to this Court between Jno. Duke, plf. against Nicolas Philips, deft. in an acion of case, the plf. in his replicacion this day demurd to the deft.'s plea and the deft. hath time to mend paying costs.

Benjamin Shepherd, his injunction in chancery depending to this Court against John Pond's judgment formerly obtaind against the said Benjamin in an acion of debt is dismisst, no cause appearing to stay the execution of the said judgment, which judgment is now confirmd and the sum menciond therein orderd to be paid with costs alies execution.

John Morrat hath judgment this day granted against Anthony Jesper in an acion of debt for the sum of £8:6:10 due by bill dated Feby. the 12th 1705/6 and is orderd to be paid with costs alies execution.

John Morrat hath judgment this day granted against Timothy Johnson in a plea of case for the sum of £3:12:11 due by account proovd in Court by the plf.'s oath and is orderd to be paid with costs alies execution.

Joseph Chermison, his acion of case depending to this Court against Oliver Perron is dismist per non prosecution.

Wm. Farbar's acion of debt depending to this Court against Timothy Johnson is dismist per non prosecution.

Wm. Farbar's acion of case depending to this Court against Timothy Johnson is dismist per non prosecution.

The suit depending to this Court between John Owen, plf. against David Robertson, mariner, in an acion of case is continued to the next Court per consent.

Thomas Mountfort's acion of case depending to this Court against Use Gibson is dismist per non prosecution.

Thomas Mountfort's acion of case depending to this Court against Edward Newman is dismist per non prosecution.

64. In the suit depending to this Court between Willm. Kaydee, plf. and Adam Galt, deft. in an acion of case declared for one white guelding of the value of £15 lent by the plf. to the deft., who detaind the same to the plf.'s damage £20, the plf. hath judgment of nihil dicit this day confirmd against the deft. and orderd that a Writ of Enquiry for damage be executed the next Court.

Thomas Mountfort, his acion of case depending to this Court against Samll. Cooper is dismisst per non prosecution.

Thomas Mountfort, his acion of case depending to this Court against Wm. Roberts is dismisst per non prosecution.

Richard Wharton, his acion of debt depending to this Court against John Redwood is continued to the next Court by consent.

Hester Sessions hath judgment this day granted against Barantine Howells in an acion of debt for the sum of £1:2:6 in sufficient country pay due by ballance of a bill dated under his hand Novr. 15th 1704 and is orderd to be paid with costs alies execution.

John Penton hath judgment this day granted against Michael Cormack in an acion of debt for the sum of £17:11:7 due by ballance of a bill dated under the deft.'s hand July 8th 1706 and is orderd to be paid with costs alies execution.

The suit depending to this Court between John Sergerton, plf. and John Nicholson, deft. in an acion of debt is dismisst for defect in the proceedings.

In the suit depending to this Court between Robt. Mynne, plf. and Andrew Young, deft. in an acion of case declared that when the said Robt. was possest of 2 hogsheads of sweet scented tobacco of the price and value of £12 as of his owne proper goods and chattles in the Parish and Co. of York, the same out of his possession aforesaid casually lost, which afterwards that is to say the same day, yeare and Parish aforesaid to the hands and possession of the said Andrew by finding came, who converted the same to his owne use, notwithstanding the severall demands of the plf. to the damage of the plf. £12. Therefore he brings suit to which the deft. by Stephen Thomson, his Attorney, pleaded not guilty and time was granted to try it this Court. Whereupon a jury being impannelld and sworn to try the issue, after a full hearing of all evidences and pleas, went out to consult their verdict, which on their return, the plf. and deft. being calld, was read (viz) We find for the deft., signd John Mihill, foreman, which on the request of the deft.'s Attorney is admitted to record.

John Duke being summond an evidence for Robt. Mynne, plf. against Andrew Young, deft. in an acion of case is orderd to be paid for 9 days attendance at 40 lbs. of tobaco per diem, 360 lbs. according to Law with costs.

Benjamin Shepherd, his acion of case against Daniel Taylor, deft. is referd to the next Court for proof of his declaracion.

It is orderd that Sarah Stanup, widow Relict and Admx. of Richd. Stanup, dec'd. return an Inventory of the said dec'd. Estate to the next Court and that the Shf. give her notice thereof.

Joseph Chermison hath judgment this day granted against Joseph Walker, Admr. of the Estate of Willm. Aylward, dec'd. in an acion of debt for the sum of £25:15:0 due by ballance of a bill dated under the dec'd. hand Sepr. 23rd 1703 and is orderd to be paid with costs alies execution.

In the acion of case damage £50 brought to this Court by Cornelius Jones, plf. against John Loyne, deft., a speciall imparlance is granted till the next Court.

Orlando Jones, his suit in chancery brought to this Court against Stephen Founce is dismisst per non prosecution.

James Bates, Assignee of John Harrison, arresting Jno. Warren to this Court in an acion of debt for the sum of £1:5 and he not appearing, order is granted against Wm. Barbar, H.S., and the next Court to be confirmd if he causeth not the deft. then personally to appeare and answer the same.

John Eaton's acion of debt against Edwd. Davis brought to this Court is dismisst per non prosecution.

65. The suit brought to this Court by Joseph Chermison, plf. against George Booker, deft. is referd till the next Court at the request of Wm. Coman, his Attorney and security.

James Wallas hath judgment this day granted against Damazinah Brown, formerly Dixon, Extx. of Richard Dixon, dec'd. in an acion of case for the sum of £4:6:0 due by account proved in Court and is orderd to be paid with costs alies execution.

In the suite brought to this Court by Elizth. Somerwell, widow, Relict and Admx. of Mungo Somerwell, dec'd., plf. against Damazinah Brown, formerly Damazinah Dixon, Extx. of Richard Dixon, dec'd. in an acion of case, oyer is granted the deft. till the next Court.

John Brooks arresting Damazinah Brown, formerly Damaz. Dixon, Extx. of Richd. Dixon, dec'd. to this Court in an acion of case and not further prosecuting, is nonsuited with costs.

In the suit brought to this Court by Thomas Pain, plf. against Damazinah Brown, formerly Damazinah Dixon, Extx. of Richard Dixon, dec'd., deft., a speciall imparlance is granted the deft. till next Court.

Samll. Seldon's acion of case against Use Gibson is dismisst per non prosecution.

Robt. Beverly hath judgment this day granted against Samll. Dickeson in an acion of seire facias for the renewing of a judgment by him obtaind Novr. 5th 1703 for the sum of 773 lbs. of tobaco and costs amounting in the whole to the sume of 855 lbs. of tobaco, and is orderd to be paid with costs alies execution.

John Penton arresting Joseph Mountfort to this Court in an acion of debt declared for the sum of £9:16 and he not appearing, order is granted against Wm. Barbar, H. Shf., the next Court to be confirmd if he causeth not the deft. then personally to appeare and answer the same.

Willm. Tunley's acion of case against John Penton is continued till next Court by consent.

Coll. Edmund Jenings arresting Isabella Broadbent, Admx. of Joshua Broadbent, dec'd. to this Court in an acion of debt declared for the sum of £16 damage and she not appearing, order is granted against Wm. Barbar, H.S., and the next Court to be confirmed if he causeth not the deft. then personally to appeare and answer the same.

Wm. Barbar, H.S., hath attachment granted against the Estate of Isabella Broadbent for the sume of £16 with costs returnable to the next Court, she failing to appear at this to answer the suit of Edmund Jenings, Esquire, in an acion of debt for the said sume.

Thomas Harton arresting James Bowman to this Court in an acion of case declared for the sum on £1 and he not appearing, order is granted against Willm. Barbar, H. Shf., the next Court to be confirmed if he causeth not the deft. then personally to appear and answer the same.

Wm. Barbar, H.S., hath attachment granted against the Estate of James Bowman for the sum of £1 with costs returnable to the next Court, he failing to appear at this to answer the suit of Thomas Harton in an acion of case for the said sume.

In the suit brought to this Court by John Cox, plf. against John Fergason, deft. in an Ejectione firmae, Wm. Gordon, Sub Sheriff, this day making oath that he deliverd a copy of the declaracion to John Drury, tenant in possession of the land in question. It is therefore orderd that unless the said tenant appeare at the next Court and confess lease entry and ouster, judgment shall go by default and he honsled[?] of possession.

Elizabeth Somerwell, widow, Relict and Admx. of Mungo Somerwell, dec'd. is orderd to make return of the Inventory & Appraisement of the said dec'd. Estate to the next Court.

Edward Parkeson, on petition showing his inability, is excused from paying levyes.

Henry Lee, orphan of Hen. Lee, dec'd., on his petition hath order granted that Lieut. Coll. Thomas Ballard pay unto him what Estate he hath in his hands belonging to the said orphan.

Charles Cox on his petition hath order granted for a Licence to keep ordinary at his dwelling house in York Town, giving bond with good and sufficient security as the Law directs.

Edwd. Malkham's acion of case against Michaell Cormack is dismisst per non prosecution.

In the suit brought to this Court by John Loynes, plf. against Hen. Hayles, deft. in an acion of case, an imparlance is granted till the next Court.

66. Whereas it was formerly orderd that the Sheriff should take and in safe custody keep the body of Barbara Hutton up till she should give Bond with good and sufficient security to appeare at this Court to answer the Informacion of John Wythe, Church Warden of York Parish, for fornicacion, and said order being by George Baskervill [?] execution and she not appearing, it is therefore orderd that unless the said George cause the said Barbara personally to appeare at the next Court to answer the said

76

Informacion, the judgment shall be awarded against the said George for her fine, which the Law prescibes for the sin of fornicacion.

The former order for Damazinah Brown to perfect the Inventory of Richard Dixon's Estate is continued till the next Court.

John Morrat on his petition hath obtain order for a License to keep ordinary at his now dwelling house in the Citty of Williamsburgh in this County, giving bond with Richd. Wharton and Joseph Chermison, his security as the Law directs.

On the Informacion of Jno. Sergenton against Mary Bryan for having a mulato bastard, she this day appearing and confessing the fact, is orderd to be by the Church Warden's of Bruton Parish after her time by Indenture be expired, sold for 5 yeares according as is prescribed by a Late Law in the case made and provided entitled Servant and Slaves.

Henry Cary, his Power of Attorney from Mary Whaly of this present date was this day proved in Court by the oaths of Michaell Archer and Christopher Jaxon and ordered to be recorded.

The Court is adjournd to the 24th of June.

Received by me, John Tyler, son of Henry Tyler of York Co. in Virginia, and grandchild of Coll. John Page, formerly of the said County in Virginia, dec'd., of John Page of the Co. of Glouster £50 of lawfull mony of England by Bills of Exchange on Micajah Perry and Comp., merchants in London at ten days sight, the said sum being due to me the said John Tyler for a legacie left me by the Last Will & Testament of the said Col. John Page, dec'd., which I do hereby acknowledge to have received and discharge and acquit the said John Page of the said Co. of Gloucester and Mary, his wife, Admrs. of Matt Page Esqr., late of the said Co. of Gloucester, dec'd., one of the Extrs. of the Last Will & Testament of the said Coll. John Page, dec'd. and hold myself fully satisfied, contented and paid. In witness whereof, I have hereunto set my hand and seal this 19th day of August 1706. Wit. Mary Whaley and Hen. Cary. Recorded June the 24th 1707.

67. Inventory & Appraisement of the Estate of Cornelius Wilson, late of York Co., dec'd., taken the 27th day of May 1707. Among other items, one negro man of no value and one negro girl, if belonging to the Estate, £25, not included in total. Total value of estate, £58:1:2. Appraised by Willm. Allen, Jno. Wythe, Bazill Wagstaf and Charles Cox.

68. Power of Attorney. John Clark of the Island of Barbados, merchant, to Thomas Nelson in York River, Virginia, merchant, my true & lawfull

Attorney to collect debts due me by John Owen of Williamsburgh, merchant. Dated the 30th day of Aprill 1707. Wit. Nathll. Tatum and Samll. Smith.

Power of Attorney. Robert Cary of London, merchant, Extr. of the Last Will & Testament of Willm. Aylward, late of Virginia, merchant, but since dec'd. in the Kingdome of France, to Joseph Walker, merchant in Virginia, his true and lawfull Attorney to collect debts due the said Estate. Dated the 20th day of February 1706. Wit. John Brisco, Joseph Buck, Thomas Bagwell Junr., Thomas Bagwell, Thos. Jones, John Marshall and Danll. Sullivan. Recorded June 24th 1707.

69. What is come to hand since the appraisement of Richd. Dixon's Estate. Total £1:18:3. June the 25th 1707.

An account of the Estate of Willm. White, late of York Co., dec'd., which was by order of the said Court sold at Outcry and the bills assignd to the Trustee, Elizabeth Jones, widow grandmother, to the said White's orphan, who by her peticion obtain the Wardship of the said orphan and his Estate into her care, she having given bond and security as the Law directs, which said Estate was collected, and the severall debts due from the said Estate was paid by me the subscriber, Attorney of the said Elizabeth Jones as followeth. A total of £161:4:6 has been paid out to John Daniells, John Bates, Elizabeth Johnson, Willm. Spencer, James Archer, Capt. Hugh Norvell, Hen. Holdcraft, George Baskervile, John Levers, Edward Thomas, Job Cockings, Timothy Pinkethman, Robt. Stephenson, Benjamin Lillingston, Edward Wiggs, Coll. Ballard and Willm. Pinkethman.

71. At a Court held for York Co. June the 24th 1707. Robt. Read, Hen. Tyler, Thomas Roberts, Capt. Thomas Nutting, Coll. Thomas Ballard, Capt. Lawc. Smith, Majr. Wm. Buckner, Capt. Willm. Timson and Willm. Pinkethman, Justices.

Thomas Haustead, Elizabeth Cook and Mary Metam, evidences on behalf of our Sovereign Lady the Queen, against Elizabeth Gordon, who hath been lately accused for the feloniously taking away of severall moneys, goods and chattles from the house of Samuell Metam of Bruton Parish in this County, and by virtue of [?] brought from Henry Tyler before this Court for examinacion, being this day sworn and examind, it is the opinion of this Court and it is therefore orderd that the Sheriff safely convey the said Elizabeth Gordon to the Publick Goale of Williamsburgh, there to be safely kept till she be from thence deliverd by due course of Law.

Thomas Hawstead, Elizabeth Cook and Mary Metam this day in Court assumed themselves holden and firmly bound unto our Sov. Lady the Queen in the sum of £10 a piece to appeare on the 4th day of the next Generall Court, then and there to give their evidence on behalf of the said Sov. Lady against Eliz. Gordon.

James Ross, Elizabeth Ross of James Citty Co. and Jno. Redwood of the Co. of York this day came into Court and assumd themselves held and firmly bound to Our Sov. Lady the Queen in the sum of £10 a piece to appeare at the next Genll. Court on the 4th day thereof, then and there to give evidence on behalf of Our said Sov. Lady the Queen against Elizth. Gordon.

Sett as a rule of this Court that no Speciall Imparlance be granted without Speciall Reasons.

It is orderd by this Court that the Sheriff gett a pillory and stocks made and the prison mended and branding irons for the use of the County.

John Page, his Deeds of Sale by way of Lease and Release bearing date under the hand and seal of Mrs. Mary Whaley the 5th and 6th day of this Instant June for 200 acres of land lying and being in this County, was this day in Court personally acknowledged by the said Mary to the said John and orderd to be committed to record.

William Kemp of the Co. of Gloucester, his Deed of Sale bearing date under the hands and seales of Lieut. Coll. Thomas Ballard and Majr. Wm. Buckner, Trustees of the Portland in York Towne in this County, this present Instant for the Port Land lott 59 was this day in Court by the said Trustees sign'd, sealed and delivered and acknowledged to the said Willm. Kemp and orderd to be committed to record.

Wm. Tunley, his Deed of Sale bearing date under the hands and seales of Lieut. Coll. Thomas Ballard and Majr. Wm. Buckner, Trustees of the Portland in York Towne in this County, this present Instant for the Port Land lot 81 was this day in Court by the said Trustees sign'd, sealed and delivered and acknowledged to the said Wm. Tunley and orderd to be committed to record.

The last Will & Testament of Thomas Feare dated the 8th day of Octr. last past being this day brought before this Court for a probat thereof, and Samuel Taylor in hehalf of himself and wife, Jane, the daughter of the said dec'd., this day objected against the probat thereof for that he says is a clandestine will, is therefore referd till the next Court.

Joseph Walker, his Power of Attorney from Robert Cary of London, merchant, as Extr. of the Last Will & Testament of Wm. Aylward, dec'd. bearing date Feb. 26th 1706 was this day proovd in Court by the oaths of

Capt. Thomas Bagwell Junr., one of the evidences thereto, and is orderd to be committed to record.

72. Thomas Nelson, his Power of Attorney from John Clark of the Island of Barbados, merchant, bearing date Aprill 30th 1707 was this day proovd in Court by the oaths of Nathll. Tatum and Samll. Smith, evidences thereto, and is ordered to be committed to record.

The Deposicion of Robt. Bullock of London, merchant, concerning a mill called Warwick River Mill before Robt. Beddingfield, Knight, Lord Major of the said Citty of London and the Alderman of the said Citty, dated under the seal of the said Citty Feb. 6th 1706 this day presented in Court by Coll. Miles Cary, was this day proved in Court by the oaths of Thomas Bagwell Junr. and Benj. French, two of the evidences present at the dispatch thereof, and is orderd to be committed to record.

John Page, his receipt bearing date under the hand and seale of John Tyler, Legatee of Coll. John Page, dec'd. Augt. the 19th 1706, was this day in Court personally acknowledged by the said John Tyler to the said John Page and orderd to be comitted to record.

It is orderd that the Creditors of Cornelius Wilson, dec'd. bring their claimes to the next Court.

An Inventory & Appraisement of Cornelius Wilson's Estate was this day returnd by the Sheriff and orderd to be comitted to record.

The complaint of Anne Duvall to the Hon. the President referred to the Court concerning the ill usage of her daughter Mary Pagett by Elizth. Moody, wife of Humphry Moody, being this day pled and considerd, is refferd till tomorrow morning at which time if the said Anne produce good and sufficient security for the payment of 600 lbs. of tobaco to the said Elizth. on the 10th of October next, the said Mary Pagett shall be dischargd from the said Elizabeth.

In the suit brought to this Court by Abell Dun, plf. against Arthur Lawe, deft. in an Ejectione firmae, Wm. Barbar, Sheriff, this day making oath that he deliverd a copy of the declaracion to Nicholas Sebrell, tenant in possession of the land in question, it is therefore orderd that unless the said tenant in possession appear at the next Court and confess the lease entry and auster, judgment shall go by default and he will be hausted[?] of possession.

In the suit formerly brought by John Cooper of London, merchant, plf. against Thomas Whitby and Mary, his wife, Extrs. of the Last Will & Testament of Thomas Collier, dec'd. in an acion of case, the said plf.

appealed to the Genll. Court against the judgment formerly passed to dismiss the suit. Whereby said appeallant obtain order for a Writt of Enquiry for damage to be executed at this Court, which writ of Enquiry is orderd to be executed the next Court and the deft. being this day at Barr accepted, the notice thereof given him.

Elizabeth Jones by her Attorney, Henry Holdcraft, this day presented to the Court an account of the Estate of Will. White, dec'd. comitted to her care, which was this day examind, adjusted and approvd by the Court and orderd to be comitted to record.

On mocion of Joseph Chermison, it is orderd that the Clerk make a schedule of the papers belonging to the Estate of John Hilliard, dec'd. and deliver the said papers to him the said Joseph to collect and pay himself out of the same for a judgment formerly obtain by the said Joseph at this Court against the said Hilliard, and return the overplus to the Court.

Benjamin Lawson, on his petition showing his sickness and inability in getting his living, is exempt from paying levyes.

Mungo Ingles, on his peticion, hath judgment this day granted against Rachell Wood for having a bastard mulato female child born of her body and she is orderd to serve the said Mungo one whole yeare after her time by Indenture or custome be expired for the trouble of his house, and it is allso orderd that afterward she be sold by the Church Wardens of Bruton Parish as the Law directs.

73. James Bowman being presented by the Grand Jury for entertaining wicked and profane persons in his house and summond to this Court to answer the same, he this day appeard, made his defence and no evidence appearing, is discharged.

John Loynes being presented by the Grand Jury for keeping a whore in his house and summond to this Court to answer the same and not appearing, is orderd to be by the Sheriff taken into custody, safely to be kept till he give good security to appear at the next Court to answer the same.

Elizth. Starnes being presented by the Grand Jury for entertaining wicked and lewd persons in her house and summond to this Court to answer the same and not appearing, is orderd to be by the Sheriff taken into custody, safely to be kept till she give good security to appear at the next Court to answer the same.

John Phips this day appearing to answer the presentment of the Grand Jury for absenting from the Church and confessing the fact, is by the Court fined

5 shillings or 50 lbs. of tobacco and orderd to pay it to the Church Wardens of York Parish for the use of the said Parish betwixt this and the laying of the said Parish next levy, otherwise to receive on his bare back the number of 10 lashes well laid on by the Sheriff.

Robt. Clark, orphan of John Clark, dec'd., on his peticion obtain order for the admittance of Thomas Rogers to be his Guardian, who this day enterd into Bond with Joseph Chermison and George Baskervile for the due performance of his trust therein, according to Law.

Thomas Wooten appearing on a summons to answer the presenting of the Grand Jury for absenting from the Church, and confessing the fact, is fin'd 5 shillings or 50 lbs. of tobaco and is orderd to pay it to the Church Wardens of York Parish for the use of the said Parish next levy, otherwise to receive on his bare back the number of 10 lashes well laid on by the Sheriff.

Henry Clark appearing on a summons to answer the presenting of the Grand Jury for absenting from the Church and confessing the fact, is fin'd 5 shillings or 50 lbs. of tobaco and is orderd to be pay it to the Church Wardens of Charles Parish for the use of the said Parish betwixt this and the laying of the said Parish next levy, otherwise to receive on his bare back the number of 10 lashes well laid on by the Sheriff.

James Everet appearing on a summons to answer the presenting of the Grand Jury for absenting from the Church and confessing the fact, is fin'd 5 shillings or 50 lbs. of tobacco and is orderd to pay it to the Church Wardens of Charles Parish for the use of the said Parish betwixt this and the laying of the said Parish next levy, otherwise to receive on his bare back the number of 10 lashes well laid on by the Sheriff.

John Mackenry appearing on a summons to answer the presenting of the Grand Jury for absenting from the Church and confessing the fact, is fin'd 5 shillings or 50 lbs. of tobacco and orderd to pay it to the Church Wardens of Charles Parish for the use of the said Parish betwixt this and the laying of the said Parish next levy, otherwise to receive on his bare back the number of 10 lashes well laid on by the Sheriff.

Willm. Jones being summond to this Court to answer the Informacion of the Grand Jury for absenting from the Church and being unable to appeare, the Informacion is dismisst.

John Pattison being summond to this Court to answer the Informacion of the Grand Jury for absenting himself from Church and not appearing, is orderd to be taken into custody till he give bond and security for his appearance at the next Court to answere the same.

82

John Comes being summond to this Court to answere the Informacion of the Grand Jury for living in fornication and not appearing, is orderd to be taken into custody till he give bond and security for his appearing at the next Court to answere the same.

Danll. Mackentash being summond to this Court to answer the Informacion of the Grand Jury for absenting himself from Church and as being a vagrant and not appearing, is orderd to be taken into custody till he give bond and security for his appearing at the next Court to answer the same.

John Sandover being summond to this Court to answer the Informacion of the Grand Jury for absenting himself from Church and he not appearing, is ordered to be taken into custody till he give bond and security for his appearing at the next Court to answer the same.

74. Benjamin Lovell being summond to this Court to answer the Informacion of the Grand Jury for absenting himself from Church and not appearing, is orderd to be taken into custody till he give bond and security for his appearance at the next Court to answer the same.

The Informacion of the Grand Jury against Willm. Ryland for absenting from the Church is continued, he being sick.

Elizabeth Thomson being summond to this Court to answer the Informacion of the Grand Jury for bastardizing and not appearing, is orderd to be taken into custody untill she give bond with good and sufficient security to appear at the next Court and answere the same.

The Informacion of the Grand Jury against Catherine Masterton for bastardizing is continued till the next Court, she being unable to appeare at this.

Adduston Rogers being summond to this Court to answer the Informacion of the Grand Jury for not keeping the rodes clear in his precinque, this day made his appearance at Court and complaind against Thomas Wooten for turning the roads. It is therefore orderd that the said Thomas Wooton make good and sufficient bridges in the road through his land sufficient for cart and horse betwixt this and the next Court, otherwise to be fined according to Law.

Jonathon Lark being summond to this Court to answer the Informacion of the Grand Jury for not clearing the roads in this precinque, this day appeared and showed his late sickness for cause, is cleared if betwixt this and the next Court he amend the roads to the french ordinary.

83

Thomas Vines being this day summond to the Court to answer the Informacion of the Grand jury for not clearing the roads in his precinques, this day appeard and showed that they are since amended, he is therefore dismisst.

Thomas Whitby, his acion of debt depending to this Court against Isaac Jamart, Admr. of Wm. Chalkhill, dec'd. is dismisst per non prosecution.

In the suit depending to this Court between Thomas Ballard, plf. and Wm. Buckner, Admr. of John Hilliard, dec'd., deft. in an acion of debt declared for the sum of £4:5 due by bill dated under the dec'd. hand and seale January the 19ᵗʰ 1705/6, the plf. hath judgment granted for the said sum and ordered to be paid with costs when assess.

In the suit depending to this Court between John Tomer, plf. and John Wells and Elizabeth, his wife, Extrs. of Thomas Harwood, dec'd. in an acion of case, the plf. this day put in his replicacion and the deft. cravd time to rejoyne.

Wm. Tunley's acion of trespass depending to this Court against John Andrews is postponed at the request of the deft.'s Attorney.

Wm. Shareman's attachment obtaind against Anthony Jesper in an acion of debt is dismisst per non prosecution.

Wm. Shareman's attachment obtaind against Anthony Jesper in an acion of debt is dismisst per non prosecution.

Wm. Shareman's attachment obtaind against Anthony Jesper in an acion of case is dismisst per non prosecution.

In the suit brought to this Court by Thomas Whitby and Mary, his wife, Extrs. of the Last Will & Testament of Thomas Collyer, dec'd., plf. against Joseph Walker, Admr. of Wm. Aylward, dec'd. in an acion of debt, the deft. hath obtaind time till next Court.

Henry Hayward Junr. having brought suit to this Court against John Dozwell Senr. in an acion of debt declared for the sum of £4:8:8 due by bill and he not appearing, order is granted against Wm. Barbar, H.S., and the next Court to be confirmd if he causeth not the deft. then personally to appear and answer the same.

Wm. Tunley's acion of case damage £60 brought to this Court against James Ming is dismisst per non prosecution.

75. Samll. Boys hath judgment this day granted against Charles Holdsworth in an acion of debt for the sum of 600 lbs. of sweet scented tobaco due by bill dated Sepr. the 6th 1705 and is orderd to be paid with costs alies execution.

Henry Holdcraft, Assignee of Thomas Green, his acion of debt against David Harbeard is dismisst per non prosecution.

Benjamin Weldon, Assignee of Robt. Bills, his acion of debt against Edwd. Young is dismisst per non prosecution.

Wm. Davis having brought suit to this Court in chancery against John Loynes and he not appearing, an attachment is granted against the respondent's body, he being by the Sheriff returnd summond to answer the said suite.

Danll. Burton's acion of debt against Willm. Thacker and Thomas Halye is dismisst per non prosecution.

Humphrey Moody's complainte against Barbara Hutton is dismisst per non prosecution.

Joshua Curl, his seire facias against Isaac Jamart, Admr. of Wm. Chalkhill, dec'd. is dismisst per non prosecution.

In the suit brought to this Court by John Owen, plf. against Isaac Jamart, Admr. of Wm. Chalkhill, dec'd., deft. in an acion of seire facias, the deft on his prayer hath time given till the next Court.

In the suit brought to this Court by Charles Chiswell, plf. against Wm. Barbar, Sheriff of York Co., deft. in an acion of case damage £100, a specialle imparlance is granted till the next Court.

In the suit brought to this Court by Mary Whaley, plf. against Henry Gilbert, deft. in an acion of debt, an imparlance is granted till the next Court.

George Baskervile, Assignee of Hugh Owen, arresting John Saunders to this Court and declared for the sum of 30 shillings, and he not appearing, order is granted against Wm. Barbar, H.S., and the next Court to be confirmd if he causeth not the deft. then personally to appeare and answer the same.

In the suit brought to this Court by Henry Cary, plf. against John Naylor, deft. in an acion of case declared that when the said Henry the 23d day of May was possesd of 48 yards of kersie, 40 yards of thickset, 1 lb. of cotton, 80 yards of ozenbriggs and 40 yards of estamines as of his owne proper goods and chattles, without of his possession he lost, and afterwards to the hands of the said John by finding came, who converted it to his owne use to the said Henry's damage £30, to which the deft. pleaded not guilty. Whereupon a jury was impannelld and sworn to try the issue, who after a full hearing of all evidences and pleas returnd for verdict in these words – Wee find for the deft., sign'd Willm. Shelden, foreman. Which on mocion of the deft.'s Attorney is admitted to record.

The Court adjournd till the hower of 9 tomorrow morning.

Power of Attorney. Thomas Rose, Chirnagson[?] of the Ship Providence [?] Kent [?], to Use Gibson, carpenter of York co., my true and lawfull Attorney. Dated the 14th day of Jany. 1706. Wit. Tho. Ravenscroft, Natt Huggins, Adam Galt and Thomas Odill.

76. At a Court held for York Co. June 25th 1707 per adjournment from the 24th Instant. Present: Robt. Reade, Henry Tyler, Lt. Col. Thomas Ballard, Capt. Lawc. Smith, Major Wm. Buckner and Wm. Timson, Justices.

Joseph Walker, his Deed of Assignment bearing date under the hand and seale of Samuell Dickson May the 24th 1707 for the Portland lot in York Towne no. 17, was this day acknowledged in Court by Willm. Tunley, Attorney for the said Samuell, whose Power together with the said deed was allso proovd by the oaths of James Archer, Philip Moody and Ralph Hubbard, evidences thereto, and orderd to be comitted to record.

James Sclater, his Deed of Assignment bearing date under the hand and seale of Capt. Daniell Taylor and Mary, his wife, this present Instant for the Portland lot in York Towne no. 25, was this day by the said Danll. and Mary personally acknowledged in Court and orderd to be comitted to record.

An Inventory & Appraisement of Cornelius Wilson's Estate was this day presented to the Court by Willm. Barbar and orderd to be cimitted to record.

Wm. March and Elizabeth, his wife, late widow and Relict of Job Cocking, dec'd., their complaint against Joseph Thrift concerning John Bartlot is dismisst, no cause of complaint, and the said John Bartlot is discharged.

The former order against George Baskervile for the non appearance of Barbara Hutton to answer the Informacion of John Wythe for fornicacion is continued till the next Court.

It is orderd that the Sheriff take and in safe custody keep the body of Elizth. Ditcher till she give bond with good and sufficient security to appear at the next Court to answer the Informacion of Peter Goodwin, Church Warden of York Parish, for fornicacion.

Damazinah Browne this day made return of the remainder of Richard Dixon's Estate, according to her former oath, which is orderd to be added to the Inventory allready on record.

The former order for Sarah Stanup, Admx. of Richard Stanup, dec'd., to return an Inventory of the said dec'd. Estate is continued till the next Court.

In the suit depending to this Court between John Duke, plf. against Nicholas Phillips, deft. in an acion of case, the plf. this day by Robt. Hyde, his Attorney, demurd generally to the deft.'s plea and the deft. hath time till next Court to mend paying costs or join in demure.

The suit depending to this Court between Jno. Owen, plf. against David Robinson, deft. in an acion of case is dismisst per non prosecution.

In the suit depending to this Court between Wm. Kaydyee, plf. against Adam Galt, deft. in an acion of case wherein the plf. declared that when he the plf. on the 19th of October last past in the Parish of Bruton in this County was possessed of one whole guelding of the value of 15 shillings as of his owne proper goods, and being so possessed the same did lend to the deft. at his instance and request in consideracion of friendship, that the said deft. should redeliver unto the plf. the said horse the day next following in as good order and well condiciond as he then received him, but the deft. not regarding his promise aforesaid, the same refused to the damage to the plf. £20, and the deft. suffering judgment to be confirmd against him per nihil dicit and order for a Writ of Enquiry for damage to be this day executed, the plf and deft. this day by consent refferd the enquiry of damage aforesaid to the Court, who this day granted judgment for the plf. against the deft. for the sume of £7 damage and it is orderd that the deft. pay it to the plf. with costs alies execution.

77. Richard Wharton, his acion of debt depending to this Court against John Redwood is continued till the next Court by consent.

The suit depending to this Court between Benjamin Shepherd, plf. against Danll. Taylor, Gent., in an acion of case, the plf. not prooving his declaracion, the suit is dismisst, the deft. denying the account sued for upon oath.

Cornelius Jones hath judgment of nihil dicit this day granted against John Loynes in an acion of case for the sum of £50 damage and the next Court to be confirmd on the like default.

John Warren did this day in Court confest judgment to James Bates, Assignee of Jno. Harrison, in an acion of debt for the sume of £1:5 due by bill dated the 30th day of Augt. 1706 and is orderd forthwith to pay it to the plf. with costs alies execution.

Joseph Chermison hath judgment of nihil dicit this day granted against George Booker in an acion of case for the sume of £8:6:6 and the next Court to be confirmd on the like default.

Elizth. Somerwell, Admx. of Mungo Somerwell, dec'd. hath judgment this day granted against Damazinah Brown, Extx. of Richd. Dixon, dec'd. in an acion of debt for the sume of £8 by protested Bills of Exchange dated April the 27th 1702, and is orderd to be paid with the damage of 15% charge of protest and costs alies execution.

Elizabeth Somerwell, Admx. of Mungo Somerwell, dec'd. hath judgment of nihil dicitt this day granted against Damazinah Brown, formerly Dixon, Extx. of Richd. Dixon, dec'd. in an acion of case for the sume of £4:16 and the next Court to be confirmd on the like default.

Thomas Pain hath judgment of nihil dicit this day granted against Damazinah Brown, formerly Dixon, Extx. of Richd. Dixon, dec'd. in an acion of case for the sume of 4,000 lbs. of tobaco damage and the next Court to be confirmd on the like default.

John Penton this day in Court confesst judgment to Wm. Tunley in an acion of case for the sume of 3,083 lbs. of tobaco due on account of Peter Gibson, signd and accepted to be paid by the said John Penton and Use Gibson, Novr. the 16th 1706, and is orderd to pay it to the plf. with costs alies execution.

John Penton's acion of debt against Joseph Mountfort is dismist per non prosecution.

Coll. Edmd. Jenings hath judgment this day granted against Izabella Broadbent, Admx. of Joshua Broadbent, dec'd. in an acion of debt for the sume of £11:13:6 and 73 lbs. of tobaco due by a judgment of Gloucester Co. dated the 18th of Sepr. 1706 and is orderd to be paid with costs alies execution.

John Loynes, his acion of case against Henry Hayles is dismisst per non prosecution.

In the suit depending to this Court between Thomas Harton, plf. against James Bowman in an acion of case, the plf. hath judgment confirrmd against the Sheriff and orderd that a Writ of Enquiry be executed the next Court.

The Ejectione firmae depending to this Court between John Cox, plf. and John Fergason, deft. is continued till the next Court for the condicionale order to be served.

Frances Hooper's acion of case against Michaell Cormack is dismisst per non prosecution.

78. Anne Duvall's suit against Humphrey Moody is dismisst, she not producing security for 600 lbs. of tobaco according to an order yesterday granted.

James Shield's acion of case against David Claxton is dismisst per non prosecution.

James Hill hath judgment this day granted against John Hall in an acion of case for the sume of £5:3:6 due by bill dated under the hand of the deft. Sepr. the 27 1706 and is orderd to be paid with costs alies execution.

Robt. Mynne's acion of case against Joseph Mountfort is dismisst per non prosecution.

John Hall's acion of trespass against Thomas Walker is dismisst per non prosecution.

Andrew Young's acion of debt damage £40 against Thomas Wamsley is dismist per non prosecution.

In the suit brought to this Court between Hen. Hayward Junr. against Joseph Walker, Admr. of Wm. Aylward, dec'd., an imparlance is granted till next Court.

John Martin's acion of debt against John Redwood is dismisst per non prosecution.

John Martin's acion of case against John Redwood is dismisst per non prosecution.

Susanah Leighton, Extx. of the Last Will & Testament of Edwd. Not, Esqr., dec'd. against John Marrot is dismisst per non prosecution.

In the suit in chancery brought to this Court by Robert Cary, Extr. of Wm. Aylward, dec'd. against Wm. Babb, time is given till the next Court for answere.

John Thruston bringing suit to this Court against James Pendergrace in an acion of case for the sum of £6:3 returnable to the next Court, he being by the Sheriff on his oath returnd non est inventus.

Gabriel Mompain arresting Ralph Hubbard to this Court in an acion of case for the sum of £3:10:7 ½ and he not appearing, order is granted against Wm. Barbar, Sheriff, and the next Court to be confirmd if he causeth not the deft. then personally to appeare and answer of the same.

Charles Handsford bringing suit in this Court against John Loynes in an acion of case for the sume of £10 damage and he not appearing, an attachment is granted against his Estate returnable to the next Court, he being by the Sheriff on oath returnd non est inventus.

In the suit brought to this Court by Joshua Curl, plf. against Isaac Jamart, Admr. of Willm. Chalkhill, dec'd., deft. in an acion of seire facias, time is given till the next Court.

Wm. Tunley arresting Joshua Curl to this Court in an acion of case for the sume of 331 lbs. of tobaco and he not appearing, order is granted against Robt. Hyde, his security, and the next Court to be confirmd if he causeth not the deft. then personally to appeare and answer the same.

Robert Hyde hath an attachment this day granted against the Estate of Joshua Curl for the sume of 331 lbs. of tobacco and costs returnable to the next Court for the non appearance of the said Joshua at this Court to answer the suite of William Tunley in an acion of case for the like sume.

John Prat arresting John Chiles to this Court in an acion of debt for the sume of £4:17:6 and he not appearing, order is granted against Wm. Barbar, Sheriff, and the next Court to be confirmed if he causeth not the deft. then personally to appeare and answer the same.

William Barbar, High Sheriff, hath an attachment granted against the Estate of John Chiles for the sume of £4:17:6 with costs returnable to the next Court for his non appearance at this Court to answer the suite of John Pratt for the like sume.

Wm. Walrond hath judgment this day granted against Wm. Kaydyee in an acion of debt for the sum of £7:15 due by bill dated Aprill the 15th 1706 and is orderd to be paid with costs alies execution.

79. Walter Butler's acion of debt against Samll. Groves is dismisst per non prosecution.

John Owen arresting Andrew Young to this Court in an acion of debt for the sum of £13:0:7 and he not appearing, order is granted against Wm. Barbar, H. Sheriff, and the next Court to be confirmd if he causeth not the deft. then personally to appeare and answer the same.

William Barbar, Sheriff, hath an attachement granted against the Estate of Andrew Young for the sume of £13:0:7 with costs returnable to the next Court for his non appearance at this Court to answer the suite of John Owen in an acion of debt for the like sum.

The suit brought to this Court by John Sergeton, plf. against John Nicholson, deft. in an acion of case is continued by consent.

John Redwood arresting Andrew Young to this Court in an acion of debt for the sum of £2:5:9 and he not appearing, order is granted against Wm. Barbar, H.S., and the next Court to be confirmd if he causeth not the deft. then personally to appear and answer the same.

Wm. Barbar, Sheriff, hath an attachment this day granted against the Estate of Andrew Young for the sume of £2:5:9 with costs returnable to the next Court for his non appearance at this Court to answer the suite of John Redwood in an acion of debt for the like sume.

In the suit brought to thsis Court by John Redwood, plf. against Wm. Kaydyee, deft. in an acion of debt, an imparlance is granted till next Court.

Adjournd to the 24th of July next. God love the Queen.

Power of Attorney. Thomas Taillor, John Taillor, William Arnold and Thomas Harwood of London, merchants, John Silke of London, butcherer[?], Thomas Moore of London, distiller, and Daniel Oley of London, haberdasher, owners of the Ship Thomas & John, whereof Robert Ransome, late was and William Marshall now is Commander, to Col. Dudley Digges of Virginia, Esqr., our true and lawful Attorney, to collect debts due us for the price of any negro slave or slaves, part of the cargo of slaves lately brought in the said Ship from Guinea to Virginia. Dated the 4th day of February 1706. Wit. Thomas Bagwell Junr. and Benjamin French. Recorded the 24th day of July 1707.

80. Power of Attorney. Thomas Carleton of Barbados, merchant, to Col. Dudley Digges, Esqr. of Virginia, my true and lawful Attorney to collect debts due unto me in the Island of Barbados. Dated the 7th day of May

1707. Wit. John Wells and William Griffin. Recorded the 24th day of July 1707.

81. Power of Attorney. Elizabeth Fear, wife of Thomas Fear of York Co., to John Smith of York Co., my true and lawfull Attorney to acknowledge this Indenture of even date being for 66 acres of land, unto John Bates. Dated the 22d of July 1707. Wit. Susanna Nash and Dionisha Unthanks. Recorded the 24th day of July 1707.

June 28th 1707, this day came Thomas Parris, merchant, and declared that in Cornelius Wilson's lifetime, he several times heard him say that the young negro girl calld Jenny was [the property of] his daughter, Rose, and that she was purchased from the produce of a cow calf given her by her Godfather. Tho. Parris.

John Andrews of York Towne and Co. deposeth upon oath that he the said John did often heare Cornelius Wilson, lately dec'd., say that the negro girle Jenny, then in his possession, did really and of right belong to his daughter Rosamond, being purchased by the produce of a calf that her Godfather gave her. Jno. Andrews. Sworne before the Court this 24th day of July 1707.

Ralph Ransford of York Town and Co. deposeth upon oath that the the said Ralph did often hear Cornelius Wilson, late of this Town, dec'd. say tht the negro girle, Jenny, then in his possession, did really and of right belong to his daughter Rosamond, being purchased ty the produce of a calf that her Godfather gave her. Ralph Ransford. Sworn before the Court this 24th day of July 1707.

The deposision of Edward Parson saith that the said deponent hath heard Cornelius Wilson say that he sold his daughter Rosamon Willson cattell and hath bought her a negro girl in the year 1704. Edward Parsons. 1707 June the 16th.

82. The deposition of Thomas Potter saith that the said deponent, when he lived with Cornelius Wilson in the year 1700, that there was a cow and two or three young cattell then that was calld Rosaman Wilson's cattel, but what increase the said cattell hath had since, your deponent cannot say. Thomas Potter. 1707 June the 16th.

At a Court held for York Co. the 24th July 1707. Present, Robert Read, Henry Tyler, Thomas Ballard, Lawrence Smith, Wm. Buckner and Wm. Pinkethman, Gents.

Philip Lightfoot Junr. presented a commission from the Hon. Edmd. Jenings, Esq. to be Clerk of this Court and has taken the oaths thereby required.

Wm. Buckner, Henry Tyler and Wm. Barbar, Gent., presented their commissions to be Coronors of this County and have taken the oaths thereby required.

Wm. Tunley, late Clerk, being ordered to deliver up the records belonging to this Court, withdrew himself, and in some short time sent a letter to the Court to this effect, that some part of the records which were demanded of him were his. The Court having just reason to suspect that they may be imbasoled if speedy care be not taken, it is therefore ordered that the Sheriff of this County forthwith take him into his custody and bring him before the Court to answer his contempt therein.

A Letter of Attorney from Thomas Carleton of Barbados, merchant, to Dudley Diggs, Esq. was this day produced in Court and proved by the oath of John Wells, one of the witnesses thereto, and at the motion of John Clayton, Attorney of the said Diggs, was ordered to be recorded.

John Clayton, Attorney of Dudley Diggs, Esq., presented a Letter of Attorney from Thomas Taylor, John Taylor and others to the said Diggs and at his the said Clayton's mocion, ordered to be recorded.

A negro boy named Robin, belonging to John Goodier, was this day brought into Court and adjudged to be 13 years old.

Wm. Buckner and Thomas Ballard, the Trustees of the Portland in York Town, presented and acknowledged their deed to Henry Hayward Junr. for one Lott in the said town and at his mocion ordered to be recorded.

Thomas Fear came into Court and acknowledged his Deeds of Lease and Release for land, as also John Smith by virtue of Letter of Attorney from Eliz., the wife of the said Thomas Fear, relinquished her the said Eliz.'s right of dower in the said lands, to John Bates and at his motion ordered to be recorded.

83. A Letter of Attorney from Eliz. Fear to John Smith was proved by the oaths of Susanna Nash and Dionisha Unthanks, witnesses thereto, and at the said Smith's mocion, admitted to record.

Major Lewis Burwell producing a judgment of the Gloucester Co. Court for £20 confirmed against John Toagle as security of Cornelius Wilson, late of this County, dec'd., whose Estate is now in the hands of the Sheriff of this

County, it is therefore ordered that the said Sheriff deliver so much of the Estate of the said Wilson to the said Burwell as will satisfy the said judgment with costs, according to the former appraisement returned.

Rosamond Wilson, daughter of Cornelius Wilson, dec'd., produced the severall depositions of Ralph Ransford, John Andrews, Thomas Parris, Edward Parsons and Thomas Potter, showing that a negro girl named Jenny, supposed to be the Estate of the said Wilson, doth properly belong to her the said Rosamond. Therefore at her request they are admitted to record.

John Loynes, according to order appearing to answer the presentment of the Grand Jury against him for keeping a whore and absenting himself contrary to Law from Church, on Examination is found guilty of absenting himself from Church. It is therefore ordered that he be fined 5 shillings or 50 lbs. of tobacco to be paid to the Church Wardens of Bruton Parish, and upon refusall of payment by distress.

Eliz. Stains appeared to answer the presentment of the Grand Jury for entertaining wicked and lude persons and it not appearing against her, is discharged.

The former order for taking John Pattison into custody to answer the presentment of the Grand Jury against him is continued till the next Court.

John Sandover this day appearing to answer the presentment of the Grand Jury against him for absenting himself from the Church and on hearing what he had to say, is discharged.

John Comes appearing to answer the presentment of the Grand Jury against him for living in fornication and he confessing the fact before the Court, it is therefore ordered that he be fined 500 lbs. of tobacco to be paid to the Church Wardens of Charles Parish at the next levy and on failure that he receive 25 lashes on his bare back well laid on by the Sheriff of this County.

The former order for taking Daniell Mackintosh into custody to answer the presentment of the Grand Jury against him for absenting himself from Church and as a vagrant is continued till the next Court.

The former order for taking Benjamin Lovell in custody to answer the presentment of the Grand Jury against him for absenting himself from Church is continued till the next Court.

The former order for taking Wm. Ryland in custody to answer the presentment of the Grand Jury against him for absenting himself from Church is continued till the next Court.

The former order for taking Eliz. Thompson in custody to answer the presentment of the Grand Jury against her for bastardizing is continued till next Court.

The former order for taking Kathn. Masterton in custody for reasons shewd to the Court, is discontinued.

Ordered the Court be adjourned to the 24th of August next.

Certificate according to Law issue out of my office of Wm. Sheldon departure out of this colony on the 10th of October 1707.

84. At a Court held for York Co. the 25th day of August 1707. Present: Thomas Barbar, Henry Tyler, Thomas Ballard, Lawrence Smith, William Buckner and W. Pinkethman, Gent., Justices.

William Robertson presented a deputation from Edmund Jenings, Esq., Secretary of Virginia, impowering him to officiate as Clerk of this Court in the room of Philip Lightfoot, who is disabled from attending, and was accordingly sworne Clerk for this Court.

The petition of Lemuel Taylor for staying the probate of the Will of Thomas Fear, dec'd., the petr. not appearing to make out his objections, is dismist.

The last Will & Testament of Thomas Fear, dec'd. was this day presented in Court by Thomas Fear, the Extr. therein named, who made oath thereto and the same being also proved by the oaths of John Smith and Susanna Nash, witnesses thereto, was admitted to record and probate thereof granted under the said Thomas Fear, the Extr.

A Letter of Attorney from Robert Cary of London, merchant, to Joseph Walker was this day proved in Court by the oath of Thomas Jones, one of the witnesses thereto, and is admitted to record.

The orders of the Last Court for the creditors of Cornelius Wilson to appear and make out their debts, on further consideration, is [?]. And it is ordered that the Sheriff of this County sell the remainder of the said Wilson's Estate in his hands by order on the 2d day of September for money or Bills of Exchange payable the 10th day of March next and that he take security of the purchasers for the payment thereof accordingly, and make report of his proceedings to the next Court.

In the ejectione firmae brought by Abel Dun, plf. against Arthur Laws, deft., George Baskerville, Under Sheriff of this County, this day made oath in Court that he served Nicholas Sebrell, the tenant in possession of the lands in question, with a copy of the conditional order in this cause. And the said Nicholas Sebrell comes by Henry Holdcraft, his Attorney, and prayd to be admitted deft. in the room of Arthur Laws, and he is admitted accordingly having ordred into rule to come to tryal of these till the next Court.

Thomas Ballard and Wm. Buckner, Gent., Trustees of the Portland in this County, come into Court, presented and acknowledged the Deed for one Lott of the said land unto Joseph Walker, Gent., and it is admitted to record.

The action on the case between John Cooper of London, merchant, plf. and Thomas Whitby and Mary, his wife, Extrs. of Thomas Collier, dec'd., on the motion of the plf.'s Attorney, is continued till next Court.

The order for Joseph Chermison's returning an account of the Estate of John Hilliard, dec'd. is continued till next Court and ordered that the Clerk make an Inventory of the papers belonging to the said Hillyard's Estate and deliver the same to the said Chermisson upon his request, for the better enabling of the said Chermison to make up the account required of him.

The action on the case between John Toomer, plf. and John Wills and Elizabeth, his wife, Extrs. of the last Will & Testament of Thomas Harwood, dec'd., by consent of both partys is continued till next Court.

In the action of debt between Thomas Whitby and Mary, his wife, Extrs. of Thomas Collier, dec'd., plf., and Joseph Walker, Admr. of Wm. Aylward, dec'd., deft. for £9 due by protested Bills of Exchange with damage according to Law, the deft. appeared and confessed judgment for the personall damages and [?] the said Bill of Exchange, whereupon it is considered by the Court that the deft. pay the same unto the plf. amounting in the whole to £10:10:6 with costs alies execution.

The action of debt between Henry Hayward Junr., plf. and John Dozwell Senr., deft., the plf. not presenting, is dismist.

In the suite in Chancery between Wm. Davis, complainant and John Loynes, respondent, on the resp.'s motion time is granted him till next Court to put in his answer, and the compl. hath time granted him till the same Court to amend his bill having entered into rule to give the respt.'s Attorney a copy of the bill as amended 10 days before the Court.

85. The suite by seire facias brought by John Owen, plf. against Isaac Jamart, Admr. of the goods, rights and credits of Wm. Chalkhill, dec'd., deft., by consent of both partys is continued till next Court.

The action in the case between Charles Chiswell, plf. and Wm. Barbar, deft., on the plf.'s motion is continued till next Court.

In the action of debt between Mary Whaley, plf. and Henry Gilbert, deft. for £61 due by bill, time being granted the deft. to try this Court to importe and being now called and not appearing, judgment by nihil dicit is granted the plf. against the said deft. for the aforesaid sum and costs unless the deft. appears at next Court and answers the said action.

Thomas Nutting, Gent. present.

In the actio of debt between George Baskerville, Assignee of Hugh Owens, plf. and John Sanders, deft. for 30 shillings due to the plf. by bill under the deft.'s hand the 17th of April 1706, wherein an order was granted against Wm. Barbar, Sheriff of this County, for the nonappearance of the deft., and the said deft. being this day called to come forth and answer the said action, who not appearing, the judgment is therefore confirmed against the said Wm. Barbar for the sum of 30 shillings and ordered that he pay the same unto the plf. with costs alies execution.

Judgment being this day confirmed against William Barbar, Sheriff of this County, for the sum of 30 shillings and costs to be paid to George Baskerville by reason of the nonappearance of John Sanders at the suite of the said Baskerville, on the motion of the said Barbar an attachment is granted him against the Estate of the said John Sanders for the said sum of 30 shillngs with costs returnable to the next Court for judgment.

Barbara Hutton being arrested to answer the Information of John Wyth, Church Warden of York Parish, for fornication and not appearing, judgment is granted the plf. and Thomas Mountfort returned security for the said Hutton, for the sum of 500 lbs. of tobacco unless he produces the body of the said Hutton at next Court to answer the said Information, and ordered that this order be served on the said Mountfort by the Sheriff.

Elizabeth Ditcher failing to appear to answer the presentment of the Grand Jury against her for fornication, ordered that the Sheriff take the said Ditcher into custody untill she give bond with good security for her personal appearance at next Court to answer the said presentment.

Thomas Ballard and Wm. Buckner, Gent., trustees of the Portland in this County, came into Court, presented and acknowledged their Deed for one Lott of the said land unto John Martin, and it is admitted to record.

William Crymes comes into Court, states under oath that the account produced by him in the suite now depending to this Court against George

Livingston is a true copy of the account which he received from the said Livingston and that he hath received no satisfaction for the same.

Thomas Nutting, Gent. presented his commission to be one of the Coroners of this County and was accordingly sworne into the said office.

Sarah Stanup failing to appear and return an inventory of the Estate of Richard Stanup, her dec'd. husband's Estate, ordered that the Sheriff take her into custody untill she give bond with good security for her appearance at next Court and returning the same.

The order of Elizabeth Somerwell's returning of Inventory & Appraisement of her dec'd. husband's Estate is continued till next Court.

In the motion on the case between John Duke, plf. and Nicholas Philips, deft., the deft. having amended his plea, on the motion of the plf. time is granted him till next Court to reply.

The action of debt between Richd. Wharton, plf. and John Redwood, deft., on the plf.'s motion is continued till next Court.

In the action on the case between Cornelius Jones, plf. and John Loynes, deft. for the sum of £50 damage by means of the deft.'s not procuring an Indian man called Peter Larabie to bond himself apprentice to the said plf. for the sume of 8 years and not paying the plf. the sum of £4 or the value thereof, nor delivering back to the plf. one negro woman slave according to his promise and assumption… the deft. having had time given him to answer the said action and being now called and not appearing to offer anything in defense of the plf.'s action, it is therefore considered by the Court that the plf. ought to have his damage against the deft. by means of the nonperformance of his promise and assumption aforesaid. But because it is unknown by the Court what damage the said plf. in that part hath sustained, therefore it is commanded that the Sheriff cause to come before Her Magesty's Justices at next Court to be held for this County a jury of 12 good and lawful men of his balywick by whose oaths dilligent enquiry may be made of the said damage of which the deft.'s Attorney hath notice given him and argued the same at the Barr.

86. The action on the case between Joseph Chermison, plf. and George Booker, deft. is continued by consent till next Court.

In the action in the case between Elizabeth Somerwell, Admx. of Mongo Somerwell, dec'd., plf. and Damazinah Brown, formerly Damazinah Dixon, Extx. of Richd. Dixon, dec'd. for £4:16 due by account, the plf. having made oath that she found the account declared for among the accounts of her dec'd. husband and that she hath received no part of satisfaction thereof, and the said deft. offering no defense or objection against the same, it is therefore ordered that the deft. pay unto the plf. the said sum with costs alies execution.

In the action in the case between Thomas Paine, plf. and Damazinah Brown, Extx. of the last Will & Testament of Richd. Dixon, dec'd., deft., the deft. having put in a plea to the plf.'s declaration, on the plf.'s motion time is granted him till next Court to reply or demur.

In the action in the case between Thomas Harton, plf. and James Bowman, deft. for 20 shillings due by account, the deft. appeared and confessed judgment for the sum. Whereupon it is ordered that the said deft. pay unto the plf. the said sum with costs alies execution.

Edward Davis being summoned an evidence for Thomas Harton against James Bowman and having attended 6 days, ordered that the said Harton pay him for the sum according to the Law with costs alies execution.

John Parish the same.

In the ejectione firmae brought by John Cox, plf. against John Ferguson, deft., Thomas Walker this day made oath in Court to the service of the conditional order on John Drury, the tenant in possession of the land in controversy, and the said John appeared and on his motion ...and by consent of the plf., is continued till next Court.

In the action on the case between Henry Hayward Junr., plf. and Joseph Walker, Admr. of Wm. Aylward, dec'd., deft. for £5:1:4 due by the said Aylward to the plf. by account, the plf. having made oath to his account and allowed a discount of the deft. paid by the decedent and the deft. not objecting against the said account, judgment is therefore granted the plf. against the said deft. for the sum of £4:17:4 ½ to be paid out of the Estate of the said Aylward when assetts come to the deft.'s hands with costs alies execution.

William Timson, Gent. present.

Elizabeth Davis being summoned an evidence for Henry Hayward Junr. against Joseph Walker and having attended 4 days, ordered that the said Hayward pay her for the same according to Law with costs alies execution.

In the suite in chancery between Robert Cary, Extr. of Wm. Aylward, dec'd., complainant and Wm. Ball, respondent, the respt. not appearing, on the compl.'s motion for an attachment is granted against the body of the said respt. for his appearance at next Court to answer the said complaint.

In the motion on the case between John Thruston, plf. and James Pendergrass, deft. for £10:3 due by account, the deft. having made oath to his account and therein allowed the deft.'s credit and the deft. showing no cause why judgment shall not pass against him for the ballance, it is therefore considered by the Court that the deft. pay unto the plf. the sum of £1:8 with costs alies execution.

The action in the case between Gabriel Mompain, plf. and Ralph Hubbard, deft., neither party appearing, is dismist.

In the action on the case between Charles Hansford, plf. and John Loynes, deft. for £7:1:8 due by account, the deft. appeared and confessed judgment for the sum of £2:7, and on the plf.'s motion judgment is granted him against the said deft. for the said sum with costs alies execution.

The suite by seire facias between Joshua Curle, plf. and Isaac Jamart, Admr. of the goods, chattels, rights and credits of Wm. Chalkhill, dec'd., deft., by consent of both partys is continued till next Court.

In the action on the case between Wm. Tunley, plf. and Joshua Curle, deft. for 361 lbs. of tobacco due by account, Wm. Gordon came into Court and assumed the payment of the debt in name of the deft. It is thereupon ordered that the said Gordon pay unto the plf. the said sum with costs alies execution.

The action of debt between Jno. Pratt, plf. and John Chiles, deft., neither party appearing, is dismist.

The action of debt between Jno. Owen, plf. and Andrew Young, deft., neither party appearing, is dismist.

87. In the action on the case between John Serjanten, plf. and John Nicholson, deft., on the deft.'s motion an imparlance is granted till next Court.

In the action of debt between John Redwood, plf. and Andrew Young, deft. for £2:5:9 due by bill under the deft.'s hand dated the 6th of November 1706, judgment being passed by the Court unto the said plf. against Wm. Barbar, Sheriff of this County, for the said sum for the nonappearance of the said Young to answer the plf.'s action, and the said Young being now called and not appearing, judgment is therefore confirmed against the said Wm.

Barbar and it is considered by the Court that he pay unto the plf. the said sum with costs alies execution.

The attachment which Wm. Barbar, Gent, Sheriff of this County, obtained against the Estate of Andrew Young for the non appearance of the said Young in the suite of John Redwood, not being yet executed, on the motion of the said Barbar is continued till next Court.

The action of debt between John Redwood, plf. and Wm. Kaidyee, deft., on the plf.'s motion is continued till next Court.

The action of debt between Mongo Ingles, plf. and Jno. Loynes, deft., neither party appearing, is dismist.

In the action of debt between John Bates, plf. and Jno. Loynes, deft. for £8:8:9 due by bill under the deft.'s hand dated the 27th of May 1707, the deft. appeared and confessed judgment for the same, whereupon it is ordered that he pay unto the plf. the said sum with costs alies execution.

The action of the case between James Phillob, plf. and Saml. Mettam, deft., neither party appearing, is dismist.

The action of the debt between Isaac Rowden, plf. and Oliver Perron, deft., neither party appearing, is dismist.

The action of the case between Isaac Rowden, plf. and Oliver Perron, deft., neither party appearing, is dismist.

The action on the case between Anthony Jasper, plf. and Wm. Sharmin, deft., neither party appearing, is dismist.

In the action of the case between John Roberts, plf. and Robert Jasper Winscomb, deft. for £1:10 due by bill under the deft.'s hand dated the 20th of Jany. 1706, the deft. being called to come forth and answer the said action and not appearing, on the plf.'s motion judgment is granted him against Francis Sharp, returned security for the deft., for the said sum unless the said deft. appears at next Court and answer the said action.

The action of debt between Saml. Hill, plf. and Thomas Lamb, deft., neither party appearing, is dismist.

In the action on the case between Stephens Thomson, plf. and Thomas Ballard, deft., the plf. not prosecuting, on the deft.'s motion it is ordered that he be nonsuited and that he pay the deft. damage according to Law with costs alies execution.

The action on the case between Stephens Thomson, plf. and Dionisia Hadley, deft., neither party appearing, is dismist.

In the action on the case between Stephens Thomson, plf. and John Myhil, deft. , the plf. not prosecuting, on the deft.'s motion it is ordered that he be nonsuited and that he pay the deft. damage according to Law with costs alies execution.

The action on the case between Stephens Thomson, plf. and Jno. Redwood, deft., neither party appearing, is dismist.

In the action on the case between Stephens Thomson, plf. and James Morris, deft. the plf. not prosecuting, on the deft.'s motion it is ordered that he be nonsuited and that he pay the deft. damage according to Law with costs alies execution.

In the action on the case between Stephens Thomson, plf. and Thomas Pinket, deft., the plf. not prosecuting, on the deft.'s motion it is ordered that he be nonsuited and that he pay the deft. damage according to Law with costs alies execution.

The action of case between Stephens Thomson, plf. and Anthony Jasper, deft., neither party appearing, is dismist.

The action of case between Stephens Thomson, plf. and Thomas Fear, deft., neither party appearing, is dismist.

The action of case between Stephens Thomson, plf. and Edwd. Foulkes, deft., neither party appearing, is dismist.

In the action of case between Jno. Roberts, plf. and Richd. Johnson, deft. for £4:2:3 due by an account, the deft. being called and not appearing nor any security returned for him, on the plf.'s motion judgment is therefore granted plf. against Wm. Barbar, Sheriff of this County, for the said sum and costs unless the said deft. appear at the next Court and answer the said action.

88. In the action on the case between John Bates, plf. and Richd. Bloxum, deft. for £1:3:1 due by an account, the deft. being called and not appearing nor any security returned for him, judgment is therefore granted the plf. against Wm. Barbar, Gent, Sheriff of this County, for the said sum and costs unless the said deft. appears at next Court and answers the said action.

The action on the case between John Bates, plf. and Thomas Stanley, deft., neither party appearing, is dismist.

The action of debt between John Bates, Assignee of John Robinson, plf. and Thomas Pinket, deft., neither party appearing, is dismist.

In the action of debt between Richd. March, plf. and James Priest, deft. for £20 damage by means of the deft. not paying unto the plf. £19:16:3 contained in a certain writing obligatory of the said James Priest... under the hand and seal of the said James produced, the said deft. being called and not appearing nor any security returned for him, on the plf.'s motion judgment is granted him for the aforesaid sum with costs against Wm. Barbar, Sheriff of this County, unless the said deft. appears at next Court and answers the said action.

Judgment being this day past unto Richd. March against Wm. Barbar, Sheriff of this County, for the sum of £20 damage by means of the nonappearance of James Priest at the suite of the said Marche, on the motion of the said Barbar an attachment is granted him against the Estate of the said Priest for the aforesaid sum with costs returnable to the next Court for judgment.

In the action on the case between Wm. Tunley, plf. and James Bowman, deft. for detaining certain bills which the plf. in his declaration saith he casually lost and the same by the hands and possession of the plf. by finding came, the deft. appeared in Court and delivered up the bills sued for, and it is thereupon ordered that the suite be dismist.

The action in the case between Stephens Thomson, plf. and Use Gibson, deft., neither party appearing, is dismist.

The action in the case between Stephens Thomson, plf. and Andrew Young, deft., neither party appearing, is dismist.

The action in the case between Stephens Thomson, plf. and Wm. Kaidyee, deft., neither party appearing, is dismist.

The action in the case between Stephens Thomson, plf. and Thomas Walker, deft., neither party appearing, is dismist.

The action in the case between Stephens Thomson, plf. and Thomas Burnham, deft., neither party appearing, is dismist.

The action in the case between Stephens Thomson, plf. and Jno. Adduston Rogers, deft., neither party appearing, is dismist.

The action in the case between Thomas Mountfort, plf. and Michael Cormack, deft., neither party appearing, is dismist.

The action in the case between Thomas Colleson, plf. and Michael Cormack, deft., neither party appearing, is dismist.

The orders for Jno. Pattison's appearing to answer the presentment of the Grand Jury is continued till next Court.

Daniel Mackentash failing to appear to answer the presentment of the Grand Jury the last Court, order against him is continued.

Benjamin Lovell the same.

William Ryland the same.

Elizabeth Thomson not appearing to answer the presentment of the Grand Jury against her, ordered that the Sheriff take her into custody untill she give bond with good security for her appearance at next Cout to answer the said presentment.

The Last Will & Testament of Robert Ranson, dec'd. was presented in Court by Dudley Diggs, Esq., the Extr., who made oath thereto, and the same being proved in Court by the oath of James Shelton, one of the witnesses thereto, on the motion of the said Extr. is ordered to remain in Court.

In the Ejectione firmae brought by Robert Faldo, plf. against Richd. Aldo, deft. for 200 acres of land, 200 acres of meadow and 200 acres of pastures with the appurtenances lying in the Parish of Charles in the Co. of York, which the said Robert in his declaration saith that Edwd. Davis and Mary, his wife and Paul Washington and Ehra, his wife demised to the plf. for a term as yet not expired, and for £100 damage by means of the deft. with force and arms entring upon the posssion of the said plf. and his ejecting, expelling and removing from the same... oath being made by Wm. Gordon, Under Sheriff of the County, that he delivered a copy of the declaration to Jno. Dozwell Junr., tenant in possession of the lands in question, with an endorsement therein in the following words July the 2d 1707 – You may perseive I am sued for the within mentioned premises and unless you or someone for you appear at the next Court held for the Co. of York to defend your title thereto, I shal suffer judgment to pass against me by default and you will be turned out of possession. Signed Richd. Aldoe. It is therefore ordered that unless the said deft. or he or they under whom his claims having legal notice of this order, shal appear at next Court and make him or themselves deft. or defts., confess lease entry and ouster and insist only on the title right at tryal, judgment shal be given against him by default...and Writ of habere facias possessionem awarded to put the plf. in possession of the premises.

89. In the action brought by Robert Corlett, Wm. Roberts and Henry Withers of Barbados, merchants and copartners, against John Owen, deft. for rendering unto them a reasonable account from the time that he was bailliff of the said plfs., on the motion of the deft. an imparlance is granted him till next Court.

In the action on the case between Baldwin Matthews, plf. and Lemuel Taylor, deft. for £7:16:3 due to the plf. by account, the deft. being called and not appearing or any security returned for him, and the plf. having made oath that his account is just and due and that he hath received no satisfaction thereof or any part thereof, judgment is therefore granted the said plf. for the aforesaid sum and costs against Wm. Barbar, Gent., Sheriff of this County, unless the said deft. appears at next Court and answers the said action.

Judgment being this day passed unto Baldwin Matthews against Wm. Barbar, Sheriff of this County, for £7:16:3 by means of the nonappearance of Leml. Taylor at the suite of the said Matthews, on the motion of the said Barbar an attachment is granted him against the Estate of the said Taylor for the aforesaid sum with costs returnable to the next Court for judgment.

In the action on the case between Richd. Bloxom, plf. and Jno. Roberts, deft., the plf. not prosecuting, on the deft.'s motion it is ordered that he be nonsuited and that he pay the deft. damage according to Law with costs alies execution.

In the action of debt between Jno. Bates, Assignee of Richd. Drury, plf. and Wm. Sherman, deft., on the deft.'s motion an imparlance is granted him till next Court.

Thomas Ballard, Gent. absent.

The action on the case between Stephens Thomson, Esq., plf. and Thomas Ballard, deft., on the plf.'s motion is continued till next Court.

Thomas Ballard, Gent. present.

The action on the case between Stephens Thomson, Esq., plf. and Jno. Myhill, deft. by consent of both partys is continued till next Court.

In the action of debt between Stephens Thomson, Esq., plf. and James Morris, deft., on the deft.'s motion, oyer is granted him of the bills entered upon till next Court.

The action of debt between Stephens Thomson, Esq., plf. and Thomas Pinket, deft. is continued by consent till next Court.

The action of case between Stephens Thomson, Esq., plf. and Edwd. Foulkes, plf., neither party appearing, is dismist.

The action of debt between Stephens Thomson, Esq., plf. and Thomas Fear, deft., neither party appearing is dismist.

Thomas Ballard and Wm. Buckner, Gents., trustees of the Portland in York Co., came into Court, presented and acknowledged their Deed for one lot of the said land unto John Dowzing and it is admitted to record.

The action of debt between John Bates, plf. and Joseph Dunbar, deft., neither party appearing, is dismist.

In the action on the case between Edwd. Davis, plf. and James Calthrop, deft., the plf. not prosecuting, on the deft.'s motion it is ordered that he be nonsuited and that he pay unto deft. damage according to Law with costs alies execution.

Thomas Nutting, Gent. absent.

In the action of debt between Thomas Nutting, plf. and Jno. Adduston Rogers and Jane, his wife, Admrs. of the Estate of Henry Andrews, dec'd., deft., on the motion of the deft., oyer of this bill entered upon is granted the deft. till next Court.

90. The action of debt between Charles Cox, plf. and Samuel Groves, deft., neither party appearing, is dismist.

In the action in the case between Wm. Kemp, plf. and Charles Cox, deft., the plf. not prosecuting, on the deft.'s motion ordered that he be nonsuited and that he pay the deft. damage according to Law with costs alies execution.

The action on the case between Henry Hayward, plf. and Francis Rogers, deft., neither party appearing, is dismist.

In the action on the case between William Crymes, plf. and George Lovingstone, deft., on the motion of the deft. an imparlance is granted him till next Court.

In the action of account render between Edmd. Jenings, Esq., Secretary of Virginia, plf. and Wm. Tunley, deft., on the deft.'s motion an imparlance is granted him till next Court.

The action in the case between Mary Whaley, plf. and Samuel Plantain, deft., by consent of both partys is continued till next Court.

The action on the case between Thomas Colleson, plf. and Samll. Dickenson, deft. is continued till next Court.

Ordered that the Court be adjourned.

Power of Attorney. Robert Cary of London, merchant, Extr. of the Last Will & Testament of William Aylward, late of Virginia, merchant, but since deceased in the Kingdom of France, to Joseph Walker, merchant in Virginia, his true and lawfull Attorney to collect debts due the said Estate. Dated the 20th day of February 1706. Wit. John Brisco, Joseph Buck, Tho. Bagwell Junr., Tho. Bagwell, Tho. Jones, John Marshall and Danl. Sullivan. Recorded the 25th of August 1707.

91. Will of Thomas Fear of Bruton Parish in York Co. dated the 8th day of October 1706. To my daughter, Jane Taylor, wife of Lemuel Taylor, one cow and one heifer. To my son Thomas Fear, all my lands and plantations…and all the remainder of my personal estate. My son, Thomas, to be my Executor. Wit. John Smith and Susanna Nash. Proved the 25th day of August 1707.

92. Two negroes, the one named Sam, the other Jenny, belonging to Jonathan Lark, were brought into Court and Sam adjudged at 13 years old and Jenny, 10 years old.

Wm. Gibs petitioning this Court as being very antient that he might pay no publick levys, which is granted and ordered that he be levy free.

The order for Wm. Barbar, Sheriff of this County, to make report against the outcry of Cornelius Wilson's Estate is at his mocion continued till the next Court.

The former order requiring Joseph Chermison to return an account of the Estate of John Hilliard, dec'd. is continued till the next Court.

The acion upon the case between Jno. Tomer, plf. and John Wills and Eliz., his wife, Extrs. of Thomas Harwood, dec'd., by consent of both partys is continued till next Court.

The suit in Chancery depending between Wm. Davis, complainant and Jno. Loynes, respondent, is dismist with costs.

The suit by seire facias brought by John Owen, plf. against Isaac Jamart, Admr. of William Chalkhill, dec'd., deft., the deft. having put in his plea to the plf.'s declaracion, at the mocion of the plf. time is given till next Court to reply.

In the ejection firmae between Abell Dun, plf. against Nicho. Sebrell, deft., the plf. declares to wit that when one Anthony Sebrell on the 3rd day of Aprill in the year 1707 at the Parish of Bruton in the Co. of York had demised to the said Abell 20 acres of land, 10 acres of woodland and 10 acres of pastures with the appurtenances... to which the deft. this day pleaded not guilty and for tryall put himself on his country and the plf. likewise. Whereupon a jury was impannelled and sworn to try the issue, joyned by names John Drowry, Jno. Doswell Senr., Jno. Doswell Junr., Wm. Sheldon, John Moss, Wm. Davis, Joseph Walker, Philip Moody, Jno. Adduston Rogers, Simon Stacy, John Toomer and Wm. Babb, who having received their charge, were sent out and in some time came again into Court and returned their verdict, which at the mocion of the deft. is recorded and is in these words. Wee the jury find for the deft., signed Wm. Sheldon. Therefore ordered that the plf. pay costs alies execution.

93. The acion in the case between Charles Chiswell, plf. and Wm. Barbar, Gent., Sheriff of York Co., deft. is by consent of both partys continued till the next Court.

In the acion of debt between Mary Whaley, plf. and Henry Gilbert, deft. for £61 by bill dated under the deft.'s hand the 22d day of May 1706, the deft. having put in his plea to the plf.'s declaracion, the plf. demurred thereto and the deft. praying time till next Court to amend his plea or joyn in demurrence, which the Court refused, adjudging the deft.'s plea [?] vitices. Therefore ordered that he pay the said sum to the plf. with costs alies execution.

The attachment which William Barbar, Gent., Sheriff of this County, obtained against the Estate of Jno. Saunders, at his mocion is continued till next Court.

The judgment which John With, Church Warden of York Parish, obtained against Thomas Mountfort for 500 lbs. tobacco for the nonappearance of Barbara Hutton to answer the Informacion against her for fornicacion is confirmed and ordered that he pay the same to the Church Wardens of York Hampton Parish at the next levy alies execution.

In the Informacion brought by Peter Goodwin, Church Warden of York Parish, against Eliz. Ditcher for fornicacion, the deft. came into Court and confessed the fact and Cornelius Jones also came and assumed the payment of her fine being 500 lbs. tobacco, which was accepted and ordered that he pay the same to the Church Wardens of York Hampton Parish at the next levy alies execution.

The order for Sarah Stanup to return an inventory of Richd. Stanup's Estate is continued till next Court and ordered that Robert Harrison, Robt. Crawley, Robt. Jackson, Thomas Buck and James Causby or any three of them, appraise the said Estate being first sworn before a Justice of the Peace for this County on the 1st day of October next if fair, if not at any other time, when they shall appoint and make report thereof to the next Court.

Benja. Lovett appearing to answer the presentment of the Grand Jury against him, on hearing what to say, is discharged.

In the acion upon the case between John Duke, plf. and Nicho. Phillips, deft., the plf. by his Attorney replyed to the deft.'s plea, and at the deft.'s mocion time is given him till next Court to rejoyn.

The acion of debt between Richd. Wharton, plf. and Jno. Redwood, deft., neither party appearing, is dismist.

In the acion upon the case between Cornelius Jones, plf. and John Loynes, deft. for the sum of £50 damage by means of the deft. not procuring an Indian man named Peter Larabie an apprentice for the term of 8 years and not paying to the plf. the sum of £4 or the value thereof, nor delivering back a certain negro woman slave according to his promise and assumption as is in the declaracion set forth, according to a rule of this Court a jury was this day sworn to inquire of damage, whose names are John Drowry, Jno. Doswell Senr., Jno. Doswell Junr., Wm. Sheldon, Jno. Moss, Wm. Davis, Jno. Walker, Nicho. Phillips, Jno. Adduston Rogers, Simon Stacy, Jno. Tomer and Wm. Babb, who after they had received their charge were sent out and in some time came again into Court, and being agreed on their verdict, returned the same in these words: The jury find £30 for the plf.. Which on the mocion of the plf.'s Attorney is recorded. It is therefore considered by the Court adjudged and accordingly ordered that the deft. pay the said sum to the plf. with costs alies execution.

94. John Hobkins being sumoned an evidence for Cornelius Jones against Jno. Loynes and having attended here 5 days, it is therefore ordered that the said Jones pay him for the same according to Law with costs alies execution.

John Godwin the same.

James Morris the same.

Thomas Cowles for the same, one day.

On reading the order past this day between Mary Whaley, plf. and Henry Gilbert, deft., the said deft. by his Attorney put in his plea in arrest of judgment and on hearing the arguments on both sides, is overruled. From which judgment the said deft. appeals to the 7th day of the next Genll. Court. James Morris and Nicho. Sebrell enter themselves security for his due prosecucion of the same according to Law.

Ordered that the Court be adjourned to the 24th day of November next.

At a Court held for York Co. the 24th day of November 1707. Present: Robert Read, Thomas Nutting, Thomas Ballard, Lawrence Smith and Wm. Timson, Gent.

Elizabeth Bloxton petitioning this Court to have the Estate of John Childs, who dyed at her house, ordered that she return an inventory thereof to the next Court.

John Crombie, Constable of York Hampton Parish, petitioning this Court as having served in the office one year and 6 months and now being disabled by the Gripes to be discharged from the same, which is granted and ordered that Charles Cox be in his stead, being first sworn before a Justice of the Peace of this County.

Present Wm. Pinkethman and Henry Tyler, Gent.

Edward Moss hath order granted him for administracion of the Estate of Tho. Gibbons, giving security according to Law. And ordered that John Wells, John Doswell Senr., Thomas Burnham and Simon Stacy, being first sworn before a Justice of the Peace for this County, appraise the said Estate on the 29th day of this Instant and return an inventory thereof to the next Court, and that Sarah Gibbons, his widdow, appear then and make oath to the same.

John Crombie on his petition hath order granted him for a Lycence to keep an ordinary at his dwelling house in York Town, giving security as the Law directs.

The petition of Thoma Mountfort for a Lycence to keep an ordinary is rejected, the Court thinking him insufficient.

A Power of Attorney from Elizabeth Fear, wife of Thomas Fear, to Thomas Cowles, was this day proved in Court by the oaths of Joseph Ashlin and Henry Holdcraft, the witnesses thereto, and ordered to be recorded.

Thomas Fear came into Court and acknowledged his Deed for land to John Bates, as also Thomas Cowles, Attorney of Eliz. Fear, wife of the said Thomas, came and relinquished her the said Eliz.'s right of dower in the same, and at the said Bates' mocion admitted to record.

On the petition of Ann Eaton for a maintenance from her husband, John Eaton, it is ordered that the Sheriff of this County summon him to appear at the next Court to answer the said petition.

On the petition of Wm. Tunly for 375 lbs. of tobacco against the Estate of James Darbishire, dec'd., by account and having proved the same by his oath, it is ordered that Capt. Lawrence Smith, who was appointed by this Court Trust for the said Estate, pay the said sum of 375 lbs. of tobacco to the said Tunly when asses with costs.

95. Humphry Moody on his petition hath order granted for a Lycence to keep an ordinary at his dwelling house in York Town.

Hump. Moody, Philip Moody and John Myhill came into Court and acknowledged their bond to our Sovereign Lady, the Queen, for his well keeping ordinary and on mocion made, is admitted to record.

It is ordered that the Sheriff of this County summon Damazinah Brown, Extx. of the Last Will & Testament of Richd. Dixon, to appear at the next Court and answer the petition of John Hunt against her.

Present, Thomas Roberts, Gent.

On the mocion of the Attorneys of the suit between John Cooper of London, merchant, and Thomas Whitby, it is ordered that all the papers relating to the said suit be delivered out to them.

James Morris came into Court and acknowledged his Deed for negroes to his son, John Morris, and at mocion made in his behalf, admitted to record.

In the acion upon the case between Wm. Crimes, plf. and George Lovingston, deft., wherein the deft. had an imparlance granted him at the last Court and being called and not appearing, judgment is therefore granted to the plf. by nihil dicit returnable to the next Court for confirmation.

The acion upon the case between Joseph Chermisson, plf. against George Booker, deft., by consent of both partys is continued till next Court.

Elizabeth Somerwell having according to an order of this Court made return of the Inventory of her dead husband, Mongo Somerwell's Estate and

111

having made oath to the same and that if any more of the said Estate shall hereafter come to her hands or knowledge that she will fully account for the same to this Court, is at her mocion admitted to record.

A Letter of Attorney from Job Wilkes to James Sclater, Minister, was this day proved by the oath of Thomas Jones, one of the witnesses thereto, and at the said Sclater's mocion admitted to record.

In the acion upon the case between Thomas Pain, plf. and Damazinah Brown, Extx. of Richd. Dixon, dec'd., deft., the partys having joyned issue, the cause is as found till next Court for tryall.

Wm. Hewit and John Hansford, Extrs. of the Last Will & Testament of Capt. Charles Hansford, dec'd. came into Court and confessed judgment to Wm. Coman for the sum of £3:10:3 and 85 lbs. of tobacco. It is therefore ordered that they pay the aforesaid sums to the said Coman out of the said Hansford's Estate together with costs alies execution.

In the suit in Chancery between Robert Cary, Extr. of Wm. Aylward, complainant and Wm. Babb, respondent, the respt. having put in his answer and made oath thereto, at the compl.'s mocion time is given him till next Court to consider the same.

The suit by seire facias brought by Joshua Curle, plf. against Isaac Jamart, Admr. of the Estate of Wm. Chalkhill, dec'd., deft., the deft. being dead, the said acion is dismist.

In the acion on the case between John Serjanton, plf. against John Nicholson, deft., wherein the deft. had an imparlance granted him last Court and now not appearing, judgment is therefore granted to the plf. by nihil dicit against the said deft. returnable to next Court for confirmation.

The attachment which Wm. Barbar, Gent., Sheriff of this County, obtained against Andrew Young's Estate for the nonappearance of the said Young at the suit of John Redwood for the sum of £2:5:9, being served on a horse of the said Young's, and the attachment returned at the request of the said Sheriff, it is ordered that Henry Hayward, Baswell Wagstaf and Robt. Sheilds, being first sworn before the Court, appraise the said horse and make return thereof to this Court.

The acion of debt between John Redwood, plf. and Wm. Kaydiee, deft., neither party appearing, is dismist.

In the acion of debt between John Roberts, plf. against Robert Jasper Winscomb, deft. for £1:10 by bill under the deft.'s hand, the plf. having obtained judgment at the last Court against Francis Sharp, security for the deft., and the said deft. being called and not appearing, the said judgment is confirmed and ordered that the said Sharp pay the said sum to the plf. with costs alies execution.

96. In the acion upon the case between John Roberts, plf. against Richd. Bloxom, deft. for the sum of £4:2:3 by account and having proved the same by his own oath as also the oath of James Roberts, it is therefore considered by the Court that he pay the same to the plf. with costs alies execution.

John Crombie, James Morris and John Doswell Senr. came into Court and acknowledged their bond to our Sovereign Lady, the Queen for the said Crombies' well keeping an ordinary, and at his mocion admitted to record.

James Roberts, an evidence for John Roberts against Richd. Bloxum, being summoned by the Sheriff and attending here 4 days, it is ordered that the said John Roberts pay him 160 lbs. of tobacco for the same with costs alies execution.

The acion of debt between Richd. March, plf. against James Preist, deft. for £19:16:3 by bill dated under the deft.'s hand the 27th of May 1707, the deft. came personally into Court and confessed judgment to the plf. for the sum, which is ordered to be paid with costs alies execution.

The attachment which Wm. Barbar, Gent, Sheriff of this County, obtained against the Estate of James Preist, the said Barbar not appearing to the same, is dismisst.

The former order made for John Pattison's appearance to answer the presentment of the Grand Jury against him is continued till next Court.

Daniel Mackintosh the same.

Wm. Ryland the same.

Eliz. Thomson the same.

The ejectione firmae depending between Robt. Faldoe, plf. against Richd. Aldoe, deft. is dismist, neither party appearing.

The acion upon the case between Robert Corlet, Wm. Roberts and Henry Withers of Barbados, merchants, plts. against John Owen, deft., at the mocion of the plf.'s Attorney time is given him till the next Court to consider the deft.'s account now put in.

In the acion on the case between Baldwin Mathews, plf. against Leml. Taylor, deft. for the sum of £7:16:3 by account, at the deft.'s mocion time is given him to make oath against the Article of Crape[?] in the said account mencioned till next Court.

The attachment which Wm. Barbar, Sheriff of this County, obtained against the Estate of Leml. Taylor for the nonappearance of the said Taylor at the suit of Baldwin Mathews is discontinued.

The acion of debt between John Bates, Assignee of Richd. Drury, plf. against Wm. Sherman, deft. is continued by consent till next Court.

In the acion upon the case between Stephens Thompson, Esq., plf. against John Mihill, deft. for £1 by account, which being put to the Court for judgment and on hearing the arguments on both sides, it is considered by the Court adjudged and accordingly ordered that he pay the same to the plf. with costs alies execution.

Saml. Hill on his petition hath order granted for a Lycence to keep an ordinary at the french ordinary.

Saml. Hill, Wm. Barbar and John Hansford acknowledged their bond to our Sovereign Lady, the Queen for a Lycence to keep ordinary and at the said Hill's mocion admitted to record.

According to an order of this Court, Henry Hayward, Baswell Wagstaff and Robert Sheild hath returned the appraisement of a horse belonging to Andrew Young's Estate, which is continued till next Court.

Ordered that the Sheriff of this County summon 24 able freeholders of this County to appear and attend at the next Court to be of the Grand Jury.

Orderd that the Court be adjourned till the 13th day of December next.

97. Bond. Humphrey Moody, Phillip Moody and John Myhill, all of the Parish of York Hampton and Co. of York, to the Queen, in the sum of 10,000 lbs. of tobacco. Securities for Humphrey Moody to renew his Lycense to keep an ordinary. Dated the 10th day of October 1707.

Bond. John Crombie, James Morris and John Dozwell Senr., all of the Parish of York Hampton in the Co. of York, to the Queen, in the sum of 10,000 lbs. of tobacco. Securities for John Crombie to renew his Lycense to keep an ordinary. Dated the 10th day of October 1707. Wit. Wal Crombie and Wm. Kaidyee.

98. Bond. Samuel Hill, William Barbar and John Hansford, all of the Co. of York, to the Queen, in the sum of 10,000 lbs. of tobacco. Securities for Samuel Hill to renew his Lycense to keep an ordinary. Dated the 10th day of October 1707.

Inventory & Appraisement of the Estate of Mongo Somerwell. Among other items, two negroes unappraised. Total value of estate, £368:11:2 ½. Presented by Eliz. Somerwell at the November Court 1707.

Revocation of Power of Attorney. Whereas on or about the 17th day of June 1700, I Job Wilks…did authorize, impower and appoint Henry Gibbs, a planter in the Parish of Mulbery Island in the Co. of Warwick in Virginia, to receive debts from several persons. Now know all men by these presents that I have revoked…the power of Authority to the said Henry Gibbs…and I do hereby appoint James Sclater, minister of the Parish of Po Colson[?] in York Co., my true and lawfull Attorney…to receive from the said Henry Gibbs all such sums collected by him on my behalf. Dated this 10th day of March 1706. Wit. Wm. Johnson, Ralph Gray, John Emett and Tho. Jones. Recorded the 24th day of November 1707.

100. Deed of Gift. James Morris of the Parish of Bruton in the Co. of York, to my well beloved son, John Morris, one negro boy named Robin, aged about 13 years and also one negro girle named Betty,about 9 year of age, both which young negroes are my own slaves…with the consent and at the request of my loving wife, Elizabeth Morris, mother of my said son. Provided that if my said son should dye before he attains the age of 21 yeares, then the said two negroes to remain to me. In case of my death or absence from this country before my said son shall attain to the age of 21 yeares, then I appoint my said wife to be Gardian or Tutor to my said son and that she have the benefit of the said negroes labour. Dated the 24th day of November 1707. Wit. Henr. Holdcraft and William Sharman. Recorded the 24th day of Nov. 1707.

101. Power of Attorney. Elizabeth Fear, wife of Thomas Fear, of the Parish of Bruton in York Co., to Thomas Cowles of James City Co., my true and lawfull Attorney to appear at York Co. Court the 24th day of November 1707 to acknowledge…a deed unto John Bates. Dated the 22nd day of November 1707. Wit. Jo. Ashlin and Henr. Holdcraft. Recorded the 24th day of November 1707.

102. At a Court held for York Co. the 18th day of December 1707 by adjournment from the 24th of November last. Present: Robert Reade, Thomas Roberts, Thomas Ballard, Wm. Buckner and Lawrence Smith, Gent.

William Gordon came into Court, presented and acknowledged his Assignment of Deed for one Lott or half acre of land in York Town to James Wallace, which together with the said deed is admitted to record.

Present, Tho. Nuting, Gent.

On consideracion of the petition of Sarah Gibbons against Edward Moss, Admr. of the Estate of Thomas Gibbons, it is ordered that he deliver to her out of the said Estate the bed appraised at £4:10, one frying pan, one iron pot, one pewter dish, two plates, three spoons and one hay, and that the former appraisers of the said Estate appraise what of the aforesaid items are not particularly valued and make report thereof to the next Court.

It is ordered that the creditors of the Estate of Thomas Gibbons, dec'd. appear at the next Court and make out their claims against the said Estate.

James Bowman came into Court, presented and acknowledged his Deed for land to Thomas Mountfort, which together with the said Bowman's bond are admitted to record.

Isabella Brodbent on her petition hath order granted her for a Lycence to keep an ordinary in York Town, giving security according to Law.

John Redwood on his petition hath order granted him for a Lycence to keep an ordinary, giving security according to Law.

The acion upon the case between Stephens Thomson, Esq., plf. against Tho. Ballard, Gent., deft. is by consent continued till next Court.

The acion upon the case between Stephens Thomson, Esq., plf. against James Morris, deft. is by consent continued till next Court.

Elizabeth Stains acquainting the Court that Ralph Rainsford, who is supposed to be drowned, left several goods at her house and praying that care might be taken therein, it is therefore ordered that the Sheriff of this County take these goods into his custody and make sale thereof on the 22nd day of this Instant by way of outcry for money or Bills of Exchange to be paid at or before the 5th of Aprill next, and the bills for the same be taken to the Sheriff and that he make report of his proceedings to the next Court.

In the acion of debt between Stephens Thompson, Esq., plf. against Thomas Pinket, deft. for the sum of £1, the deft. appeared this day and confessed judgment to the plf. for the said sum, which is ordered to be paid with costs of suit alies execution.

In the acion of debt between Thomas Nuting, plf. against John Adduston Rogers and Jane, his wife, Admrs. of the Estate of Henry Andrews, dec'd., deft. for the sum of £50:6:7, wherein oyer of the bill was granted in last Court and the deft. being called and not appearing, now judgment by nihil dicit is therefore granted to the plf. for the aforesaid sum with costs returnable to the next Court as usuall.

In the acion of account between Edmund Jenings, Esq., Secretary of Virginia, plf. against Wm. Tunly, deft. for £150 damage by means of the deft. not rendering unto the plf. a reasonable account of 80,000 lbs. weight of tobacco due and owing for fees and business done by the said deft. as Deputy Clerk of York Court as is set forth in the declaracion, wherein an imparlance was granted in August Court and being called and not appearing, now judgment by nihil dicit is therefore granted to the plf. for the aforesaid sum with costs returnable to the next Court as usual.

In the acion upon the case between Mary Whaly, plf. against Saml. Plantain, deft. for £20 damage by means of the deft. damnifying and spoiling 2,700 lb. weight of tobacco belonging to the plf., wherein the deft. had time given in August to plead and being now called and failing to do the same, judgment is therefore granted to the plf. by nihil dicit for the sum with costs returnable to the next Court for confirmacion.

103. In the acion upon the case between Richard Bloxum, plf. against John Roberts, deft. for the sum of £2:16 by account, the Sheriff having made oath that he left a copy of this acion at his house, and not appearing, at the mocion of the plf. an attachment is therefore granted him against the deft. for the aforesaid sum with costs returnable to the next Court for judgment.

The acion of debt between Henry Hales, plf. against John Bates, deft., neither party appearing, is dismist.

In the acion upon the case between Thomas Collison, plf. against Saml. Dickenson, deft. for £2:9:11 ½, the deft. by his Attorney confessed judgment to the plf. for the said sum. Therefore ordered that he pay the same with costs of suit alies execution.

In the acion upon the case between Archobald Blair, plf. against Charles Cox, deft., the deft. came personally into Court and confessed judgment to the plf. for the sum of £21:1 ½, which is ordered to be payd with costs alies execution.

The acion of debt between Charles Thurman, plf. and Edwd. Foulkes, deft., neither party appearing, is dismist.

The acion of trespass on the case between John Seawell, plf. against Morris Jones, deft., neither party appearing, is dismist.

The acion of debt between Mary Rice, plf. against Thomas Rogers, deft., neither party appearing, is dismist.

Richard Bloxum being sumoned an evidence for John Seawell against Morris Jones and having attended here 3 days, it is ordered that the said Seawell pay him 120 lbs. of tobacco for the same with costs alies execution.

The acion on the case between Archabald Blair, plf. against David Stoner, deft., neither party appearing, is dismist.

In the acion upon the case between Thomas Roberts Junr., plf. against Charles Cox, deft., the plf. failing to prosecute, at the mocion of the deft. it is ordered that he be nonsuited and that he pay the sum according to Law with costs alies execution.

The acion upon the case between John Tomer, plf. against John Wills and Eliz., his wife, Extrs. of Thomas Harwood, dec'd., deft., the plf. not prosecuting, is therefore discontinued.

The suit brought by seire facias by John Owen, plf. against Isaac Jamart, Admr. of Wm. Chalkhill, dec'd., deft., the deft. being dead is dismist.

The acion upon the case between Cha. Chiswell, plf. against Wm. Barbar, Gent. Sheriff of York Co., deft., is discontinued by consent.

The attachment which Wm. Barbar, Gent., Sheriff of this County, obtained against the Estate of John Saunders at his mocion is discontinued.

The order for Sarah Stanup to return and make oath to the Inventory of her husband's Estate is continued till next Court to do the same.

In the acion upon the case between John Dukes, plf. against Nicho. Phillips, deft., wherein the deft. had time given at September Court to rejoyn to the plf.'s replycacion and now having done the same, the tryal of the issue is refered by consent till the next Court.

The acion upon the case between Peter Caudery, plf. and Cha. Holdsworth, deft. is dismist, neither party appearing.

In the acion of debt between Wm. Faulkner, plf. against Wm. Sherman, deft., the deft. on his mocion hath oyer of the bill declared on till next Court.

In the acion upon the case between Wm. Robertson, plf. against Wm. Sherman, deft., on the mocion of the deft.'s Attorney an imparlance is granted him till the next Court.

The acion of debt between Henry Duke, Esq., plf. against Antho. Jasper, neither party appearing, is dismist.

The acion of debt brought by Nicho. Sebrell, plf. against Alexander Bonymond, deft., neither party appearing, is dismist.

In the acion of debt between Stephens Thomson, Esq., plf. against Edward Foulks, deft. for £1, the Sheriff having made oath that he left a copy of this acion at his house and not appearing, at the mocion of the plf. an attachment is granted him against the said deft.'s Estate for the sum with costs returnable to the next Court for judgement.

104. In the action upon the case between Stephens Thomson, plf. against Edward Foulks, deft. for the sum of £2:10:1 due on ballances of accounts, the deft. being called and not appearing and the Under Sheriff making oath that he left a copy of the acion in this cause at the deft.'s house, at the mocion of the plf., an attachment is granted him against the deft.'s Estate for the aforesaid sum with costs returnable to the next Court for judgment.

The acion upon the case brought by John Seawell, plf. against Morris Jones, deft., neither party appearing, is dismist.

In the acion of debt between Isaac Rowden, plf. against Oliver Peron, otherwise called Oliver Perron, deft. the Under Sheriff having made return that he hath no residence in his bailywick, at the mocion of the plf. by his Attorney an attachment is therefore granted against the deft.'s Estate for £25 with costs, being the sum sued for, returnable to the next Court for judgment.

In the acion upon the case between Isaac Rowden, plf. against Oliver Peron, deft., the Under Sheriff having made return that he hath no residence in his balywick, at the mocion of the plf.'s Attorney an attachment is granted against the deft.'s Estate for the sum of £79:3 with costs returnable to the next Court for judgment.

In the acion upon the case between Charles Cox, plf. against Oliver Peron, deft. for the sum on £1:7:6, the deft. being returned by the Sheriff of this County that he hath no residence in his balywick, at the plf.'s mocion an attachment is therefore granted him for the aforesaid sum with costs returnable to the next Court for judgment.

The acion on the case brought by Lucy Burton against John Redwood is dismist, neither party appearing.

The Informacion brought by Robt. Ambrose who sues as well for our Sovereign Lady, the Queen as himself against John Marott, the plf. not prosecuting, is dismisst.

In the acion of trespass brought by Wm. Davis, plf. against John Loynes, deft., the deft. by his Attorney appearing and at his mocion hath an imparlance granted him till the next Court.

In the acion of trespass between Wm. Forbush, plf. against James Morris, deft., the deft. appearing and on his mocion hath an imparlance granted him till the next Court.

The acion of debt brought by Thomas Hansford, plf. against Edward Foulks, deft., neither party appearing is dismist.

In the acion of debt between Henry Hales, plf. against David Stoner, deft. for the sum of £34:5 and as an endorser to a protested Bill of Exchange with damage and charge of protest, the Sheriff having made oath that he left a copy of the acion in this suit at the deft.'s house and he not appearing, at the mocion of the plf.'s Attorney an attachment is granted against his Estate for the aforesaid sum, damage and charge of protest with costs returnable to the next Court for judgment.

In the acion of debt between James Waite, plf. and Abra. Martin, deft. for £33:11, the deft. being called and not appearing nor any security returned for him, and Jno. Clayton entering into rules to pay what costs and damage shall be adjudged against the plf. in this suit, on his mocion judgment is therefore granted to the plf. against Wm. Barbar, Sheriff of this County, for the aforesaid sum with costs unless the said deft. appears at the next Court and answers the said acion.

Judgment being this day passed unto James Waite against Wm. Barbar, Gent., Sheriff of this County, for £33:11 by means of the nonappearance of Abra. Martin at the suit of the said Waite, on the mocion of the said Barbar, an attachment is granted him against the Estate of the said Martin for the aforesaid sum with costs returnable to the next Court for judgment.

In the acion of debt between Thomas Hansford, Assignee of Andrew Young, plf. against Henry Dukes, deft. for 20 shillings, the deft. being called and not appearing nor any security returned for him, on the plf.'s mocion judgment is therefore granted him against Wm. Barbar, Sheriff of this County, for the aforesaid sum with costs unless the said deft. appears at the next Court and answers the said action.

105. Judgment being this day passed unto Thomas Hansford, Assignee of Andrew Young, against Wm. Barbar, Gent., Sheriff of this County, for 20 shillings by means of the nonappearance of Henry Duke at the suit of the said Hansford, at the mocion of the said Barbar an attachment is therefore granted him for the aforesaid sum with costs against the deft.'s Estate returnable to the next Court for judgment.

The acion upon the case between Hump. Ball, plf. against Wm. Breton, deft., neither party appearing, the said acion is dismisst.

The acion of debt between Robt. Porteus, plf. against Wm. Breton, deft., neither party appearing, is dismist.

In the suit brought by seire facias by John Hansford, plf. against Henry Atkinson, deft. to renew a judgment of York Co. Court dated the 24th day of February 1704[?] for £1:12 and also the sum of 51 lbs. of sound tobacco for the costs in the said suit, the deft. being summoned by the Sheriff and not appearing or showing any cause why the said judgment may not be renewed, it is therefore considered by the Court that the said judgment be renewed to the plf. and accordingly ordered that the deft. pay the aforesaid sums with costs of suit alies execution.

The acion upon the case between Michl. Cormack, plf. against Henry Akins, deft., neither party appearing, is dismist.

The acion of debt between John Penton, plf. against Andrew Young, deft., neither party appearing , is dismist.

The action upon the case between John Penton, plf. against Andrew Young, deft., neither party appearing, is dismist.

The action of debt between Thomas Grayham, plf. against Andrew Young, deft. is at the request of the deft.'s sister refered till the next Court.

In the action of trespass on the case between Frederick Jones, plf. against John Penton, deft., the deft. being arrested by the Sheriff and not appearing nor any security returned for him, at the mocion of the plf. judgment is therefore granted him against Wm. Barbar, Sheriff of this County, for the sum sued for in the declaracion or what thereof shall appear due at the next Court, unless the said deft. appears then and answers the said acion.

The acion upon the case between Saml. Seldon, plf. against Phi. Smith, deft., at the plf.'s mocion it is continued till the next Court.

The acion of debt between John Eaton, plf. against Michl. Cormack, deft., neither party appearing, is dismist.

The acion of debt between Thomas Mountfort, plf. against James Bowman, deft., neither party appearing, is dismist

The acion of debt between Johanna Atkins, plf. and Cha. Cox, deft., neither party appearing, is dismist.

The acion of debt between Thomas Walker, plf. against Andrew Young, deft., neither party appearing, is dismist.

The acion of debt between Katherine Sparrow, plf. against John Eaton, deft., neither party appearing, is dismist.

In the acion of trespass on the case between Thomas Cheesman, plf. against Adduston Rogers, deft. for £50 damage by means of the deft. with force and armes committing a trespass on the plf.'s land at the Parish of York Hampton and Co. of York as is set forth in the declaracion, to which the deft. pleads that he is not guilty and puts himself on the Country and the plf. likewise, whereupon it is ordered that the Surveyor of this County with an able jury of the antient freeholders of the vicinage, who are no ways concerned by afinity, consanguinity, or interest to the land in controversy nor lyable to any other just exception, to be summoned by the Sheriff and sworn before a Justice of the Peace of this County, go upon the land on the 22nd day of this Instant if fair, if not the next fair day and survey and lay out the same according to the most known antient and reputed bounds thereof, having regard to all Patents and Evidence that shall be produced by the plf. and deft. relating thereto, and if they find the deft. a trespasser, the jury are to value the damage and to the end there may be no delay therein. It is ordered that if but one of the partys with the Surveyor and jury meet at the time appointed, they proceed to perform this order and make report of their proceedings to the next Court and it is further ordered that the Surveyor fail not of the Survey and return a plat of the land accordingly to the next Court.

106. On the acion upon the case between Adduston Rogers, plf. against John Sutherland, deft., the deft. having put in his plea to the plf.'s declaracion, the cause is as found till the next Court for tryal.

In the acion of debt between Col. Wm. Wilson, plf. against Damazinah Brown, Extx. of the Last Will & Testament of Richard Dixon, dec'd., deft. for £31:3:5, the Under Sheriff having made oath that he left a copy of the acion in this cause at the deft.'s house and she not appearing, an attachment is therefore granted to the plf. against her Estate for the aforesaid sum with costs returnable to the next Court for judgment.

In the acion upon the case between Lucy Burton, plf. against Damazina Brown, Extx. of the Last Will & Testament of Richd. Dixon, dec'd., deft., at mocion of the deft.'s Attorney an imparlance is granted her till the next Court.

The seire facias brought by Henry Cary, plf. against Damazinah Brown, Extx. of the Last Will & Testament of Richd. Dixon, dec'd. is dismist, neither party appearing.

In the acion of debt between John Crombie, plf. against Ephraim Cocket, deft., at the deft.'s mocion an imparlance is granted till the next Court.

The acion upon the case between John Crombie, plf. against James Shelton, deft., neither party appearing, is dismist.

The acion upon the case between Charles Cox, plf. against Lucy Burton, deft., the Court adjudging that there is no cause of acion is therefore dismist.

The acion of Detinue brought by Charles Cox, plf. against James Potushalgingle, deft., neither party appearing, is dismist.

The acion of debt between Barentine Howles, plf. and Henry Floyd, deft., neither party appearing, is dismist.

On the petition of George Saunders against Wm. Sherman for wages due to him for one twelve months service, it is ordered that the Sheriff summon him to appear at the next Court to answer the said petition.

John Marot on his petition hath order granted him for a Lycence to keep an ordinary at Wmsburgh giving security according to Law.

The petition of Use Gibson for keeping an ordinary in York Town is continued till the next Court for the Court to consider thereof.

Wm. Forbush on the Holy Evangelist made oath before the Court that he gos in danger of his life or bodyly harm from James Morris, and praying that the said Morris may be bound to the peace, it is therefore ordered that the Sheriff of this County forthwith take him into his custody and there securely to keep him untill he enters into bond before some one of her Majesty's Justices of the Peace of this County in the penal sum of £50 to

123

our Soverign Lady, the Queen, that he shall keep the peace towards all our subjects and more especially towards William Forbush.

The severall petitions of John Wells and Cha. Cox for a Lycence to keep ferry over to Tindals point is at the said Cox's mocion continued for a fuller Court.

Ordered that the Court be adjourned to the 24th day of January next.

107. At a Court held for York Co. the 24th day of January 1707. Present: Thomas Barbar, Henry Tyler, Thomas Ballard, Thomas Nuting, Wm. Buckner, Wm. Timson and Lawrence Smith, Gent.

Wm. Taylor, son and heir of John Taylor, this day came into Court, presented and acknowledged his Deed of Lease and Release for land to Josh. Chermison, which at his mocion are admitted to record.

Wm. Taylor, son and heir of John Taylor, this day presented and acknowledged his bond to Joseph Chermison for performance of covenants, and at the said Chermison's mocion admitted to record.

John Sanders and Edward Sanders came into Court, presented and acknowledged their Deeds of Lease and Release for land as also Geo. Baskervile by virtue of a Power of Attorney from Mary Sanders, wife of the said John, relinquished her the said Mary's Right of Dower therein to Wm. Barbar, Gent, which are at his mocion admitted to record.

A Power of Attorney from Mary Sanders, wife of John Sanders to Geo. Baskervile was this day proved in Court by the oaths of John Mihill, Richd. Kendall and Wm. Davis, the witnesses thereto, and at the said Baskervile's mocion admitted to record.

A Power of Attorney from Michl. McCormack to Wm. Davis was this day proved in Court by the oaths of Wm. Shelton and James Priest, the witnesses thereto, and at the said Davis' mocion admitted to record.

Wm. Davis by virtue of a Power of Attorney from Michl. Cormack this day appeared, presented and acknowledged his the said Cormack's Deed for half of his lot or half acre of land in York Town to John Brookes and at his mocion is admitted to record.

A Letter of Attorney from Danl. Mackintosh to Henry Clark was this day proved in Court by the oaths of Elias Love and Silas Love, the witnesses thereto, and at his mocion admitted to record.

Henry Clark by virtue of a Power of Attorney from Danl. Mackentosh this day appeared, presented and acknowledged his the said Mackentosh's bond to John Drury, which at his mocion is admitted to record.

Jean Marot, Joseph Chermison and Richd. Wharton came into Court, presented and acknowledged their bond to our Sovereign Lady, the Queen for a Lycence for the said Marot keeping an ordinary at Wmsburgh, which was admitted to record.

A Letter of Attorney from Hannah Bates, wife of John Bates to Henry Holdcraft was this day proved in Court by the oaths of Edward Young and Thomas Fear, the witnesses thereto, and admitted to record.

John Bates came this day into Court, presented and acknowledged his deed for land as also Henry Holdcraft by virtue of a Power of Attorney from Hannah Bates, wife of the said John, appeared and relinquished for the said Hannah's Right of Dower therein to Wm. Forbar, which at the said Forbar's mocion is admitted to record.

John Wills on his petition hath order granted him for a Lycence for to keep an ordinary at his dwelling house in York Town, giving security according to Law.

Elizabeth Blaxton according to an order of this Court made return of the Inventory of the Estate of John Chiles, dec'd., and having made oath thereto is admitted to record.

A Letter of Attorney from Hannah, the wife of James Sheilds, to Wm. Robertson was this day proved in Court by the oath of Wm. Metheion, the witness thereto, and admitted to record.

James Sheilds as also Wm. Robertson by virtue of a Power of Attorney from Hannah Sheilds, wife of the said James, presented and acknowledged their Deed for land of John Marot, which at his mocion is admitted to record.

108. Edward Moss and John Moss came into Court, presented and acknowledged their bond to the worshipful the Justices of York Court for the said Mosses duly administering on the Estate of Thomas Gibbons, dec'd., and is admitted to record.

Simon Stacy exhibiting an account against the Estate of Thomas Gibons, dec'd. amounted to the sum of £1:1:9 and it appearing to the Court that there is due to the said Estate from the Estate of Tho. Hill, dec'd. 250 lbs. of tobacco, it is ordered that the said Stacy be paid the same out of the said Hill's Estate.

Sarah Gibbons, according to a former order, this day appeared and made oath to the Justices of her dead husband, Thomas Gibbons' Estate, that she had truly accounted for what part thereof hath come to her knowledge in words or writing to the Court is admitted to record.

Robert Sheilds hath judgment this day granted for the sum of £3:10 due for the rent of a plantacion belonging to him against Edward Moss, Admr. of the Estate of Thomas Gibbons, dec'd., which is ordered to be paid out of the said Estate in the specie alies execution.

Thomas Cheesman Senr. hath judgment this day granted him for the sum of £5:10:5 due by a protested Bill of Exchange against Edwd. Moss, Admr. of the Estate of Thomas Gibbons, dec'd., which is ordered to be paid out of the said Estate in the specie alies execution.

Philip Moody hath judgment this day granted him against Edward Moss, Admr. of the Estate of Thomas Gibbons, dec'd. for the sum of £8 due by bills under the hand of the decedent, which is ordered to be paid out of the Estate in the specie alies execution.

Ann Eaton petitioning the Court and seting forth in her said petition that her husband, John Eaton, will not suffer her to live peaceably or quietly with him nor allow her a separate maintenance, and the Court having fully heard the whole matter are of opinion that she ought to be allowed a maintenance from her said husband and accordingly ordered that she be allowed the rent of her plantacion in Cha. Parish to be yearly paid her by her said husband.

On the mocion of Edward Moss that the Court would assign a day for the creditors of the Estate of Thomas Gibbons, dec'd. to receive the debts allowed by the Court, do assign the 2nd day of Feby. next and that the said Moss give the said creditors timely notice of this order to appear then at his house and receive the same.

The petition of John Hunt against Damaz. Brown, Extx. of Richd. Dixon, dec'd. for the said Brown to return a further inventory of the said Estate is by consent refered till the next Court.

In the acion upon the case between Wm. Crimes, plf. against George Lovinstone, deft. for £50 due upon ballance of an account wherein judgment past at the last Court by nihil dicit and being now called and not appearing, the said judgment is confirmed and ordered that a Writ of Enquiry of damage be executed at the next Court, of which the plf. gave the deft.'s Attorney notice and accepted the same at the Barr.

Joseph Walker, foreman, Wm. Hansford, Ralph Hubard, John Laiton, Wm. Sherman, Tho. Fear, Cha. Collier, Wm. Davis, Robert Jackson, Wm. Lee, Mathew Peires, John Adduston Rogers, were this day sworn a Grand Jury for the body of this County, and they having finished their presentments are discharged.

Upon the mocion of Richd. Wharton in behalf of Joseph Man, son and orphan of Joseph Man, dec'd., that the Court would be pleased to appoint a Guardian to take care of the Estate of the said orphan, it is considered by the Court that Capt. Lawrence Smith be appointed Guardian to the said orphan to take care of the Estate left him by his said father.

In the acion of trespass between Thomas Cheesman, plf. against Adduston Rogers, deft., wherein a survey with a jury was ordered at the Last Court, which order not being performed, it is continued. Ordered that the said order be performed on the 12th day of February next or the next fair day and that reports and returns be made according to the said former order.

109. John Wills, Wm. Sheldon and Simon Stacy came into Court, presented and acknowledged their bond to our Sovereign Lady, the Queen for the said Will's well keeping an ordinary in York Town and is admitted to record.

John Wills on his petition for a Lycence to keep ferry over York River hath order granted him for the same, giving security according to Law.

John Redwood, Wm. Hansford and James Morris came into Court, presented and acknowledged their bond to our Sov. Lady the Queen for the said Redwood's Lycence to keep ordinary in the City of Wmsburgh and is admitted to record.

John Wills, Wm. Sheldon and Simon Stacy came into Court, presented and acknowledged their bond to our Sov. Lady, the Queen for the said Will's Lycence to keep ferry over York River to Tindals Point and it is admitted to record.

Ordered that the Court be adjourned to the 24th day of February next.

Bond. John Wills, William Sheldon and Simon Stacy, to the Queen, in the sum of 10,000 lbs. of tobacco. Dated the 24th day of January 1707. Sureties to John Wills for his Lycence to keep an ordinary at York Town for the ensueing year.

Bond. John Wills, William Sheldon and Simon Stacy, to the Queen in the amount of ₤20. Dated the 24th day of January 1707. Sureties to John Wills for for Lycence to keep a ferry from York Town to Tindalls Point.

110. Bond. John Redwood, William Hansford and James Morris, to the Queen, in the sum of 10,000 lbs. of tabocco. Dated this 15th day of December 1707. Sureties to John Redwood for his Lycense to keep ordinary at his dwelling house in Williamsburgh.

Bond. John Marott, Joseph Chermison and Richard Wharton, to the Queen, in the sum of 10,000 lbs. of tobacco. Dated the 24th day of January 1707. Sureties to John Marot for his Lycence to keep an ordinary at Williamsburgh for the ensueing year. John Marrott signs his name "Jean" on the bond.

111. Bond. Edward Moss and John Moss, both of the Parish of York Hampton, Co. of York, to the Justices of said County, in the sum of £100. Dated the 26th day of November 1707. Sureties for Edward Moss as Admr. of the Estate of Thomas Gibbons. Wit. Richd. Archer and Willm. Kemp. Recorded at January Court, 1707.

An Inventory of the Estate of Thomas Gibbons dated the 29th day of November 1707. Total value of Estate, £42. Appraised by John Wills, Tho. Binnam, Simon Stacy and John Dozwell Senr. and presented by Sarah Gibbons.

112. An Inventory of the Estate of John Chiles, dec'd. Few items are listed and none are valued. Presented by Elizabeth Blaxton at January Court 1707.

Power of Attorney. Mary Sanders, wife of John Sanders, to George Baskervyle of York co., my true and lawfull Attorney to acknowledge unto William Barbar of the said County all my right title or interest to a certain tract which my said husband hath sauld to him the said Barbar. Dated this 17th day of January 1707. Wit. Jno. Mihill, Richd. Kendall, William Davis.

Power of Attorney. Hannah Bates, the wife of John Bates of the Parish of Bruton in the Co. of York, to my friend Henry Holdcraft of the Co. of New Kent, my true and lawful Attorney to acknowledge my relinquishment of dower to a certain tract…100 acres…sold by my said husband to William Forbar for £62. Dated this 29th day of December 1707. Wit. Edward Young and Thomas Fear.

Power of Attorney. Hannah Sheils, the wife of James Sheils of James City Co., taylor, to William Robertson, my true and lawfull Attorney to relinquish my right of dower in one certain Lott of ground lying the the City of Williamsburgh and mencioned and comprised in one Indenture of Bargain and Sale bearing even date with these presents. Dated this 24th day of January 1707. Wit. William Metheven

113. Power of Attorney. Michael Mackormack of the Parish and Co. of York, to my friend William Davies of the same County, my true and lawfull Attorney to acknowledge at Court one Indenture of Bargain and Sale of the one moiety or halfe part of my Lott or parcel of land being Portland lying in the Parish aforesaid and known by the number 31...to James Brooks of said Parish and County, taylor. Dated the 20th day of January 1707. Signed, Michael Cormack. Wit. Samuel Rowland, James Shelton and James Priest.

Power of Attorney. Daniell Mackentosh of York Co., to my friend Henry Clark of the abovesaid County, my true and lawfull Attorney...to acknowledge in York Co. Court this bond by me granted to John Druitt Senior. Dated this 17th day of December 1707. Wit. Elias Love and Silas Love.

114. At a Court held for York Co. the 21st day of February 1707. Present, Thomas Barbar, Wm. Buckner, Robt. Read, Henry Tyler, Thomas Ballard and Wm. Timson, Gents.

Upon representacion of the Church Wardens of Bruton Parish that the road to Church from the upper parts of Bruton Parish in this County, as also to the ferry and other places, is made unpassable by reason of the entry buildings, and praying directions might be given for a new road to be made, therefore the Court doth think fit and accordingly order that the Surveyor of the highways in that precinct clear and make a fair road through Whaley's Quarter field over the branches above the bridge on the back side of Pages and so to the former road uses.

John Dowzing petitioning this Court and seting forth that he took up two Lotts of Portland in this town and complyed with the Law in building upon the same, which building was by a tempestuous wind blown down and praying a record might be made thereof of his complyance with the Law, do admit the same to record.

The Last Will & Testament of Humphry Moody, dec'd was presented in Court by Eliz. Moody, widow and Extx. therein named, and proved by the oaths of Wm. Barbar, Gent. and Mathew Tiplady, two of the witnesses thereto. Admitted to record and probate thereof granted to Eliz. Moody, his Extx.

The several depositions of Henry Gibbs, John Goulding and James Hill relating to the clearing and planting of 550 acres of land belonging to Tho. Redman Senr. were swore to in Court, and at his mocion admitted to record.

When the Court is informed that the place of Constable is vacant in the City of Wmsburgh, do hereby think fit and accordingly order that John Marot do officiate there, being first sworn before a Justice of the Peace for this County.

Robert Harrison this day appeared, presented and acknowledged his Deed for land unto Richd. Kendall and Frances, his wife, and at their mocion admitted to record.

The acion upon the case between Joseph Chermisson, plf. against George Booker, deft. is by consent of both partys continued till the next Court.

In the acion upon the case between Thomas Pain, plf. and Damazinah Brown, Extx. of Richd. Dixon, deft. for 4,000 lbs. of tobacco damage by means of the said Richd. not rendering to the plf. the ninth part of the sider made on the deft.'s plantacion in Gloucester Co. as by Articles of Agreement made between the plf. and the said Richd. and not paying 2000 lbs. of tobacco for breech of the said Articles as in the declaracion is set forth, and the said Damasinah by Jno. Clayton comes and defends the force and injury when he saith the plf. his acion aforesaid against her ought not to have because protesting that the plf. hath not performed all and every the said articles, clauses, covenants and agreements made and contained in the said Articles of Agreement on his part to be performed. For plea the said deft. saith that the said Richard did allow the plf. the full ninth part of the cider made upon the said plantacion in the time aforesaid according to the true meaning form and effect of the Articles, and of this she puts herself upon the Country and the plf. likewise. Whereupon a jury was impanneled and sworn to try the issue joyned by name Robt. Crawley, Thomas Cheesman Junr., Tho. Edmons, Wm. Lee, Jno. Doswell Senr., Francis Sharpe, Jno. Hansford, Wm. Davis, John Moss, Jno. Wills, Wm. Farbar and Jno. Doswell Junr. It being put to the Court for judgment who the proof of breach of the Articles lay on, are of the opinion that it lyeth on the plf. and the jury having issued their charge was sent out and after some time came again into Court and returned the verdict, which upon the deft.'s mocion is recorded in these words: We find for the deft. It is therefore ordered that the plf. pay costs alies execution.

Present, Thomas Roberts and Lawrence Smith, Gents.

Thomas Ballard and Wm. Buckner, Gents., Trustees for the Portland in York Town, presented and acknowledged their Deed for one Lot of the said land unto John Dunbar, and at his mocion admitted to record.

The Last Will & Testament of Jno. Fergason, dec'd. was presented in Court by Eliz. Fergason, widow and Extx. therein named, and proved by the oaths of Jno. Hayward, Ann Ellis and Richd. Slater, the witnesses thereto. Admitted to record and probate thereof granted to Eliz. Fergason, the Extx.

130

The Last Will & Testament of Wm. Garro, dec'd. was this day presented in Court by Eliz. Garro, widow and Extx. therein named, and proved by the oaths of Tho. Chapon and Wm. Sheldon, witnesses thereto. Admitted to record and probate thereof granted to Eliz. Garro, the Extx.

Ordered that Jno. Moss, Wm. Sheldon, Peter Goodwin and Adduston Rogers or any three of them, being first sworn before a Justice of the Peace for this County, inventory and appraise the Estate of Wm. Garro, dec'd. as shall be shown to them by Eliz. Garro, widdow, on the 4th day of March next if fair, if not the next fair day and make return of their proceedings to the next Court, and that Eliz. Garro appear then and make oath to the inventory.

Thomas Woodfield being summoned an evidence for Damazinah Brown, Extx. of Richd. Dixon at the suit of Tho. Pain and having attended 7 days, it is ordered that the said Brown pay him 280 lbs. of tobacco for the same with costs alies execution.

115. Thomas Atkins being this day brought before this Court by virtue of mittimus under the hands of Wm. Buckner, Gent., one of her Majesty's Justices of the Peace for this County, directed to the Sheriff of the said County relating to the death of a negro belonging to James Pressie and on hearing the evidence, the Court are of opinion that the said Atkins be discharged out of custody.

Hugh Norvell, one of the trustees for the land appropriated for the building the City of Wmsburgh, came into Court, presented and acknowledged his Deeds of Lease and Release for two Lotts of land in the said City to Wm. Robertson.

The ejectione firmae between Jno. Cox, plf. and Jno. Fergeson, deft. is by consent discontinued.

In the suit in Chancery depending between Robt. Cary, Extr. of Wm. Aylward, complainant and Wm. Babb, respondent, the respt. praying time till next Court for witnesses to be examined dodimus, which is granted, and by the consent of bothy partys it is ordered that a comission issue directed to Henry Tyler and Wm. Timson, Gents. or either of them to take the affidavits of such persons as shall be brought before them by either party and return the same to the next Court.

In the acion upon the case between Jno. Serjanton, plf. against Jno. Nicholson, deft., the deft. by her Attorney demurred to the plf.'s declaracion, and at plf.'s mocion he hath time granted till next Court to joyn or amend.

In the acion of account render between Robt. Corlet, Wm. Roberts and Henry Withers of Barbados, merchants, plfs. and John Owen, deft., the plfs. by their Attorney moved that auditors might be appointed to audit and settle accounts between the plfs. and deft.. Do hereby order and appoint that Joseph Walker, Archibald Blair, Tho. Jones and Richard Bland, Gents. or any three of them meet at John Redwood's in Wmsburgh some time before the next Court to audit, rate and settle all accounts between plfs. and deft. and make report thereof to the next Court.

The acion upon the case between Baldwin Mathews, plf. and Leml. Taylor, deft., neither party appearing, is dismist.

The acion of debt between John Bates, Assignee of Richd. Drury, plf. against Wm. Sherman, deft. is continued by consent till the next Court.

According to an order of this Court made, Henry Howard, Basall Wagstaf and Robt. Sheild having appraised and made their report of a horse belonging to the Estate of Andrew Young valued at £3:10 for the said Young's suffering judgment to pass against Wm. Barbar, Gent. at the suit of Jno. Redwood for the sum of £2:5:9, judgment is therefore granted to the said Barbar for the said sum of £2:5:9 with costs to be paid out of the said appraisement.

The acion upon the case between Stephens Thompson, Esq., plf. and Tho. Ballard, deft. is by consent continued till the next Court.

The acion of debt between Stephens Thomson, Esq., plf. and James Morris, deft. is by consent continued till the next Court.

In the accion of debt between Thomas Nuting, plf. against Jno. Adduston Rogers and Jane, his wife, Admrs. of the Estate of Henry Andrews, dec'd., defts., the defts. having joyned issue, the cause is refered for tryal to the next Court.

In the acion of account render between Edmund Jenings, Esq., Secy. of Virginia, plf. and Wm. Tunly, deft. for £150 damage by means of the deft. not rendering to the plf. as his bailiff a reasonable account of 80,000 lbs. weight of tobacco due and owing for fees for business [?] by the said deft. as Deputy Clerk of York Court and set forth in the declaracion, to which the deft. pleaded that he never was bayliff or receiver to the plf., and thereupon both partys put themselves on the Country for tryal. A jury was impannelled and sworn to try the issue, joyned whose names are Robt. Crawly, Thomas Cheesman Junr., Tho. Edmons, Wm. Lee, John Doswell Senr., Fra. Sharp, Jno. Hansford, Wm. Davis, Jno. Moss, Jno. With, Wm. Farbar and Jno. Adduston Rogers, the plf. producing as evidence a commission from Chichly Corbin Thacker, Deputy Secretary, to Wm. Tunley, Clerk of York Court, an obligacion from Wm. Tunly to the plf. for rendering an account of all fees due to him as Clerk of the said office as also a letter from the said Tunly to the plf. which obligacion and letter the deft. acknowledged in Court to be subscribed by his own hand, the deft. demurring to the plf.'s evidence and the plf. joyning therein, each party withdrew a jury, by consent the cause is referred till the next Court to argue the demurrence.

On the petition of Mongo Ingles seting forth that a white servant of his named Rachel Wood is delivered of a bastard child, therefore ordered that the Sheriff of this County summon her to appear at the next Court to answer the said petition.

Mongo Ingles, Gent., one the the trustees for the land appropriated for the building the City of Wmsburgh, appeared this day, presented and acknowledged is Deeds of Lease and Release for two Lotts of land in the said City to Wm. Robertson, Gent. and at his mocion was admitted to record.

116. In the acion upon the case between Mary Whaley, plf. and Saml. Plantain, deft. for £20 damage by means of the deft. negligently carrying in a boat, spoiling and damnifying three hogsheads of tobacco containing 2,700 lbs. weight as in the declaracion is set forth, to which the deft. pleaded not guilty. Whereupon a jury was impanneled and sworn to try the issue, joyned whose names are Robt. Crawley, Thos. Cheesman Junr., Thos. Edmons, Wm. Lee, John Doswell Senr., Jno. Hansford, Wm. Davis, John Moss, Jno. With, Wm. Farbar, Jno. Adduston Rogers and Nicho. Phillips and they having received their charge, were sent out and after some time came again into Court and being agreed on their verdict returned the same, which verdict at the plf.'s mocion is recorded and it is in these words: We find one hogshead returned in the condition received, the other two very much damnifyed to the value of the hole tobacco, which we judge to be £7:10 for the plf. Therefore considered by the Court adjudged and accordingly ordered that the deft. pay the aforesaid sum of £7:10 by the jurors aforesaid assessed to the plf. with costs alies execution.

The acion upon the case depending between Richd. Bloxum, plf. agaist John Roberts, neither party appearing, is dismist.

A Power of Attorney from Henry Bolch, chairmonger[?] to John Bates was this day proved in Court by the oath of Griffon Phillips as also by the solemn affirmacion of Wm. Cant, two of the witnesses thereto, and admitted to record.

James Hassell, an evidence for Mary Whaley against Saml. Plantain, having attended here 5 days on the said suit, it is therefore ordered that the said Whaly pay him 200 lbs. of tobacco for the same with costs alies execution.

Jonathan Lark, Surveyor of the highways of the upper precincts of York Hampton Parish, on his mocion is discharged from the said office and Richd. Burt is hereby appointed in his stead and place.

Ordered that the Court be adjourned till nine o clock tomorrow morning.

February the 25th 1707. Present, Thomas Barbar, Henry Tyler, Thomas Ballard, Wm. Buckner and Lawrence Smith, Gents.

On reading the order passed yesterday in the suit between Thomas Pain, plf. against Damazinah Brown, Extx. of Richd. Dixon, deft., the plf. by his Attorney moved for an appeal to the 7th day of the next Genl. Court, which is granted. Robert Hide together with the said Thomas Pain entered into bond in the sum of £10 to the said Damasinah Brown, Extx. of Richd. Dixon, for the said Pain's due prosecucion of the said appeal according to Law.

The order of the last Genl. Court requiring this Court to return their reasons for not complying with the former order of the said Genl. Court made in the appeal between Jno. Cooper of London, merchant, appellant and Thomas Whitby, appellee, this Court not having the said order, do continue the hearing thereof untill the next Court, that a copy of the said order may be had.

The Inventory of the Estate of Richd. Stanup, dec'd. was this day brought into Court by Sarah, his widow, being dead before oath was made thereto, the Court considering the same will be usefull, do admit it to record.

The acion upon the case between John Duke, plf. against Nicho. Phillips, deft., at plf.'s mocion is continued till the next Court.

In the acion of debt between Wm. Faulkner, plf. and Wm. Sherman, deft., wherein the deft. had an imparlance granted at the last Court and now not appearing, judgment is therefore granted to the plf. by nihil dicit returnable to the next Court for confirmacion.

In the acion upon the case between Wm. Robertson, plf. and Wm. Sherman, deft., wherein the deft. had an imparlance granted in December Court and now not appearing, judgment is therefore granted by nihil dicit returnable to the next Court as usual.

In the acion of debt between Stephens Thomson, plf. and Edwd. Foulks, deft., the attachment which the plf. claimed against the deft.'s Estate not being served, is continued at mocion till the next Court.

In the acion on the case between Stephens Thomson, plf. and Edward Foulks, deft., wherein the plf. obtained in December Court last an attachment against the deft.'s Estate, which not being served is at his mocion continued till the next Court.

The acion of debt between Isaac Rowden, plf. and Oliver Peron, otherwise called Oliver Perron, deft., neither party appearing, is dismist.

The acion upn the case between Isaac Rowden, plf. and Oliver Peron, deft., neither party appearing, is dismist.

In the acion on the case between Cha. Cox, plf. and Oliver Peron, deft., on the plf.'s mocion, the attachment which he obtained against the deft.'s Estate is continued till the next Court.

In the acion of trespass between Wm. Davis, plf. and John Loynes, deft. for £50 damage by means of the deft. with force and armes counting a trespass on lands of the plf. in Bruton Parish in this County… to which the deft. pleads that he is not guilty, and both partys putting themselves on the Country for tryal, whereupon it is ordered that the Surveyor of the County with an able jury of the antient freeholders of the Vicinage, who are not concerned by affinity, consanguinity, or interest to the land in controversy nor lyable to any other just excepcion, be summoned by the Sheriff and sworn in before a Justice of the Peace of this County, goe upon the land in dispute on the 29th day of March next if fair, if not the next fair day and survey and lay out the same according to the most known antient and reputed bounds thereof, having regard to all patents and evidences that shall be produced by plf. or deft. relating thereto, and if they find the deft. a trespasser, the jury are to value the damage and to the end there may be no delay therein. It is ordered that if but one of the partys with the Surveyor and jury meet at the time appointed, they proceed to perform this order and make report of their proceedings to the next Court and it is further ordered that the Surveyor fail not of the survey and return a plat of the land before the said next Court.

117. In the acion of trespass between Wm. Forbush, plf. and James Morris, deft., wherein the deft. had an imparlance granted at the last Court and now not appearing, judgment is therefore granted to the plf. by nihil dicit returnable to the next Court as usual.

In the acion of debt between Henry Hales, plf. and David Stoner, deft. for £94:5 as an endorser of a protested Bill of Exchange drawn by Jno. Higgason Junr. on Micajah Perry and Comp., merchants in London, with damage and charge of protest, the deft. came into Court and confessed judgment to the plf. for the aforesaid sum. Whereupon it is ordered that he pay the same with damage and charge of protest, the whole amounting to £39:11:6 to the plf. with costs alies execution. Execution not to issue untill the first May next.

The acion of debt between James Waite, plf. and Abra. Martin, deft. is continued till the next Court at plf.'s mocion.

The attachment which Wm. Barbar, Gent. obtained against the Estate of Abra. Martin for his nonappearance at the suit of James Waite is dismist.

Present, Wm. Timson, Gent.

In the acion of debt between Thos. Hansford, plf. and Henry Duke, deft., for the sum of 20 shillings by bill under the deft.'s hand, the deft. appeared at the Barr and confessed judgment for the said sum, whereupon it is ordered that he pay the same to the plf. with costs alies execution.

The attachment which Wm. Barbar, Gent., Sheriff, obtained against the Estate of Henry Duke for his nonappearance at the suit of Thos. Hansford is on his appearing, now dismist.

Ordered that the creditors of the Estate of Cornelius Wilson appear at the next Court to make out their claims against the said Estate, a distribucion being then to be made.

In the acion of debt between Thomas Grayham, plf. and Andrew Young, deft., wherein the deft. had at the last Court an imparlance granted and now not appearing, judgment is therefore granted to the plf. by nihil dicit returnable as usual.

The acion of trespas on the case between Fredk. Jones, plf. and Jno. Penton, deft. is continued by consent till the next Court.

The acion of the case between Saml. Seldon, plf. and Phi. Smith, deft. is by consent continued till the next Court.

In the acion upon the case between Adduston Rogers, plf. and Jno. Southerland, deft. for £10 damage by means of the deft. keeping an unlawfull bull, which bull kill the plf.'s riding horse and the deft. refusing to make him satisfacion for the said horse… to which the deft. pleaded not

136

guilty and both partys putting themselves on the Country for tryal, a jury was impanneld and sworn to try the issue, joyned whose names are Tho. Prisman Junr., Jno. With, Jno. Moss, Thomas Hansford, Jno. Hansford, Saml. Cooper, Henry Dyer, Wm. Lee, Nicho. Phillips, John Gibbons, Thomas Walker and Wm. Davis, who having heard the evidence of Thos. Edmons, Jno. Lawson, James Lawson and Edward Worley and received their charge, were sent out and in some short time came into Court and returned their verdict, which at the deft.'s mocion is recorded and is in these words: We find no cause of acion. Therefore ordered that the plf. be nonsuited and that he pay the same to the deft. with costs alies execution.

Thomas Edmons, an evidence for Adduston Rogers against Jno. Southerland being summoned and attended here 5 days, on his mocion it is ordered that the said Rogers pay him 200 lbs. of tobacco for the same with costs alies execution.

Edward Worley being summoned an evidence for Adduston Rogers against Jno. Southerland and having attended here 5 days, on his mocion it is ordered that the said Rogers pay him 200 lbs. of tobacco for the same with costs alies execution.

John Lawson being summoned an evidence for Adduston Rogers against Jno. Southerland and having attended here 3 days, on his mocion it is ordered that the said Rogers pay him 120 lbs. of tobacco for the same with costs alies execution.

118. John Lawson being summoned an evidence for Adduston Rogers against Jno. Southerland and having attended here 3 days, on his mocion it is ordered that the said Rogers pay him 120 lbs. of tobacco for the same with costs alies execution.

In the acion of debt between Col. Wm. Wilson, plf. and Damasinah Brown, Extx. of the Last Will & Testament of Richd. Dixon, dec'd., deft. for £31:3:5 due by bills under the Testator's hand, the deft. by her attachment appeared and confessed judgment for the aforesaid sum, which is ordered to be paid with costs alies execution. Execution not to issue untill first of May next.

In the acion of debt between John Crombie, plf. and Ephraim Cockit, deft., wherein the deft. had at the last Court an imparlance granted and now not appearing, judgment is therefore granted to the plf. by nihil dicit returnable as usual.

Ordered that the Sheriff summon Wm. Sherman to appear at the next Court to answer the petition of George Sanders against him.

Wm. Barbar, Gent., Sheriff of this County, according to an order of this Court this day reported and returned the outcry of Cornelius Wilson's Estate, which is admitted to record.

The acion of debt between Mongo Ingles, plf. and Jno. Loynes, deft., neither party appearing, is dismist.

In the acion on the case between John Bates, plf. and Thomas Rogers, deft. for £10, the Sheriff having made oath that he left a copy of the acion in this suit at the deft.'s house and he being called and not appearing, on the plf.'s mocion an attachment is therefore granted him against the deft.'s Estate for the aforesaid sum and costs or what thereof shall appear to be due, returnable to the next Court for judgment.

The acion on the case between Cha. Cox, plf. and Timo. Johnson, deft., neither party appearing, is dismist.

In the acion of debt between Nicho. Phillips, plf. and Jno. Redwood, deft., the deft. by his Attorney appeared and on his mocion hath an imparlance granted him till the next Court.

The acion on the case between Jno. Marot, plf. and Stephen Penton, deft., neither party appearing, is dismist.

In the acion upon the case between James Morris, plf. and Robt. Hide, deft., the deft. appeared and prayd an imparlance, which is granted him till the next Court.

The acion on the case between Tho. Jones, plf. and Richd. Turner, deft., neither party appearing, is dismist.

The acion on the case between Philip Moody, plf. and Thos. Bryan and Sarah, his wife, Admrs. of Richd. Stanup, deft., neither party appearing, is dismist.

The acion of debt between Hugh Norvell, plf. and Thos. Bryan and Sarah, his wife, Admrs. of Richard Stanup, deft., neither party appearing, is dismist.

In the acion of debt between Thomas Hansford, plf. and Mathew Jefferys, deft. for £8:9 due by bills under the deft.'s hand, Wm. Barbar, Gent., Sheriff, made oath that he left a copy of the acion in this suit at the deft.'s common place of residence and he not appearing, at the plf.'s mocion an attachment is therefore granted him against the deft.'s Estate for the aforesaid sum with costs returnable to the next Court for judgment.

The acion of debt between Jno. Eaton, plf. and Mathew Jefferys, deft., neither party appearing, is dismist.

In the acion of Assault & Battery between Jno. With, plf. and Wm. Lee, deft., the deft. joyned issue and the cause refered till the next Court for tryal.

The acion on the case between Cha. Cox, plf. and Richd. Jobey, deft., neither party appearing, is dismist.

In the acion on the case between Col. Dudley Diggs, plf. and Damazinah Brown, Extx. of Richd. Dixon, deft., the deft. appeared by her Attorney and hath an imparlance granted till the next Court.

The acion on the case between Simon Stacy, plf. and Robt. Canaday, deft., neither party appearing, is dismist.

The acion of debt between Phi. Moody, plf. and Edwd. Moss, Admr. of Tho. Gibbons, deft., neither party appearing, is dismist.

The action on the case between Cha. Cox, plf. and Edwd. Moss, Admr. of Tho. Gibbons, deft. neither party appearing, is dismist.

The acion of debt between Jno. Morris, plf. and Edwd. Moss, Admr. of Thomas Gibbons, deft., neither party appearing, is dismist.

The acion of debt between Thos. Chisman Senr., plf. and Edwd. Moss, Admr. of Tho. Gibbons, deft., neither party appearing, is dismist.

The acion of debt between Jno. Adduston Rogers and Jane, his wife, Admrs. of the Estate of Henry Andrews, plf. and Thomas Woodfield, deft., the plf. not prosecuting, is dismist.

The acion of debt between James Preist, plf. and Jos. Sledd, deft. neither party appearing, is dismist.

119. The acion of debt between Wm. Allen, plf. and Jos. Sledd, deft. is dismist, neither party appearing.

The acion of debt between Henry Hayward, plf. and Anthony Franklin, deft., neither party appearing, is dismist.

The acion on the case between Cha. Cox, plf. and Chris. Jackson, deft., neither party appearing, is dismist.

In the acion of debt between Barontine Howles, plf. and Henry Floyd, deft. for 200 lbs. of tobacco by bill under the deft.'s hand and being called and not appearing nor any security returned for him, judgment is therefore granted to the plf. for the aforesaid sum and costs against Wm. Barbar, Gent., Sheriff of this County, unless the said deft. appears at the next Court and answers the said acion.

Judgment being this day passed unto Barontine Howles against Wm. Barbar, Gent., Sheriff of this County, for 200 lbs. of tobacco and costs by means of the nonappearance of Henry Floyd at the suit of the said Howles, at the mocion of the said Barbar an attachment is granted him against the Estate of the said Floyd for the aforesaid sum and costs returnable to the next Court for judgment.

The acion on the case between John Doswell Junr., plf. and Geo. Bell, deft., neither party appearing, is dismist.

The acion on the case between Thos. Walker, plf. and Danl. Mackentosh, deft., neither party appearing, is dismist.

The acion of debt between Cha. Parish, plf. and David Holloway, deft., neither party appearing, is dismist.

In the acion of debt between Thos. Nelson, plf. and Michl. McCormack, deft. for £8:8:6 by bill under the deft.'s hand, the deft. appeared at the Barr and confessed judgment for the sum of £7:10:6, which said sum is ordered to be paid to the plf. with costs alies execution.

In the acion on the case between Wm. Tunly, plf. and Michl. McCormack, deft., the deft. appeared and on his mocion hath an imparlance granted him till the next Court.

The acion of debt between Jno. Crombie, plf. and James Shelton, deft. is dismist, the plf. not prosecuting.

Damazinah Brown, Extx. of the Last Will & Testament of Richd. Dixon, according to the prayer of John Hunt against her, brought into Court an account of the Estate of the Testator, the consideracion whereof is continued till the next Court.

The acion on the case between Wm. Crimes, plf. and Geo. Lovingston, deft. is by consent continued till the next Court and then to be first called.

In the acion on the case between Edward Whitwick, plf. and John Sanders, deft., the deft. by his Attorney appeared at his mocion hath an imparlance granted till next Court.

In the mocion of trespass on the case between Thomas Chisman, plf. and Adduston Rogers, deft. for £50 damage by means of a trespass comitted by the deft. on the lands of the plf., the surveyor and jury having made a survey and returned their verdict in the said suit, the deft. by his Attorney put in a plea to stay judgment thereon, which on the plf.'s mocion and by consent of the deft. is continued till the next Court.

In the acion on the case between Mary Whaley, plf. and Francis Sharp, deft. for £10 damage by means of the deft. not complying with his promise and assumcion in erecting and building substancially and in worklike manner a dwelling house of clapboards for the plf., and on the deft. being called and not appearing nor any security returned for him, judgment is therefore granted to the plf. for the aforesaid sum and costs against Wm. Barbar, Gent., Sheriff of this County, unless the said deft. appears at the next Court and answers the said acion.

The acion of debt between Josh. Chermison, plf. and Alexr. Bonymond, deft. neither party appearing, is dismist.

The acion of debt between Jno. Redwood, plf. and Jno. Gibb, deft. is continued till the next Court.

In the acion of debt between Henry Tyler and David Bray, Church Wardens of Bruton Parish, plfs. and Wm. Coman, deft. for 2,200 lbs. weight of tobacco damage by means of his not rendering to the plfs. 2,128 lbs. weight of tobacco for arrears of his Parish levys due from the deft. for himself, servants and slaves, and the deft. being arrested and not appearing or any security returned for him, judgment is therefore granted to the plfs. for the aforesaid sum and costs against Wm. Barbar, Gent., Sheriff of this County, unless the said deft. appears at the next Court and answers the said acion.

In the acion of debt between Henry Tyler and David Bray, Church Wardens of Bruton Parish, plfs. and Edwd. Thomas, deft., the deft. being arrested by the Sheriff and not appearing nor any security returned for him, judgment of therefore granted to the plfs. against Wm. Barbar, Gent, Sheriff of this County, for the sum sued for in the declaracion or what thereof shall appear to be due at the next Court, unless the said deft. appears then and answers the said acion.

In the acion of debt between Henry Tyler and David Bray, Church Wardens of Bruton Parish, plfs. and John Bates, deft., the deft. being arrested by the

Sheriff and not appearing nor any security returned for him, judgment is therefore granted to the plfs. for the sum of 9,600 lbs. weight of tobacco and costs against Wm. Barbar, Gent., Sheriff of this County, unless the said deft. appears at the next Court and answers the plfs.' mocion.

In the acion of debt between Henry Tyler and David Bray, Church Wardens of Bruton Parish, plfs. against James Bates, deft., the deft. being arrested by the Sheriff and not appearing nor any security returned for him, judgment is therefore granted to the plfs. against Wm. Barbar, Gent., Sheriff of this County, for 800 lbs. weight of tobacco and costs the sum sued for or what thereof shall appear to be due at the next Court, unless the said deft. appears then and answers the plfs.' acion.

120. The suit by seire facias brought by Henry Hales, plf. against John Bedford, deft. is at the deft.'s mocion continued till the next Court.

The suit in Chancery brought by Joseph Dunbarr, complainant and James Bowman, respondent, the respt. on his mocion hath time till next Court to answer.

In the acion of debt between Henry Gill, plf. against Cha. Holdsworth, deft. for £5:10:7 by bill under the deft.'s hand, and the Sheriff having under oath that he left a copy of the acion in this cause at the deft.'s comon place of residence, and he not appearing, at the plf.'s mocion an attachment is therefore granted to the plf. against the deft.'s Estate for the aforesaid sum and costs returnable to the next Court for judgment.

The acion of Trespass and Detinue between Alexr. Bonyman, plf. and Tho. Rogers, deft., neither party appearing, is dismist.

In the acion on the case between Harwood Cary, plf. and Wm. Sears, deft., the deft. appeared by Richd. Wharton, his Attorney, and at his mocion hath a Special imparlance granted him till next Court, saving all advantages.

The acion on the case between Nathl. Hook, plf. and Simon Stacy, deft., neither party appearing, is dismist.

In the acion of account render brought by Wm. Tunly, plf. against John Dozwell Junr., deft., the deft. appeared and at his mocion hath a special imparlance granted him till next Court.

In the acion of account render brought by Wm. Tunly, plf. against Wm. Sheldon, deft., the deft. appeared and at his Attorney's mocion hath a special imparlance granted till next Court.

In the acion of account render brought by Wm. Tunly, plf. against Henry Tyler, deft., the deft. appeared and at his Attorney's mocion hath a special imparlance granted till next Court.

In the acion of debt between Damh. Brown, Extx. of Richd. Dixon, plf. and James Sclater, deft., neither party appearing, is dismist.

In the acion of debt between Jno. Doswell, plf. and Tho. Walker, deft. for 695 lbs. of good sound merchantable sweet scented tobacco due by bill under the deft.'s hand and being called and not appearing nor any security returned for him, judgment is therefore granted to the plf. against Wm. Barbar, Gent., Sheriff of this County, for the aforesaid sum and costs, unless the said deft. appears at the next Court and answers the plf.'s acion.

In the acion of debt between John Doswell Junr., plf. and Tho. Walker for £12:10 due by bond obligatory under the deft.'s hand and seal, the deft. being called and not appearing nor any security returned for him, judgment is therefore granted to the plf. against Wm. Barbar, Gent., Sheriff of this County, for the aforesaid sum and costs, unless the said deft. appears at the next Court and answers the plf.'s acion.

The acion on the case between Geo. Holloway, plf. and Henry Floyd, deft., neither party appearing, is dismist.

In the acion of debt between John Crombie, plf. and Wm. Sheldon, deft., the deft. appeared and at his mocion hath an imparlance to the next Court.

In the acion of account render brought by Wm. Tunly, plf. against Wm. Gordon, deft., the deft. appeared and at his Attorney's mocion hath a special imparlance granted till next Court.

In the acion of account render brought by Wm. Tunly, plf. against Wm. Barbar, deft., the deft. appeared and at his Attorney's mocion hath a special imparlance granted till next Court.

The acion on the case between Tho. Mountfort, plf. and Jno. Sanders, deft., neither party appearing, is dismist.

Ordered that the Sheriff of this County sumon the Surveyor of the Highway in Charles Parish to answer the presentment of the Grand Jury against him for not repairing the highway according to Law to appear at the next Court to answer the same.

143

Ordered that the Sheriff sumon Thomas Walker to appear at the next Court to answer the presentment of the Grand Jury against him for absenting himself from Church contrary to Law.

The same against Wm. Ryland for absenting the Church contrary to Law.

The same against Elizth. Blackstone, widdow, for having a bastard.

The same against the Church Wardens of Charles Parish for not repairing the Church and payling in the Church Yard.

The same against the Vestry in the Upper Precinct of York Hampton Parish for no processioning of land according to Law.

The same against John Coombs for living in fornication.

The same against Ann Williams for bastardizing.

The same against John Rogers for absenting himself from Church.

The same against the Church Wardens of the Upper Precinct of York Hampton Parish for not payling in the Church Yard.

121. The same against John Loynes for absenting himself from Church.

The same against Judith Moody for having a bastard.

The same against the Worshipfull Justices of York Court for not maintaining a pillory stock and dunking stool according to Law.

The same against Richard Shoare for absenting himself from Church.

The same against Robt. Jones for absenting himself from Church.

The same against Thomas Driver for absenting himself from Church.

The same against Jno. Rhoades for absenting himself from Church.

The same against Robt. Hyde for absenting himself from Church.

The same against Thomas Tyler for absenting himself from Church.

The same against Stevens Thomson, Esq. for absenting himself from Church.

The same against Richd. Burt for absenting himself from Church.

Memorandum. That Major Wm. Buckner hath with the Court this day agreed for the consideracion of 6,000 lbs. tobacco to build a good substancial office of 16 feet square to be weather boarded with feather edged plank or good oak boards larthed[?] and plastered to be sealed with the stain and with good window will glayed[?] to be sot in such place as by the Court shall be appointed as also good stocks and pillory and other necessary and thereto with a porch to the Courthouse door of 7 foot square to joyn to the house, which he doth hereby promise to perform as soon as nails and other necessary may be had in order thereto.

Ordered that the Court be adjourned untill the 24th day of March next.

Power of Attorney. Henry Bolch of Ratcliffe in the Parish of Stepney in the Co. of Middlesex, cheesmonger, to my friend John Bates of York co, merchant, my true and lawfull Attorney to collect due me from John Graves and Henry Tandy and all other persons in Virginia or Maryland or any other places in America. Dated the last day of March 1707. Wit. William Cant, Griffin Phillips and James Randell.

122. Will of Humphry Moody of York Hampton Parish. All my wordly estate to my loving wife, Elizabeth Moody. My wife, Elizabeth , to be sole Extx. Dated this 25th day of September 1707. Wit. Wm. Barbar, Tho. Smith and Mathew Tiplady. Proved the 24th of February 1707/8.

Will of John Fergason. To my son, John Fergason, all that plantation whereon Wm. Trotter now lives by estimation 50 acres…when he attains to the age of 21 years. In case he should dye before he comes to age or without lawfull issue, then the said land to returne to my son, William Fergason. And if both of them dye without lawful issue, then to my daughter, Mary Fergason. To my son William, all that plantation whereon I now live…when he comes to the age of 21. In case he should dye before he comes to age or without lawfull issue, to my son John Ferguson, and if both of them dye, then to my daughter, Mary. To my daughter, Mary, £10 to be paid her immediately after her marriage or at the age of 21 yeares. To my wife, Elizabeth Fergason, one negro man named Walter. In case she marries, then to my son William. Ballance of Estate to be divided among my wife and all my children. My wife to be my sole Extx. Dated this 24th day of January 1707/8. Wit. John Heyward, Anne A. Ellis and Richard Slater. Proved February Court 1707/8.

123. Will of William Garro of York Co. dated the 16th day of January 1707. To my loving wyfe, my best bed and furniture and my old pasing horse. To my daughter, Elizabeth Garro, one cow and other livestock. To my son,

John Garro, one cow and negro. Ballance of Estate to be divided among my wyfe and daughter and son. My daughter to remain with her mother till she comes to the age of 16 or marries. My wife to be my Extx. Wit. Thomas Classon and Wm. Sheldon. Proved in February Court 1707/8.

Inventory & Appraisement of the Estate of Richard Stanup, dec'd. Among other items listed is one negro man valued at £30. Total value of Estate, £77:5:6. Appraised October 1st, 1707 by Robt. Harrison, Robert Jaxson and Thomas Buck.

124. An Account of the Estate of Cornelius Willson, late of York Co, sold for and to whom. Purchasers include Wm. Sheldon, Jno. Crombie, Tho. Wade, Jno. Eaton, Cha. Cox, Jo. Morris, Jo. Brook, Thos. Mountfort, and James Boman.

The deposition of John Goulding, aged about 70 years, saith that about 26 years agone, Your depondent saw a parcell of land cleared on a certaint tract of land of 550 acres belonging to Thomas Chisman Senr., the said land being cleared in the Bushy Ponds near John Gibbs his plantation, and he further saith that to his certain knowledge, there was planted and tended on the said land 4,000 tobacco plants or thereabouts and farther saith not. Dated February Court 1707/8.

So saith Henry Gibbs, aged about 48 years.

So saith James Hill, aged about 41 years.

125. At a Court held for York Co. the 24th day of March 1707. Present, Thomas Barbar, Henry Tyler, Robt. Reade and Lawrence Smith, Gents.

On the petition of Jane Park seting forth that she hath land on both sides of the main road by her dwelling house [?] out by a corn field and praying leave to tend the same, it is ordered that she have liberty to tend the same the ensueing year and that none molest her therein.

A negro girl named Jane belonging to Thomas Nelson was this day brought into Court and adjudged to be 12 years old, ordered to be entered.

A Power of Attorney from Joseph Martin of London to Dudley Diggs, Esq. was this day proved in Court by the oaths of Wm. Blackburn, one of the witnesses thereto.

Present, Tho. Ballard, Tho. Nuting and Wm. Buckner, Gents.

The Last Will & Testament of Rebecca Pinkethman was this day produced by Geo. Baskervile, one of the Extrs. therein named, and proved in Court by the oaths of Wm. Taylor, Edward Nelson and Jno. Steward, admited to record and probate thereof granted to the Extrs. accordingly.

Thomas Ballard and Wm. Buckner, Gents., Trustees for the Portland in York Town, presented and acknowledged their Deed for one lot of the said land to Thomas Nelson and admitted to record.

Thomas Ballard and Wm. Buckner, Gents., Trustees for the Portland in York Town, presented and acknowledged their Deed for one lot of the said land to Jno. Dowzing and admitted to record.

On the petition of Josias Bourn, a New England Indian, it is ordered that the Sheriff summon Wm. Jackson to appear at the next Court to answer the said petition.

Thomas Ballard and Wm. Buckner, Gents., Trustees for the Portland in York Town, presented and acknowledged their Deed for one lot of the said land to John Wills and admitted to record.

The Deeds of Lease and Release for land from John Loynes to Jno. Bates were this day produced in Court and proved by the oaths of George Sitwell, Henry Holdcraft and Thomas Fear, the witnesses thereto, and admitted to record.

John Loynes' bond for performance of covenants to John Bates was this day proved in Court by the oaths of Geo. Sitwell, Henry Holdcraft and Thomas Fear and admitted to record.

John Martin appeared in Court and presented an account against the Estate of John Hunt, dec'd. and made oath thereto, and at his mocion admitted to record.

A Letter of Attorney from Frances Wilkinson to Geo. Baskervile was this day proved in Court by the oath of Edwd. Foulks and admitted to record.

Tho. Wilkinson appeared, presented and acknowledged in Court his Deed for land, as also Geo. Baskervile by virtue of a Power of Attorney from Frances, the wife of the said Thomas, relinquished her the said Frances' right of dower therein to Francis Sharp and admitted to record.

John Loynes not appearing to answer the presentment of the Grand Jury against him, ordered that the Sheriff of this County take him into custody and there safely to keep him untill he gives good security for his appearance at the next Court to answer the same.

Robert Jones, the same.

Stephens Thomson, the same.

Richard Shore, the same.

Judith Moody being presented by the Grand Jury for having a bastard and since the same hath absented and gone out of the County, therefore ordered that the Sheriff of this County (if he can at any time find her in the County) take her into his custody and there securely to keep her untill she shall give good security for her appearance at the next Court to be held for this County and answer the said presentment.

Robert Hide, presented by the Grand Jury for absenting the Church contrary to Law, this day appeared and the Court on hearing his argument, do consider and accordingly order that he be fined 50 lbs. tobacco or £5 to the vestry of York Hampton Parish for the use of the Parish and he pay the same alies execution.

Thomas Driver, the same.

Ordered that the Sheriff summon Tho. Tyler to appear at the next Court to answer the presentment of the Grand Jury against him for absenting the Church contrary to Law.

126. The Surveyor of the Highways in Cha. Parish being presented by the Grand Jury for not repairing the same, appeared and informed the Court that he was about it. The said presentment is dismist.

The Grand Jury having presented Thomas Walker for absenting the Church contrary to Law, he appeared and confessed the same to be true. The Court doth therefore order that he be fined 50 lbs. tobacco or £5 to the vestry of Charles Parish and that he pay the sum for the use of the Parish alies execution.

John Rogers appeared to answer the presentment of the Grand Jury against him, and on hearing his argument the said presentment is dismissed.

The Grand Jury having presented Ann Williams for bastardizing and she by a note confessed the crime and Giles Taverner appeared and assumed to the Court the payment thereof being 500 lbs. of tobacco, as also that he would the Parish of Charles harmless and indemnifyed keep from the said child, it is therefore ordered that the said Taverner's aforesaid assumption be allowed and that he pay the sum of 500 lbs. of tobacco for the use of the aforesaid Parish alies execution.

In the acion upon the case between Wm. Crimes, plf. and George Lovinston, deft. for £50 damage by means of the deft. not paying £32:3:1 due upon ballance of account, wherein judgment was cofirmed at the last Court by nihil dicit according to a rule of this Court, a jury was this day sworn to enquire into damage, whose names are Wm. Sheldon, John Dozwell Junr., Thomas Edmons, Jno. Adduston Rogers, Wm. Sherman, Tho. Holliday, Tho. Fear, Robt. Peters, Wm. Babb, Adduston Rogers, Thos. Walker and Henry Hayward Senr., having received their charge were sent out to consult their verdict and after some time came into Court and returned the same in these words: We find for the plf. £35:3:1 damage. Signed, Henry Hayward, which at the plf.'s mocion is recorded and ordered the deft. pay the aforesaid sum of £35:3:1 to the plf. with costs alies execution.

The acion on the case between Jos. Chermison, plf. and Geo. Booker, deft. is by consent of the Attorneys on both sides continued till the next Court.

The suit in Chancery depending between Robt. Cary, Extr. of the Last Will & Testament of Wm. Aylward, dec'd., complainant and Wm. Babb, respondent, is by consent continued till the next Court.

In the acion on the case between Jno. Serjanton, plf. and Jno. Nicholson, deft. for the sum of £10 damage by means of the deft. not rendering to the plf. the sum of £5:6, the deft. having at the last Court demurred generally and the plf. now joyning therein, the Court on hearing the arguments fully on both sides do adjudge the plf.'s declaracion insufficient and at the deft.'s mocion, it is ordered that he be nonsuited and that he pay the same to the deft. with costs alies execution.

A Power of Attorney from Job Wilkes to James Sclater was this day proved in Court by the oath of Wm. Johnson, one of the witnesses thereto.

In the acion of account render between Robt. Corlet, Wm. Roberts and Henry Withers of Barbados, merchants, plfs. and John Owen, deft. for £1,000 damage by means of the deft. not rendering to the plfs. a reasonable account for the time that he was bayliff to the plfs. and receiver of their goods, and as in the declaracion expressed wherein auditors were appointed at the last Court to state and settle the accounts between plfs. and deft., which order not being performed by reason of the deft. not appearing before the auditors, it is therefore further ordered by consent of both partys that Joseph Walker, Richd. Bland, Arch Blair and Tho. Jones or any three of

them meet on the 9ᵗʰ day of Aprill next or the next fair day at the house of
John Redwood in Wmsburgh, audit, state and settle the accounts in
difference between plfs. and deft. and report their proceedings to the next
Court, of which the deft.'s Attorney had notice and accepted the same at the
Barr.

Mary Garro, according to an order of this Court, returned and made oath to
the Inventory of her dec'd. husband's Estate which at her mocion is
admitted to record.

In the acion of debt between John Bates, Assignee of Richd. Drury, plf. and
Wm. Sherman, deft. for £10 by bill, the deft. having pleaded a discount of 6
shillings, it is therefore considered by the Court adjudged and accordingly
ordered that the said deft. pay the sum of £9:14 to the plf. with costs alies
execution.

The acion on the case depending between Stevens Thomson, Esq., plf. and
Thomas Ballard, deft. is continued at the plf.'s mocion till next Court.

The acion on the debt depending between Stevens Thomson, Esq., plf. and
James Morris, deft. is continued at the plf.'s mocion till next Court.

Wm. Barbar, Gent., Sheriff, according to order this day returned an account
of the Estate of Ralph Ransford, dec'd. and it was admitted to record.

In the acion of debt between Thomas Nuting, plf. and Jno. Adduston Rogers
and Jane, his wife, Admrs. of the Estate of Henry Andrews, dec'd., defts.
for £50:6:7, which the said Henry Andrews at the time of his death was
indebted to the plf. by a protested Bill of Exchange with damage and charge
of protest included, and as in the declaracion set forth, to which the deft.
pleaded that the said Henry was not indebted to the said Thomas at the time
of his death as above in the declaracion set forth and of this the defts. put
themselves on the Country and the plf. likewise, whereupon a jury was
impanneled and sworn to try the issue, joyned whose names are Wm.
Sheldon, Thomas Edmons, Thomas Holliday, Tho. Fear, Robt. Petters, Wm.
Babb, Tho. Walker, Henry Hayward Senr., Wm. Lee, Jno. With, John Drury
and Fra. Sharp, who having heard the evidence and received their charge
were sent out and in some time came again into Court and returned their
verdict which at the plf.'s mocion is recorded and is in these words: We find
for the plf. £50:6:7. Therefore considered by the Court and accordingly
ordered that the deft. pay the aforesaid sum to the plf. with costs alies
execution.

127. The acion of account render between Edmd. Jenings, Esq., Secy. of Virginia, plf. and Wm. Tunly, deft., is at the plf.'s Attorney's mocion continued till the next Court.

Edmd. Curtis, on his petition seting forth that he hath served in the office of headborough one whole year, is discharged from his said office.

On the mocion of Mongo Ingles, his petition against Rachl. Wood is continued till the next Court.

The acion on the case between Jno. Duke, plf. and Nicho. Phillips, deft., is postponed till tomorrow morning.

In the acion of debt between Wm. Faulkner, plf. and Wm. Sherman, deft., the deft. came personally into Court and confessed judgment for the sum of £6:10. Therefore considered by the Court that the plf. recover the aforesaid sum of the deft. with costs alies execution.

The acion on the case between Wm. Robertson, plf. and Wm. Sherman, deft., the deft. brought in a discount and at his mocion and by consent of the plf. hath time till the next Court to prove some articles therein.

Richd. Slaughter, an evidence for Thomas Nuting against Jno. Adduston Rogers and being summoned and attended one day on the said suit, on his mocion it is ordered that the said Nuting pay him 40 lbs. of tobacco for the same with costs alies execution.

Thomas Kirby, an evidence for Thomas Nuting against Jno. Adduston Rogers and Jane, his wife, being summoned by the Sheriff and attended one day on the said suit, on his mocion it is ordered that the said Nuting pay him 40 lbs. of tobacco for the same with costs alies execution.

In the acion of debt between Stevens Thomson, Esq., plf. and Edward Foulks, deft. for £1 by bill, the deft. appeared and confessed judgment for the said sum. Therefore ordered that he pay the said sum of £1 to the plf. with costs alies execution.

The acion on the case between Stevens Thomson, plf. and Edward Foulks, deft. is by consent continued till the next Court.

Dudly Diggs, Esq. made oath this day to his account against the Estate of Richd. Dixon, dec'd., that he hath received no part or satisfaccion thereof.

Richd. Wharton and James Morris came into Court, presented and acknowledged their bond to Our Sovereign Lady the Queen for Isabella

Brodbent's well keeping an ordinary in York Town, and it was admitted to record.

Ordered that the Court be adjourned till tomorrow morning 8 o'clock.

March the 25th, 1708. Present, Tho. Barbar, Wm. Buckner, Robt. Read, Tho. Nutting, Tho. Roberts and Law. Smith, Gents.

The acion on the case between Cha. Cox, plf. and Oliver Peron, deft., neither party appearing, is dismist.

In the acion of trespass between Wm. Davis, plf. and John Loynes, deft., wherein a survey with a jury was ordered at the last Court, which survey in pursuance of the order being made and a verdict returned, and therein having found the deft. no trespasser, at the deft.'s mocion the said verdict is orderd to be recorded, the suit dismist and that the plf. pay costs alies execution.

Thomas Ballard and Wm. Buckner, Gent., Trustees for the Portland in York Town, presented and acknowledged their Deed for one lot of the said land to John Wills and admitted to record.

In the acion of trespass between Wm. Forbush, plf. and James Morris, deft., the deft. put in his plea to the plf.'s declaracion, and at plf.'s mocion hath time till next Court to reply.

The acion of debt between James Wayte, plf. and Abra Martin, deft., neither party appearing, is dismist.

Wm. Barbar, Gent., Sheriff of this County, exhibited an account against the Estate of Cornelius Wilson, dec'd. for his sallary for his case about the said Estate amounting to £3:17, which is allowed and ordered that he retain the same in his hands.

Wm. Tunly's account against Cornelius Wilson's Estate allowed and orderd that Wm. Barbar pay him 15 shillings out of the bills taken at the outcry alies execution.

128. George Baskervile hath judgment granted against the Estate of Cornelius Wilson, dec'd. for levys amounting to 38 lbs. of tobacco and ordered that Wm. Barbar pay him out of the bills taken at the outcry 3 shillings and 10 pence alies execution.

Philip Lightfoot, on his mocion hath judgment granted him against the Estate of Cornelius Wilson, dec'd. for 11 shillings and 6 pence, and ordered that Wm. Barbar pay him the said sum out of the bills taken at the outcry alies execution.

Eliz. Somerwell hath judgment this day granted her against the Estate of Cornelius Wilson for the sum of £17:9 due from the said Estate by a protested Bill of Exchange, and ordered that Wm. Barbar, Gent., pay the said Somerwell the aforesaid sum out of the bills taken at the outcry alies execution.

Doctor Phi. Moody hath judgment granted him against the Estate of Cornelius Wilson, dec'd. for 18 shillings, and ordered the Wm. Barbar, Gent. pay him the said sum out of the bills taken at the outcry alies execution.

There being part of the Estate of Cornelius Wilson, dec'd. left undisposed of, the Court finding there is severall debts of equal dignity, thought fit to refer the disposall thereof till the next Court and accordingly it is refered.

In the acion upon the case between John Duke, plf. and Nicho. Phillips, deft. for £8 for diverse sums of money by the plf. at the deft.'s special instance and request laid out and expended as in the declaracion is set forth, to which the deft. pleaded acion not be because that a bill or writing for the sum mencioned was entred into by the deft. to the plf. on certain conditions, and the plf. replys and saith that he by anything by the said deft. in his plea alledged might not to be precluded or barred and this he prays may be enquired by the Country and the deft. likewise. Whereupon a jury was impannelled and sworn to try the issue joyned by name Robt. Crawley, Wm. Lee, Adduston Rogers, Tho. Edmons, Tho. Walker, Francis Sharp, Jos. Mountford, Thomas Chisman Junr., Wm. Sheldon, Jno. Moore, Jno. Drury and John Dozwell Junr., who after having heard the evidence and received their charge, went out to consult their verdict and in some time came again into Court and returned the same in these words: We find the plf. sold a slave mulatto woman to the deft. for £29 and we found £20 of it paid, £8 remaining still unpaid. Signed, Tho. Chisman Junr. Which verdict at the plf.'s mocion was recorded and considered by the Court that the plf. recover the aforesaid sum against the deft. with costs alies exeuction.

In the petition of Stevens Thomson seting forth that he is a creditor of Cornelius Wilson, dec'd., and that one Rosamond Wilson, daughter of the said Cornelius, has without administracion granted to her taken into her custody great part of said Estate to which rum, cash, gold and negroes, and has sold and disposed of the same without rendering any account thereof, on his mocion it is ordered that the Sheriff of this County sumon her the said Rosamond to appear at the next Court to answer the same.

The acion of debt between Thomas Grayham, plf. and Andrew Young, deft., the deft. came personally into Court and confessed judgment for the sum of £4. Therefore considered by the Court and accordingly ordered that the deft. pay the said sum to the plf. with costs alies execution.

In the acion of trespass on the case between Frederick Jones, plf. and Jno. Pinton, deft., both partys appeared and consented it should be continued till the next Court.

The acion on the case between Saml. Seldon, plf. and Phi. Smith, deft. is dismist, the plf. not prosecuting.

The acion of debt between Jno. Crombie, plf. and Ephraim Cockit, deft., neither party appearing, is dismist.

George Saunders not prosecuting his petition against Wm. Sherman, it is therefore dismist.

The acion on the case brought by John Bates, plf. against Thomas Rogers, deft. is dismist, the deft. being dead.

In the acion of debt brought by Nicho. Philips, plf. against John Redwood, deft. for £36:13:9 due by a protested Bill of Exchange with charge and damage of protest included, wherein the deft. had an imparlance at the last Court and now being called and not appearing, judgment is therefore granted to the plf. by nihil dicit returnable to this next Court for confirmacion.

In the acion on the case between James Morris, plf. and Robt. Hide, deft., wherein the deft. had an imparlance at the last Court and now not appearing, judgment is therefore granted to the plf. by nihil dicit returnable to the next Court as usual.

In the acion of debt between Thos. Hansford, plf. and Mathew Jefferys, deft., the attachment not being served, on the plf.'s mocion the former order is continued with the attachment returnable to the next Court.

In the acion upon the case between Dudly Diggs, Esq., plf. and Damazinah Brown, Extx. of the Last Will & Testament of Richd. Dixon, dec'd., wherein the deft. had an imparlance granted at the last Court and now being called and not appearing, judgment is therefore granted to the plf. by nihil dicit returnable as usuall.

129. In the acion of debt between Barontine Howles, plf. and Henry Floyd, deft. for the sum of 200 lbs. of sweet scented tobacco due by bill under the

deft.'s hand, judgment being past at the last Court unto the said plf. against Wm. Barbar, Gent., Sheriff of this County, for the sum with costs for the nonappearance of the said Floyd to answer the plf.'s acion, and the said Floyd being now called and not appearing, judgment is confirmed against the said Barbar and it is considered that he pay the sum of 200 lbs. of sweet scented tobacco to the plf. with costs alies execution.

The attachment which Wm. Barbar, Gent., Sheriff of this County, obtained against the Estate of Henry Floyd for his nonappearance at the suit of Barontine Howles, not being served, is continued till the next Court.

In the acion upon the case between Wm. Tunly, plf. and Michl. MacCormack, deft. for 250 lbs. of tobacco by account, and having proved the same by his oath and allowed the deft.'s discount, therefore ordered that the deft. pay 200 lbs. of tobacco or 20 shillings to the plf. with costs alies execution.

On the petition of John Hunt seting forth and praying that Damazinah Brown, Extx. of the Last Will & Testament of Richd. Dixon, might be compeld to return a further account of the Testator's Estate, hath done the same and the Attorney's on both sides agreed to put the said account to auditors. This Court doth think fit and also desires Robt. Read, Wm. Buckner, Law. Smith, Gents. and Tho. Nelson or any three of them to meet at Jno. Wills' in York Town on the 3d day of May next or the next fair day and audit, state and settle the accounts in difference and make report thereof to the next Court, of which the Attorneys on both sides took notice of at the Barr.

In the acion upon the case between Edward Wightwick, plf. and John Sanders, deft. for £80 damage by means of the deft. not paying to the plf. the sum of £57:12:6 due by account, wherein the deft. had time at the last Court to plead and now not appearing, judgment is therefore granted to the plf. by nihil dicit for the said sum with costs unless the deft. appears at the next Court and answers the plf.'s acion.

In the acion of debt between Jno. Redwood, plf. and John Gybb, deft., time being given at the last Court for the deft. to imparle and he not appearing, judgment is therefore granted to the plf. by nihil dicit for the sum of £4:7:7 with costs unless returnable to the next Court for confirmacion.

In the acion of debt between Henry Tyler and David Bray, Church Wardens of Bruton Parish, plfs. and Wm. Comon, deft., the deft. by his Attorney appeared and at his mocion hath a reference till the next Court.

In the acion of debt between Henry Tyler and David Bray, Church Wardens of Bruton Parish, plfs. and Edward Thomas, deft., the deft. by his Attorney appeared and at his mocion hath a reference till the next Court.

In the acion of debt between Henry Tyler and David Bray, Church Wardens of Bruton Parish, plfs. and Jno. Bates, deft., the deft. by his Attorney appeared and at his mocion hath a reference till the next Court.

In the acion of debt between Henry Tyler and David Bray, Church Wardens of Bruton Parish, plfs. and James Bates, deft., the deft. by his Attorney appeared and at his mocion hath a reference till the next Court.

In the suit brought by seire facias by Henry Hales, plf. against Jno. Bedford, deft., the plf. on his mocion hath leave to amend his declaracion, having paid costs, and by consent the cause is refered till the next Court.

In the suit in chancery depending between Joseph Dunbarr, complainant and James Bowman, respondent, the respt. failing to put in his answer, at the compl.'s mocion an attachment is granted against the body of the respt. for his appearance to answer the compl.'s bill returnable to the next Court.

The acion of debt between Henry Gill, plf. and Cha. Holdsworth, deft., neither party appearing, is dismist.

In the acion upon the case between Harwood Cary, plf. and Wm. Sears, deft. for £20 damage by means of the deft. carelessly losing and destroying a gelding saddle and bridle of the plf.'s and wherein the deft. had at the last Court a special imparlance granted and now not appearing, judgment by nihil dicit is therefore granted to the plf. for the aforesaid sum with costs returnable to the next Court for confirmacion.

In the acion of account render between Wm. Tunly, plf. and Jno. Dozwell Junr., deft., the deft. by his Attorney appeared and at his mocion the suit is continued till the next Court.

In the acion of account render between Wm. Tunly, plf. and Wm. Sheldon, deft., the deft. by his Attorney appeared and at his mocion the suit is continued till the next Court.

In the acion of account render between Wm. Tunly, plf. and Henry Tyler, deft., the deft. by his Attorney appeared and at his mocion the suit is continued till the next Court.

In the acion of debt between Jno. Crombie, plf. and James Shelton, deft. for £1:3 by bill under the deft.'s hand, wherein the deft. had time at the last

Court to plead and now not appearing, judgment by nihil dicit is therefore granted to the plf. for the aforesaid sum with costs returnable to the next Court for confirmacion.

In the acion of account render between Wm. Tunly, plf. and Wm. Gordon, deft., the deft. by his Attorney appeared and at his mocion the suit is continued till the next Court.

130. In the acion of account render between Wm. Tunly, plf. and Wm. Barbar, deft., the deft. by his Attorney appeared and at his mocion the suit is continued till the next Court.

In pursuance of an order of the Hon. The Genl. Court requiring this Court to return their reasons why they did not pursue the direccions of a former order of the said Court made in a difference depending between John Cooper of London, plf. and Tho. Whitby and Mary, his wife, defts., it is ordered that the Clerk of this Court copy all such orders as relates to the said suit and return the same to the first day of the next Genl. Court, that thereby their Hon. may perceive that this Court had proceeded regularly in the said suit.

Whereas by Law it is required that all Courts within this colony shall sometime between the last of January and the last day of March yearly recommend three fit and capable persons to execute the Office of Sheriff, in pursuance thereof, this Court nominates and recommends Tho. Roberts, Thomas Nuting and Lawrence Smith, Gents. as fit and capable persons to execute the said Office for the ensueing year.

The former rates of liquors for ordinary keepers is continued.

In the acion of debt between John Bates, plf. and John Loynes, deft. for £200 in lawfull money of England by bond obligatory under the deft.'s hand and seal, the Sheriff having made oath that he left a copy of the acion at the deft.'s comon place of residence and he not appearing, at the plf.'s mocion an attachment is granted him against the deft.'s Estate for the aforesaid sum with costs returnable to the next Court for judgment.

In the acion of debt between John Bates, plf. and John Marot, deft. for the sum of £12:11:7 ½ and 126 lbs. of tobacco by a judgment obtained in the James City Co. Court, the deft. not appearing or any security returned for him, judgment is therefore granted to the plf. against Wm. Barbar, Gent., Sheriff of this County, for the aforesaid sum with costs unless the said deft. appears at the next Court and answers the plf.'s acion.

In the acion upon the case between Saml. Seldon, plf. and John Loynes, deft. for £6 by account, the Sheriff having made oath that he left a copy of the acion in this suit at the deft.'s comon place of residence and he not appearing, at the plf.'s mocion an attachment is therefore granted him against the deft.'s Estate for the aforesaid sum with costs returnable to the next Court for judgment.

In the acion upon the case between Cha. Cox, plf. and Timothy Johnson, deft., the plf. failing to produce the bill whereon he declared, at the deft.'s mocion it is ordered that he be nonsuited and that he pay dammage according ot Law with costs alies execution.

The acion of debt between John Morris, plf. and Wm. Thacker, deft., neither party appearing, is dismist.

In the acion upon the case between Cha. Cox, plf. and Andrew Young, deft., the deft. appeared and on his mocion hath an imparlance till the next Court.

The acion on the case between Joanna Atkins, plf. and Rosamond Wilson, deft., neither party appearing, is dismist.

The acion of debt between Gabl. Maupin, plf. and Tho. Haly, deft. is dismist, neither party appearing.

In the acion of debt between Henry Holdcraft and John Marot, deft. for 108 lbs. of tobacco, which to him he oweth by a judgment of James City Co. Court as evidence for the deft., the deft. being called and not appearing nor any security returned for him, on the plf.'s mocion judgment is therefore granted him against Wm. Barbar, Gent., Sheriff, for the aforesaid sum with costs unless the said deft. appears at the next Court and answers the plf.'s acion.

In the acion of debt between Dudly Diggs, Esq., plf. and Thomas Fear, deft. for £34:14 by a protested Bill of Exchange with charge and damage of protest included, the deft. being called and not appearing nor any security returned for him, on the plf.'s mocion judgemnt is granted him against Wm. Barbar, Gent., Sheriff, for the sum with costs unless the said deft. appears at the next Court and answers the plf.'s acion.

In the acion of debt between Joseph Chermison, plf. and Silas Smith, otherwise called Silas Smith of the Parish of Burton in the Co. of York, taylor, deft., for £140 by bond under the deft.'s hand and seal, the Sheriff having made oath that he left a copy of the Writ at the deft.'s common place of residence, on the mocion of the plf.'s Attorney an attachment is granted him against the deft.'s Estate for the aforesaid sum with costs returnable to the next Court for judgment.

In the acion of debt between John Gybb, plf. and Peter Finny, deft., neither party appearing, is dismist.

In the acion on the case between Richd. Wharton, plf. and James Sclater, deft., the deft. appeared and on his mocion hath a special imparlance till the next Court.

In the acion of debt between Robt. Mynn, plf. and John Duke, deft. for £12:10 by bill under the deft.'s hand, the deft. being called and not appearing nor any security returned for him, on the plf.'s mocion judgment is granted him against Wm. Barbar, Gent., Sheriff, for the said sum with costs unless the said deft. appears at the next Court and answers the plf.'s acion.

131. Judgment being passed this day to Robt. Mynn against Wm. Barbar, Gent., Sheriff, for the sum of £12:12 by means of the nonappearance of John Duke at the suit of the said Mynn, on the mocion of the said Barbar an attachment is granted him against the said Duke's Estate for the aforesaid sum with costs returnable to the next Court for judgment.

In the acion of debt between Edward Moss, plf. and Wm. Drury, deft., Wm. Gordon, Sub Sheriff, having returned a retraxit and neither party appearing, is dismist.

In the acion upon the case between Samuel Seldon, plf. and Use Gibson, deft. for £7 by account, both partys submiting themselves to the Court for tryal, on hearing the arguments do adjudge and accordingly order that the said deft. pay the sum of £5 to the plf. with costs alies execution.

In the acion on the case between Richd. Morton, plf. and Eliz. West, deft. for £1:5 by account, the deft. being arrested and not appearing nor any security returned for her, on the plf.'s mocion, judgment is granted him against Wm. Barbar, Sheriff, for the said sum with costs, unless the deft. appears at the next Court and answers the plf.'s acion.

In the acion on the case between Wm. Tunly, plf. and James Bowman, deft., the deft. being arrested by the Sheriff and not appearing nor any security returned for him, judgment is granted to the plf. for the sum sued for with costs against Wm. Barbar, Gent., Sheriff, unless the deft. appears at the next Court and answers the plf.'s acion.

Judgment being passed this day aagainst Wm. Barbar, Sheriff, for the sum of 324 lbs. of tobacco with costs by means of the nonappearance of James Bowman at the suit of Wm. Tunley, on the said Barbar's mocion an attachment is granted him against the said Bowman's Estate for the said sum with costs returnable to the next Court for judgment.

In the acion of Assault & Battery between Thomas Haly, plf. and Jno. Morris, deft., neither party appearing, is dismist.

In the acion of debt between Thomas Cowles Junr., plf. and Cha. Cox, deft. for the sum of 51 shillings, the deft. being arrested by the Sheriff and not appearing nor any security returned for him, judgment is therefore granted to the plf. against Wm. Barbar, Sheriff of this County, for the said sum with costs unless the deft. appears at the next Court and answers the plf.'s action.

In the acion of debt between Thomson Stapley, plf. and Cha. Cox, deft. for £8:15 by bill under the deft.'s hand, he being arrested by the Sheriff and not appearing nor any security returned for him, judgment is therefore granted to the plf. for the aforesaid sum with costs against Wm. Barbar, Gent., Sheriff of this County, unless the said deft. appears at the next Court and answers the plf.'s action.

In the acion on the case between Wm. Davis, plf. and Michl. McCormack, deft., the plf. failing to file his declaracion, at the deft.'s mocion it is ordered that he be nonsuited and that he pay the deft. damage according to Law with costs alies execution.

In the acion on the case between Jno. Morris, plf. and Richd. Cheshire, deft., neither party appearing, is therefore dismist.

In the acion of trespass between Wm. Stoakes, plf. and Geo. Rogers, deft., the plf. not prosecuting, is therefore dismist.

On the mocion of Thomas Hansford, an evidence for John Duke against Nicho. Philips, having attended two days on the said suit, it is ordered that the said Duke pay him 80 lbs. of tobacco for the same alies execution.

The acion of Assault & Battery between Jno. With, plf. and Wm. Lee, deft. is dismist, the plf. not prosecuting.

The acion of trespass between Tho. Chesman, plf. and Adduston Rogers, deft. is by consent continued till the next Court.

In the acion upon the case between Mary Whaly, plf. and Francis Sharp, deft. for £10 damage by means of the deft. not complying with his promise and assumption in erecting and building substantially and in workman like manner a dwelling house for the plf. as in the declaracion, both party's agreed to put the said work to viewers and the plf. having made choice of

John Turner and the deft. of Richd. Bloxum, it is therefore ordered that the said Turner and Bloxum meet on the first day of Aprill next or the next fair day at the house in difference and view and value the same. It is also further agreed between the said partys that in case the said viewers cannot agree, at their discretion, are to make choice of an umpire and that they make report of their proceedings to the next Court.

Thomas Hansford being sumoned an evidence for John With against Wm. Lee and having attended 5 days on the said suit, at his mocion it is ordered that the said With pay him 200 lbs. of tobacco for the same with costs alies execution.

Sarah Hansford allowed for 3 days attendance, 120 lbs. of tobacco as above.

John Carter being sumoned an evidence for Francis Sharp at the suit of Mary Whaly and having attended three days on the said suit, at his mocion it is ordered that the said Sharp pay him 120 lbs. of tobacco for the same with costs alies execution.

132. In the acion of debt between John Doswell, plf. and Thomas Walker, deft., the deft. appeared and at his mocion hath time till next Court to plead when he is to come peremtorily to tryal.

In the acion of debt between John Dozwell Junr., plf. and Thos. Walker, deft., the deft. appeared by his Attorney and at his mocion hath time till next Court to plead when he is to come peremtorily to tryal.

In the acion upon the case between Eliz. Moody, Extx. of the Last Will & Testament of Humphry Moody, dec'd., plf. and Robt. Crawley, deft. for £1:4:7 ½ by account, the deft. having exhibited a discount, both partys agreed to refer the said accounts to be adjusted by auditors. The Court doth think fit and accordingly order that Thomas Ballard, Gent. and Thos. Nelson or either of them meet at the plf.'s house on the 3d day of May next or the next fair day, then and there audit, state and settle the accounts in difference and return their proceedings therein to the next Court, the deft. having had notice of the same at the Barr.

In the acion on the case between Robt. Crawley, plf. and Eliz. Moody, Extx. of the Last Will & Testament of Humphry Moody, dec'd., deft. for £19:10:11 ½ by account and bill, the deft. put in her discount to the same, and both partys consented to refer the said accounts to be adjusted by auditors. The Court thinks fit and accordingly orders that Tho. Ballard, Gent. and Tho. Nelson or either of them meet on the 3d day of May next or the next fair day at the deft.'s house and audit, state and settle the accounts in difference and make report of their proceedings to the next Court, the deft.'s Attorney having had notice of the same at the Barr.

In the acion of debt between Robert Mynn, plf. and Joseph Mountfort, deft. for £6:12:8 by bill under the deft.'s hand, he being arrested by the Sheriff and not appearing nor any security returned for him, at the plf.'s mocion judgment is granted him against Wm. Barbar, Sheriff, for the aforesaid sum with costs, unless the said deft. appears at the next Court and answers the plf.'s acion.

Judgment being this day passed against Wm. Barbar, Sheriff, in the sum of £6:12:8 by means of the nonappearance of Joseph Mountfort at the suit of Robt. Mynn, at the said Barbar's mocion an attachment is granted him against the said Mountfort's Estate for the aforesaid sum with costs returnable to the next Court for judgment.

The suit by partition brought by Saml. Cooper, plf. against Thos. Edmonds and Kath., his wife, is dismist, neither party appearing.

In the acion of debt between John Dozwell Senr., plf. and Thomas Walker, deft., the deft. by his Attorney appeared and on his mocion hath an imparlance till the next Court.

Ordered that the Court be adjourned till the 24th day of May next.

Power of Attorney. Frances Wilkinson, wife of Thomas Wilkinson, to my friend George Baskervyle, my lawfull Attorney in all cases and acion whatsoever. Dated this 22nd day of March 1707/8. Wit. Letitia Armstrong and E. Foulkes.

Certificate according to Law was granted to John Martin to depart this Colony on the 29th day of March 1708.

Bond. Isabella Brodbent and Richard Wharton, both of the Parish and Co. of York, and James Morris of the same County and Parish of Bruton, to the Queen in the sum of 10,000 lbs. of tobacco. The 15th day of December 1707. Sureties for Isabella Brodbent to obtain a Lycence to operate an ordinary.

Will of Rebecca Pinkethman, widow of Bruton Parish. To my daughter, Mary Pinkethman, my negro girle named Phota. To my loving son, Thomas Pinkethman, my negro boy named Jomoy. To my daughter, Sarah Pinkethman, my negro girle named Moll. To my aforesaid son and daughters, my negro girle named Choragio to be equallie divided amongst them, but in case my said son or daughters should lose their negro before they arrive to the age of 18, then the said negro girle to return to he or she that so lost their negro. To my son-in-law William Pinkethman, one cow calf. To my daughter-in-law Mary Pinkethman, £5. To my goddaughter, Sarah Batten, one heifer. To my godchildren beside, each of them a cow calf. To my cozen, William Batten, 20 shillings to be paid him now in his necessitie. My negro woman Juda and the rest of my Estate to be sold to satisfye my debts, and what remains to be divided among my aforesaid children, Thomas, Mary and Sarah. My brother George Baskervile and my brother-in-law Thomas Cripps to be my Extrs. My brother-in-law Thomas Cripps to take into his care and charge my children with their Estates. Dated this 12th day of March 1707/8. Wit. William Taylor, Edward Nelson and Jno. Steward. Proved in March Court 1707/8.

Inventory & Appraisement of the Estate of William Garro. Among other items, one servant boy valued at 8 shillings 6 pence. Total value of Estate, £29:4:8. Appraised by John Moss, Adduston Rogers and Wm. Sheldon and proved by Mary Garro, the widdow and Extx of Wm. Garro, dec'd., March 24th 1707.

135. Capt. John Hunt, dec'd., his account. £128:16:4 paid out for debt. Cash received for the sale of 4 negros and one child and debt collected, £92:10. Dated this 4th of March 1707/8 by Jno. Martin.

136. At a Court held for York Co. this 24th day of May 1708. Present, Thomas Barbar, Henry Tyler, Thomas Ballard, Lawrence Smith, William Buckner and Wm. Pinkethman, Gents.

Wm. Pinkethman, Gent. is hereby appointed in the Upper Precinct of Bruton Parish in this County to take the List of Tithables for the year ensueing, and ordered that he make return thereof according to Law.

Henry Tyler, Gent. is hereby appointed in the Lower Precinct of Bruton Parish in this County to take and receive the List of Tithables for the year ensueing, and ordered that he give notice of his appointment and make return of the said List according to Law.

Wm. Barbar, Gent. in the Upper Precinct of York Hampton Parish in this County.

Wm. Buckner, Gent. in the Lower Precinct of York Hampton Parish in this County.

Thomas Nuting, Gent. in the Lower Precinct of Charles Parish in this County.

Thomas Roberts, Gent. in the Upper Precinct of Charles Parish in this County.

Ordered that the Sheriff of this County sumon 24 able freeholders of this County to appear here and attend at the next Court to be of the Grand Jury.

Thomas Bournham being sumoned an evidence and having attended 2 days on the appraisement of the Estate of Thomas Gibbons, dec'd., on his mocion it is ordered that Edward Moss, the Admr., pay him 80 lbs. of tobacco out of the said Estate with costs alies execution.

Simon Stacy, the same.

The petition of Josias Bourn against William Jackson is dismist, the petr. not prosecuting.

The acion in the case between Joseph Chermison, plf. and George Booker, deft. is by consent continued till the next Court.

In the suit in Chancery between Robt. Cary, Extr. of Wm. Aylward, complainant and Wm. Babb, respondent, on the mocion of the compl. the suit is continued till the next Court, he having assumed the payment of the costs occasioned by this delay.

John Keen came personally into Court, presented and acknowledged his Deed for land as also Henry Holdcraft by virtue of a Power of Attorney from Obedience Keen, the wife of the said John, and relinquished her the said Obedience's right of dower in the said lands to Daniel Park, Esq. and admited to record.

John Keen came this day into Court and acknowledged his bond to Danl. Park, Esq. for performance of covenants and at mocion made it was admited to record.

The Power of Attorney from Obedience Keen to Henry Holdcraft was this day proved in Court by the oaths of the witnesses thereto and admited to record.

Wm. Tunly appeared in Court, presented and acknowledged his Assignment of a Deed for one lott or half acre of land in York Town to Charles Cox, which deed and assignment at the said Cox's mocion were admited to record.

Thomas Poynter came personally into Court and presented a Deed of land from Martin Goodwin to him the said Poynter as also Barbara Goodwin, wife of the said Martin, appeared and relinquished her right of dower in the said lands unto the said Poynter, and at his mocion admited to record.

In the acion of account render between Robert Corlet, Wm. Roberts and Henry Wither of Barbados, merchants, plfs. and John Owen, deft., wherein auditors was appointed at the last Court to state and settle the accounts in difference, which order not being performed, it is therefore continued and ordered that it be performed on the 10th day of June next if fair, if not the next fair day, of which the deft.'s Attorneys took notice at the Barr.

In the acion on the case between Stevens Thomson, Esq., plf. and Thos. Ballard, deft., both partys appeared and consented the cause should be refered till the next Court.

In the acion of account render between Edmund Jenings, Esq., Secretary of Virginia, plf. and Wm. Tunly, deft. for £150 damage by means of the deft. not rendering to the plf. as being his bayliff and receiver a reasonable account of 80,000 lbs. weight of tobacco due and owing for fees for business done by the said deft. as deputy Clerk of York Court as is set forth in the declaracion , which the deft. pleaded that he never was bailiff or receiver to the plf., and the plf. having at February Court produced some papers as evidence to which the deft. demurred and the plf. joyning therein was referred till this Court to be argued. On hearing the arguments on both sides, the Court are of opinion that the deft.'s demurrence be overruled and ordered that he account for the usuall sallary allowed the Secy. for holding the Office of Clerk of York Court for the time that the deft. was Clerk thereof, and at the plf.'s mocion it is further ordered that Joseph Walker, Thomas Nelson and John Wills or any two of them meet on the 9th day of June next if fair, if not the next fair day at John Wills' house in York Town, then and there to audit, state and settle the accounts in difference and make report of their proceedings to the next Court.

137. On the petition of John Marot seting forth that a servant woman belonging to him named Sarah Barefoot hath been absent and runaway from his service… for the space of 6 months and ten days, and praying that he may be allowed as by case it is directed and for his charges in apprehending her amounting to 230 lbs. of tobacco, the said Barefoot being before the Court and did not deny what was alledged against her, it is therefore ordered that she serve her said Master after the time of her service by indenture is expired one year and four months according to Law.

The acion on the case between Wm. Robertson, plf. and Wm. Sherman, deft. is at the deft.'s mocion continued till the next Court.

165

The acion on the case between Stevens Thomson, plf. and Edward Foulks, deft., at the plf.'s mocion continued till the next Court

In the acion of trespass between William Forbush, plf. and James Morris, deft., the plf. put in his replicacion to the deft.'s plea, and the deft. on his mocion hath time till the next Court to consider it.

John Loynes, who was presented by the Grand Jury for absenting himself from Church contrary to Law, this day appeared to answer the same, and on hearing his arguments the Court do order that he be fined 5 shillings or 50 lbs. of tobacco to the Church Wardens of Bruton Parish to be payd at the next levy alies execution.

The petition of Stevens Thomson against Rosamond Wilson is dismist, the petr. not prosecuting.

The acion of trespass on the case between Frederick Jones, plf. and John Pinton, deft. is by consent of both partys continued till the next Court.

In the acion of debt between Nicho. Phillips, plf. and John Redwood, deft. for £36:13:9 by protested Bill of Exchange with charge of protest and damage according to Law included, wherein judgment past at the last Court by nihil dicit and the deft. being now called and not appearing, the said judgment is confirmed and ordered that the deft. pay the aforesaid sum to the plf. with costs alies execution.

In the acion upon the case between James Morris, plf. and Robert Hide, deft., the deft. put in his plea to the plf.'s declaracion, and the plf. on his mocion hath time till the next Court to consider it.

The acion of debt between Thomas Hansford, plf. and Mathew Jefferys, deft., neither party appearing, is dismist.

In the acion on the case between Dudly Diggs, Esq., plf. and Damazinah Brown, Extx. of Richd. Dixon, dec'd., deft. for £10:15:9 by account and the plf. having provd the same by his oath, judgment being past at the last Court to the plf. by nihil dicit and the deft. now called and not appearing, the said judgment is therefore confirmed and ordered that the deft. pay the aforesaid sum to the plf. with costs alies execution.

At the mocion of Wm. Barbar, Gent., Sheriff of this County, the attachment which he obtained against the Estate of Henry Floyd is dismisst.

In the suit between John Hunt, plf. and Damazinah Brown, Extx. of the Last Will & Testament of Richd. Dixon, dec'd. for the said Brown to account for the Estate of the dec'd., wherein auditors were appointed at the last Court to audit, state and settle the accounts in difference, which order not being performed by reason of the deft. not meeting the auditors at the time appointed, it is therefore continued and ordered to be performed on the 9ᵗʰ day of June next if fair, if not the next fair day and that return by made thereof to the next Court and it is further ordered that if the deft. do not meet at the time appointed that the auditors proceed to state and settle what accounts shall be produced by the plf. and that the deft. pay all costs that shall occur occasioned by such delay, of which time the deft. had notice at the Barr.

On the peition of Mongo Ingles seting forth that a servant white woman named Rachl. Wood belonging to him is lately delivered of a mulatto bastard child and praying the benefit of the Law in that case made, it is therefore considered by the Court adjudged and accordingly ordered that the said Rachl. Wood serve her said Master one whole year after her time by indenture, custom or former order is expired according to Law.

In the acion in the case between Edward Wightwick, plf. and John Saunders, deft., the plf. failing to prosecute, at the deft.'s mocion it is ordered that he be nonsuited and that he pay the deft.'s damage according to Law with costs alies execution.

In the acion of debt between John Redwood, plf. and John Gibb, deft. for £4:7:7 by bill under the deft.'s hand, wherein judgment past at the last Court by nihil dicit and the deft. being now called and not appearing, the said judgment is confirmed and ordered that he pay the aforesaid sum to the plf. with costs alies execution.

Mary Whaley came personally into Court, presented and acknowledged her Deed for land in this County to Francis Sharp and at his mocion admitted to record.

138. In the acion of debt between Henry Tyler and David Bray, Church Wardens of Bruton Parish, plfs. and Wm. Coman, deft., the deft. put in his plea to the plf.'s declaracion, and the plfs. at their mocion hath time till the next Court to consider it.

In the acion of debt between Henry Tyler and David Bray, Church Wardens of Bruton Parish, plfs. and Edward Thomas, deft., both partys appeared and at the mocion of the deft. the cause is continued till the next Court.

The acion of debt between Henry Tyler and David Bray, Church Wardens of Bruton Parish, plfs. and John Bates, deft. is continued till the next Court at the deft.'s mocion to prove his discount.

167

In the acion of debt between Henry Tyler and David Bray, Church Wardens of Bruton Parish, plfs. and James Bates, deft., the deft. put in his plea to the plf.'s declaracion, and by consent the cause is refered to the next Court for tryal.

In the suit brought by seire facias by Henry Hales, plf. and John Bedford, deft., the deft. put in his plea to the plf.'s declaracion, and at the plf.'s mocion is continued till the next Court for him to consider it.

In the suit in Chancery depending between Joseph Dunbarr, complainant and James Bowman, respondent, the order for attachment not being served nor the respt. answering, at the compl.'s mocion the said order is continued till the next Court.

In the acion upon the case between Harwood Cary, plf. and Wm. Sears, deft., the deft. having put in his plea to the plf.'s declaracion, the plf. on his mocion hath time granted till the next Court to consider it.

John Hall, on his petition seting forth that he is very antient and past his labour, is discharged from paying any levys.

The acion of account render between Wm. Tunly, plf. and Jno. Dozwell Junr., deft., neither party appearing, is dismist.

The acion of account render between Wm. Tunly, plf. and Wm. Sheldon, deft., is dismist, neither party appearing.

The acion of account render between Wm. Tunly, plf. and Henry Tyler, deft., is dismist, neither party appearing.

In the acion of debt between John Crombie, plf. and James Shelton, deft. for £1:3 by bill under the deft.'s hand, wherein judgment passed at the last Court by nihil dicit and the deft. being now called and not appearing, it is therefore considered that the plf. recover of the deft. the aforesaid sum with costs alies execution.

The acion of account render between Wm. Tunly, plf. and Wm. Gordon, deft., is dismist, the plt. not prosecuting.

The acion of account render between Wm. Tunly, plf. and Wm. Barbar, deft., is dismist, the plt. not prosecuting.

The acion of debt between John Bates, plf. and John Loynes, deft. is dismist, neither party appearing.

The acion of debt between John Bates, plf. and John Marot, deft. is dismist, neither party appearing.

In the acion on the case between Saml. Seldon, plf. and John Loynes, deft., the plf. at the last Court having obtained an attachment against the deft.'s Estate, which not being served, is at his mocion continued till the next Court.

The acion on the case between Charles Cox, plf. and Andrew Young, deft. is dismisst, neither party appearing.

In the acion of debt between Henry Holdcraft, plf. and John Marot, deft. for 468 lbs. of tobacco due to the plf. by a judgment of James City Co. Court granted him for 11 days attendance as an evidence for the deft., wherein judgment past at the last Court against Wm. Barbar, Sheriff of this County, for the nonappearance of the said Marot to answer the plf.'s acion, and the said Marot now being called and not answering, the said judgment is therefore confirmed against the said Barbar and ordered that he pay the aforesaid sum to the plf. with costs alies execution.

Judgment being this day confirmed unto Henry Holdcraft against Wm. Barbar, Gent., Sheriff of this County, for the sum of 468 lbs. of tobacco with costs by means of the nonappearance of John Marot at the suit of the said Holdcraft, on the mocion of the said Barbar an attachment is granted him against the Estate of the said Marot for the aforesaid sum with costs returnable to the next Court for judgment.

The acion of debt between Dudley Diggs, Esq., plf and Thos. Fear, deft., neither party appearing, is dismist.

In the acion of debt between Joseph Chermison, plf. and Silas Smith, otherwise called Silas Smith of the Parish of Bruton in the County of York, deft. the attachment which the plf. obtained against the deft.'s Estate at the last Court not yet being served is at his mocion continued till the next Court.

In the acion on the case between Richd. Wharton, plf. and James Sclater, deft. for £2 by account, the deft. having had at the last Court a special imparlance and being now called and failing to answer, judgment is therefore granted to the plf. by nihil dicit for the aforesaid sum with costs returnable to the next Court for confirmacion.

In the acion of debt between Robert Mynn, plf. and John Duke, deft., the attachment not yet being served, at the plf.'s mocion it is continued till the next Court.

The attachment which Wm. Barbar, Gent., Sheriff, obtained against the Estate of John Duke for his nonappearance at the suit of Robt. Mynn not yet being served is on his mocion continued till the next Court.

139. In the acion on the case between Richd. Morton, plf. and Eliz. West, deft., both partys appeared and at the plf.'s mocion the said suit is continued till the next Court.

The acion on the case between Wm. Tunly, plf. and James Bowman, deft., neither party appearing, is dismist.

The attachment which Wm. Barbar, Gent., Sheriff of this County, obtained against the Estate of James Bowman for his nonappearance at the suit of Wm. Tunly, is dismist.

In the acion of debt between Thomas Cowles Junr., plf. and Charles Cox, deft. for 51 shillings by bill under the deft.'s hand dated the 24th day of November 1707, the deft. came personally into Court and confessed judgment to the plf. for the said sum, whereupon it is considered by the Court that the deft. pay unto the plf. the aforesaid sum with costs alies execution.

The acion of debt between Thomson Stapley, plf. and Cha. Cox, deft., neither party appearing, is dismist.

The acion of trespas between Thomas Chisman, plf. and Adduston Rogers, deft., is by consent continued till the next Court and then to be the first acion on the docquet for that Court.

In the acion on the caset between Mary Whaley, plf. and Francis Sharp, deft. for £10 damage by means of the deft. not complying with his promise and assumption in erecting and building substancially and in a work like manner a dwelling house for the plf. as in the declaracion, wherein viewers were at the last Court appointed to view the said work and report their proceedings to this Court, which being done and therein having found for the deft., therefore on the deft.'s mocion the said report is admitted to record and ordered that the plf. be nonsuited and that she pay the deft. damage according to Law with costs alies execution.

In the acion of debt between John Dozwell, plf. and Thos. Walker, deft., neither party appearing, is dismist.

The acion of debt between John Dozwell Junr., plf. and Thomas Walker, deft., neither party appearing, is dismist.

In the acion upon the case between Eliz. Moody, Extx. of the Last Will & Testament of Humphry Moody, dec'd., plf. and Robt. Crawley, deft., auditors being appointed at the last Court to state and settle the accounts in difference, and having done the same and returned their report and therein having found to be due to the plf. £1:7:4 ½, at the plf.'s mocion the report is admitted to record. Whereupon it is considered by the Court adjudged and accordingly ordered that the deft. pay the said sum to the plf. with costs alies execution.

The acion upon the case between Robt. Crawley, plf. and Eliz. Moody, Extx. of the Last Will & Testament of Humphry Moody, dec'd., deft. neither party appearing, is dismist.

The acion of debt between Robt. Mynn, plf. and Joseph Mountfort, deft., neither party appearing, is dismist.

At the mocion of Wm. Barbar, Gent., Sheriff of this County, the attachment which he obtained against Jos. Mountfort's Estate for the nonappearance of the said Mountfort at the suit of Robt. Mynn is dismist.

The acion of debt between Jno. Dozwell Senr., plf. and Thomas Walker, deft., neither party appearing, is dismist.

The former order for disposal of the remainder of the Estate of Cornelius Wilson, dec'd. is continued and ordered that the Clerk of this Court draw up and exhibit an account of the Estate for the next Court.

Robt. Jones, according to sumons, appeared this day to answer the presentment of the Grand Jury against him for absenting himself from Church, and on hearing what he had to say, is discharged.

Eliz. Blaxton appeared on the presentment of the Grand Jury against her for having a bastard child and confessed the fact. The Court thinks fit and accordingly orders that she be fined 500 lbs. of tobacco to be paid to the Church Wardens of York Hampton Parish at the next levy alies execution.

Thos. Ballard and Wm. Buckner, Gents., Trustees for the Portland in York Town, presented and acknowledged their Deed for one lot or half acre of the said land to Joseph Walker and at his mocion admitted to record.

Thos. Ballard and Wm. Buckner, Gents., Trustees for the Portland in York Town, presented and acknowledged their Deed for one lot or half acre of the said land to Richd. Chesshire and at his mocion admitted to record.

In the acion of debt between Wm. Palmer, plf. and Saml. Seldon, deft. for £24 by bill under the deft.'s hand dated the 25th of June 1707, the deft. came personally into Court and confessed judgment to the plf. for the said sum. Whereupon it is considered by the Court that the deft. pay unto the plf. the aforesaid sum with costs alies execution. Execution not to issue till the next Court.

In the acion of debt between Henry Hayward, plf. and Wm. Newberry, deft. for tobacco by a note drawn by John Merry and John Tignal and accepted by the said deft. as is set forth in the declaracion, the deft. being called and not appearing, on the mocion of the plf. judgment is granted against Saml. Seldon, security returned for the deft., for the said sum with costs unless the deft. appears at the next Court and answers the plf.'s action.

The acion of debt between Charles Cox, plf. and John King, deft., neither party appearing, is dismist.

In the Informacion exhibited by Wm. Sheldon, Church Warden of York Hampton Parish, against Anne Blackley for having a bastard child contrary to Law, and she being sumond and not appearing, it is ordered that the Sheriff of this County take her into his custody and there securely to keep her untill she shall give good and sufficient security for her appearance at the next Court to answer the said Informacion.

In the acion of debt bnetween Gawin Corbin, plf. and Torence Webb of York Co., deft. for £17:12, the deft. appeared and exhibited a discount amounting to £7:10 and made oath that it was just and true and the plf. not objecting against the same, whereupon it is considered by the Court that the plf. recover of the deft. the sum of £10:2 being the ballance of the above account with costs alies execution.

140. The acion on the case between John Pinton, plf. and Obediah Merrit, deft., neither party appearing, is dismist.

In the acion of debt between Sampson Darrell, plf. and Andrew Hamilton, deft. for £8:14:7 by a judgment of Gloucester Co. recovered by reason of the deft. having transported out of the said County without certificate one David Ross, who was indebted to the said plf. the said sum as also the sum of 156 lbs. of tobacco for the costs of the said suit, the deft. being called and not appearing, at the mocion of the plf. judgment is granted unto him against Wm. Robertson, security returned for the deft., for the aforesaid sums with costs unless the said deft. appears at the next Court and answers the plf.'s acion.

172

In the acion on the case between Thomas Woodfield, plf. and Thos. Roberts and Damazinah, his wife, Extx. of Richd. Dixon, dec'd., defts. for 600 lbs. of sweet scented tobacco with cash by account, the defts. by their Attorney appeared and on his mocion hath a special imjparlance granted to the next Court.

The acion upon the case between Eliz. Blaxton, plf. and Richd. Worledge, deft., neither party appearing, is dismist.

The acion on the case between Eliz. Blaxton, plf. and Adduston Rogers, deft., neither party appearing, is dismist.

In the acion of trespass between Henry Lightfoot, plf. and Wm. Davis, deft. for £10 damage by means of the deft. with force and armes making assault on the body of the said plf. and him beating, wounding and evilly intreating, the deft. being called and not appearing nor any security returned for him, on the mocion of the plf. judgment is granted him against Wm. Barbar, Gent., Sheriff of this County, for the aforesaid sum with costs unless the said deft. appears at the next Court and answers the plf.'s acion.

The acion on the case between John Fisher, plf. and John Dozwell, deft., neither party appearing, is dismist.

In the acion of debt between James Taylor, Gent., plf. and Christopher Smith, deft. for £22:18:6 and 3 farthings, the same being due for principal, charge of protest and damage according to Law upon a Bill of Exchange drawn by the deft. as is set forth in the declaracion, the deft. being called and not appearing nor any County security returned for him, on the plf.'s mocion judgment is granted him against Wm. Barbar, Gent., Sheriff of this County, for the aforesaid sum with costs unless the deft. appears at the next Court and answers the plf.'s acion.

In the acion of debt between Lewis Burwell, Gent., plf. and Robert Jones of Hampton Parish, deft. for £12:12:6 by bill under the deft.'s hand, the said deft. being called and not appearing nor any security returned for him, at the plf.'s mocion judgment is granted him against Wm. Barbar, Gent., Sheriff of this County, for the aforesaid sum with costs unless the deft. appears at the next Court and answers the plf.'s action.

The acion on the case between Simon Hollier of Eliz. City Co., plf. and Thos. West of King Wm. Co., deft., neither party appearing, is dismist.

The acion on the case between Richd. Whaley, plf. and Mary Whaley, Extx. of James Whaley, deft. for £500, neither party appearing, is dismist.

In the acion of debt between Henry Atkinson, Assignee of Alexr. Bonyman, plf. and James Morris, deft., the deft. appeared and on his mocion hath oyer of the bill declared on granted till the next Court.

In the acion of trespass between John King, plf. and Wm. Forbush, deft., the deft. on his mocion hath a special imparlance granted him till the next Court.

The acion of debt between John Prat, plf. and Thos. Hansford, deft., neither party appearing, is dismist.

The acion on the case between Charles Cox, plf. and Timothy Johnson, deft., neither party appearing, is dismist.

In the acion on the case between Henry Lightfoot, plf. and Daniel Israel, deft. for £7 for certain sums of money by the said plf. for the said deft. and at his special instance and request laid out and expended as in the declaracion is expressed, the deft. being called and not appearing, at the plf.'s mocion judgment is granted him against John Redwood, security returned for the deft., for the aforesaid sum with costs unless the said deft. appears at the next Court and answers the plf.'s acion.

The acion on the case between Thos. Jones, plf. and John Emmery, deft., neither party appearing, is dismist.

In the acion of debt between Dudley Diggs, Esq., plf. and John Marot, deft. for £18 by bill under the deft.'s hand, and he being called and not appearing nor any security returned for him, at the mocion of the plf. judgment is granted him against Wm. Barbar, Gent., Sheriff of this County, for the aforesaid sum with costs unless the said deft. appears at the next and answers the plf.'s acion.

Judgment being passed this day to Dudley Diggs, Esq. against Wm. Barbar, Gent, Sheriff of this County, for £18 with costs for the nonappearance of John Marot at the suit of the said Diggs, on the mocion of the said Barbar an attachment is granted him against the Estate of the said Marot for the aforesaid sum with costs returnable to the next Court for judgment.

141. In the acion of debt between Joshua Curle, plf. and Wm. Sherman, deft. for £11:14 by a protested Bill of Exchange with charge of protest and

damage included, the deft. appeared and on his mocion hath oyer of the bill declared on till the next Court.

In the acion of debt between Susannah Leighton, Extx. of the Last Will & Testament of Edward Nott, Esq., dec'd., plf. and John Redwood and Robert Harrison, defts. for £39:1 lawfull money by bill under the deft.'s hands and seals (John Clayton in behalf of the plf. enters into this rule to pay the condemnacion of the Court in case the plf. be cost in this acion), the defts. by their Attorney appeared and on his mocion hath oyer of the bill declared on granted him till the next Court.

In the acion on the case between Stevens Thomson, plf. and John Redwood, deft., on the mocion of the plf. the said suit is continued till the next Court.

Lawrence Smith, Gent., this day produced a comission under the hand of Edmund Jenings, Esq., the President of Her Majesty's Councill of Virginia, to be Sheriff of this County and having together with Robert Read and Wm. Buckner entred into bond in the sum of £1,000 to our Sovereign Lady, the Queen for his due executing the said office and acknowledged the same in open Court and ordered to be recorded was accordingly sworn and admitted Sheriff of this County.

Wm. Sheldon and Francis Tyler having taken the oaths to her Majesty as also the oath of a Sub Sheriff, they accordingly were admitted Sub Sheriffs of this County.

Ordered that the Court be adjourned till the 24th day of June next.

Power of Attorney. Obedience Keene, now wife of John Keene of Blisland Parish in New Kent Co., to Henry Holdcraft, my true and lawfull Attorney at York Co. Court to relinquish all my rite of power of 62 acres of land lying in the said County to Mrs. Jeane Parke, wife and Attorney to the Hon. Danll. Parke, Esq. Dated the 22nd day of May 1708. Wit. George Keeling and Cornelius Joanes.

Bond. Lawrence Smith, Robert Read and William Buckner, to the Queen, in the sum of £1,000. Dated this 24th day of May 1708. Sureties for Lawrence Smith as Sheriff of York co.

175

INDEX

108, 113, 114, 115, 119,
121, 122, 125, 130, 133,
137, 138, 139, 141, 142,
143, 144, 146, 151, 153,
154, 155, 156, 158, 159,
160, 161, 163, 164, 167,
169, 170, 171, 172, 174,
175
Barefoot: Sarah, 166
Barker: Charles, 62, 70
Bartelot: Charles, 43, 56,
68
Bartlet: Charles, 24
Bartlett: Jno., 71
Bartlot: John, 87
Baskervile: Geo., 14, 125,
147, 148; George, 1, 7,
39, 40, 78, 82, 85, 87,
153, 164
Baskervill: George, 76
Baskerville: George, 56,
96, 97
Baskervyle: George, 129,
163
Bass: Thomas, 18, 38, 58
Bates: Hannah, 125, 126,
129; James, 74, 88, 143,
157, 168; Jno., 106, 148,
157; John, 24, 25, 37,
41, 43, 44, 47, 48, 57, 59,
68, 69, 78, 92, 94, 101,
103, 106, 111, 114, 116,
118, 125, 126, 129, 133,
134, 139, 142, 146, 148,
151, 155, 158, 168, 169
Batten: Sarah, 164;
William, 164

Bean: Martin, 15
Beddingfield: Robert, 62;
Robt., 80
Bedford: Jno., 157; John,
42, 55, 143, 169
Bee: Robert, 53; Robt., 14
Bell: Geo., 141
Benett: James J., 5
Bennet: James, 6, 40, 56
Bennett: Richard, 29
Bentwell: Wm., 50
Berkley: Edmund, 33
Bernald: Joseph, 63
Beverly: Robt., 75
Bills: Robt., 85
Binnam: Tho., 129
Bird: Willm., 71; Wm., 58
Blackburn: Wm., 40, 147
Blackhurst: James, 47
Blackley: Anne, 173
Blackstone: Elizth., 145
Blair: Arch, 150;
Archabald, 118;
Archibald, 19, 133;
Archobald, 118
Bland: Richard, 133;
Richd., 150
Blaxton: Eliz., 172, 174;
Elizabeth, 126, 129
Bloxom: Richd., 105, 113
Bloxton: Elizabeth, 110
Bloxum: Richard, 118;
Richd., 103, 113, 134,
161
Bolch: Henry, 134, 146
Boman: James, 147
Bonyman: Alexr., 143,

175
Bonymond: Alexander,
119; Alexr., 142
Booker: Geo., 150;
George, 74, 88, 99, 112,
131, 165
Bottick: Joseph, 3, 15, 17
Botwick: Joseph, 20
Bourn: Josias, 165
Bournham: Thomas, 165
Bowman: James, 8, 23,
26, 29, 43, 47, 49, 64, 70,
76, 81, 89, 99, 103, 117,
122, 143, 157, 160, 169,
171; Mary, 49
Boys: Samll., 85
Brack: George, 41;
Margt., 41
Bradford: James, 2
Bray: David, 142, 143,
156, 157, 168; James,
33, 48, 54, 64
Breton: Wm., 121, 122
Brice: John, 25; Jon., 44
Brisco: John, 78, 107
Broadbent: Isabella, 10,
75; Izabella, 33, 89;
Joshua, 10, 33, 34, 75,
89
Broadnex: Willm., 14
Brodbent: Isabella, 117,
152, 163
Brook: Jo., 147
Brookes: John, 125
Brooks: James, 129;
John, 61, 75; Jon., 36
Broster: Elizabeth, 6;

James, 40, 56; John, 6,
30, 40, 47, 51, 60, 66;
Lidia, 60; Lydia, 5, 30,
47, 51, 66; Lydye, 51
Brown: Damasinah, 138;
Damaz., 127; Damazina,
123; Damazinah, 30, 32,
46, 47, 57, 60, 63, 68, 74,
75, 77, 88, 99, 112, 123,
131, 132, 135, 140, 141,
155, 156, 167; Damh.,
144; John, 11; Richard,
32, 33, 47; William, 10;
Wm., 17, 51
Browne: Damazina, 26;
Damazinah, 26, 35, 60,
87; Richard, 26; Richd.,
26
Bryan: Mary, 77; Sarah,
139; Thos., 139
Buck: Joseph, 78, 107;
Thomas, 109, 147
Buckner: William, 8, 30,
44, 176; Willm., 28, 35,
61, 67; Wm., 8, 9, 10, 31,
35, 44, 55, 59, 72, 79, 84,
93, 96, 98, 106, 131, 132,
145, 148, 153, 156, 164,
172, 176
Bullock: Robert, 62;
Robt., 80
Burnam: Thomas, 48
Burnham: Thomas, 18,
26, 104, 111; Thos., 13
Burt: Richd., 135, 145
Burton: Daniell, 31;
Danll., 35, 85; George,

Junr., 108, 110, 131;
Jno. Senr., 108, 110,
131; John, 162; John
Junr., 141, 144; John
Senr., 111, 113, 133, 134
Douglas: Thomas, 18, 23
Dowzing: John, 29, 106,
130
Dowzings: John, 9
Dozwell: Jno. Junr., 105,
157, 169; Jno. Senr.,
172; John, 53, 171, 174;
John Junr., 15, 32, 33,
38, 50, 143, 150, 154,
162, 171; John Senr.,
23, 33, 37, 38, 43, 49, 55,
56, 61, 67, 84, 97, 115,
129, 163; Jon. Senr., 23
Dramond: W., 26
Draper: Josiah, 40, 56
Drewry: John, 6, 60;
Richard, 47
Driver: Thomas, 145, 149
Drowry: John, 108, 110
Druit: Jonathan, 69
Druitt: John Senr., 130
Drury: Jno., 42, 154;
John, 42, 76, 125, 151;
Richd., 106, 114, 133,
151; Wm., 160
Duke: Henry, 27, 44, 119,
121, 137; Jno., 72, 152;
John, 18, 26, 39, 64, 74,
87, 98, 109, 135, 154,
160, 161, 170, 171
Dukes: Henry, 51, 121;
John, 48, 119

Dun: Abel, 96; Abell, 80,
108
Dunbar: John, 131;
Joseph, 49, 106
Dunbarr: Joseph, 143,
157, 169
Duvall: Anne, 80, 89
Dwite: Diana, 41;
Dionitia, 56; Joseph, 41,
42, 56, 67
Dwyte: Joseph, 42, 46, 55,
62
Dyer: Henry, 137

Eaton: Ann, 111, 127;
Jno., 139, 147; John, 58,
74, 111, 122, 123, 127
Edmonds: Kath., 163;
Thos., 163
Edmons: Tho., 131, 133,
154; Thomas, 138, 150,
151; Thos., 134, 138
Ellenor: Thomas, 26
Elliot: Charles, 36, 52, 66
Ellis: Ann, 131; Anne A.,
146
Emerson: Henry, 28, 48,
64
Emett: John, 116
Emmery: John, 175
Erotten: Wm., 33
Everet: James, 82
Everett: Francis, 4
Everit: James, 70
Everitt's: Frances, 20

Faircloth: Jane, 5

Hubard: Ralph, 127
Hubbard: James, 40;
Martha, 32; Ralph, 70,
86, 90, 100; Thomas, 32
Hudson: Margaret, 5
Huggens: Nathll., 27, 41
Huggins: Nathaniell, 48;
Natt., 86
Huite: Willm., 17
Hunt: Elizabeth, 29; Jno.,
27; John, 28, 29, 31, 49,
112, 127, 141, 148, 156,
164, 167; John Junr.,
46; John Senr., 1;
Rebecca, 29
Hutton: Barbara, 50, 76,
85, 87, 97, 109;
Barbary, 65
Hyde: Robert, 11, 12, 30,
33, 52, 55, 90; Robt., 60,
87, 90, 145

Indians: Charles, 60;
Josias Bourn, 148; Peter
Larabie, 98, 109
Ingles: Mongo, 101, 134,
139, 152, 168; Mungo,
81
Israel: Daniel, 175
Ivory: Robert, 41

Jackling: Edward, 62
Jackman.: Jos. Jno., 5
Jackson: Chris., 140;
Christr., 62; Robert,
127; Robt., 109;
William, 165; Wm., 148

Jamart: Isaac, 10, 11, 12,
16, 17, 19, 30, 33, 37, 52,
54, 67, 84, 85, 90, 97,
100, 108, 113, 119
Jasper: Antho., 119;
Anthony, 101, 102
Jaxon: Christopher, 77;
Daniel, 4; Lawce, 1;
Robt., 70
Jaxson: Robert, 147
Jeff: John, 16
Jefferson: Thomas, 36, 54,
58
Jefferys: Mathew, 139,
155, 167
Jenings: Edmd., 89, 93,
107, 151; Edmund, 75,
95, 117, 133, 166, 176
Jesper: Antho., 69;
Anthony, 17, 38, 48, 58,
59, 64, 69, 72, 84; Anto.,
68; Antony, 12, 68
Joanes: Cornelius, 176
Jobey: Richd., 140
Jobie: Richard, 7
Johnson: Elizabeth, 78;
Richd., 103; Tillett[?],
59; Timo., 139;
Timothy, 27, 48, 49, 64,
65, 72, 159, 175; Wm.,
116, 150
Jones: Corn., 14;
Cornelius, 74, 88, 98,
109, 110; Elizabeth, 1,
78, 81; Frederick, 122,
155, 167; Fredk., 137;
Job, 32; Jonathan, 14;

Mackentosh: Daniell, 130;
  Danl., 125, 141
Mackintosh: Daniel, 114;
  Daniell, 95; Danl., 125
Mackormack: Michael,
  129
Maclanan: Nathll., 43
Maclanen: Nathll., 24
Maclaney: Nathaniel, 68
Malkham: Edwd., 76
Mallory: Elizabeth, 37
Man: Joseph, 127
Mann: Edward, 1
Manson: Peter, 49
Maratt: John, 48
March: Elizabeth, 87;
  Elizth., 71; Richd., 103,
  114; Willm., 71; Wm.,
  87
Marenburgh: Arthur, 3
Marot: Jean, 125; Jno.,
  139; John, 124, 126,
  130, 158, 159, 166, 169,
  170, 175
Marott: John, 120, 128
Marrat: John, 48
Marratt: John, 48
Marrot: John, 64, 90
Marshall: John, 20, 25,
  62, 78, 107; William, 92
Martin: Abra., 121, 137,
  153; J.W., 59; John, 23,
  26, 27, 29, 41, 45, 47, 50,
  61, 90, 98, 148, 163;
  Joseph, 147; Martin,
  164; Nicholas, 6;
  Nicolas, 5

Masterton: Catherine, 83;
  Katherin, 70;
  Katherine, 16, 17;
  Kathn., 95
Mathews: Baldwin, 114,
  133; Mary, 63
Matthews: Baldwin, 105
Maupin: Gabl., 159
Maynard: John, 17
McCormack: Michl., 125,
  141, 161
Merick: James, 34
Merrit: Obediah, 173
Merry: John, 173
Metam: Mary, 78;
  Samuell, 78
Metheion: Wm., 126
Metheven: William, 129
Mettam: Saml., 101
Mihill: Jno., 129; John, 7,
  30, 34, 74, 114, 125
Mihille: John, 53
Miller: Alex, 5;
  Alexander, 7, 24, 43, 57,
  68; Samll., 3, 20
Ming: James, 19, 39, 85
Mompain: Gabriel, 90,
  100
Moody: Eliz., 130, 162,
  172; Elizabeth, 34, 61,
  146; Elizth., 80; Hump.,
  111; Humphrey, 85, 89,
  115; Humphry, 44, 80,
  111, 130, 146, 162, 172;
  Humpr., 14; Judith,
  145, 149; Phi., 140, 154;
  Philip, 63, 86, 108, 111,

Sullivan: Danl., 107;
Danll., 78
Sutherland: John, 123

Taillor: John, 91;
Thomas, 91
Tandy: Henry, 146
Tatum: Nathll., 78, 80
Taverner: Giles, 149
Taylor: Daniel, 35, 74;
Daniell, 55, 67, 86;
Danll., 5, 32, 71, 88;
James, 174; Jane, 79,
107; John, 93, 125;
Leml., 105, 114, 133;
Lemuel, 95, 105, 107;
Mary, 86; Samuel, 79;
Thomas, 93; William,
164; Willm., 22; Wm.,
14, 125, 147
Thacker: Chichly Corbin,
133; William, 31;
Willm., 34, 60, 62, 63,
85; Wm., 46, 159
Thisfickle: Wm., 22
Thomas: Edward, 78, 156,
168; Edwd., 142; John,
23, 43
Thompson: Eliz., 95;
Stephens, 5, 11, 12, 37,
38, 39, 43, 114, 117, 133
Thomson: Eliz., 114;
Elizabeth, 70, 83, 104;
Stephen, 74; Stephens,
7, 27, 30, 41, 48, 53, 56,
67, 102, 103, 104, 106,
117, 119, 120, 133, 135,

136, 148; Stevens, 145,
151, 152, 154, 166, 167,
176
Thouston: J.W., 29
Thrift: Joseph, 71, 87
Thruston: John, 90, 100
Thurman: Charles, 118
Tignal: John, 173
Tiler: Henry, 27
Timson: John, 2; William,
7; Willm., 71; Wm., 10,
46, 51, 132
Tiplady: Math., 20;
Mathew, 70, 130, 146
Toagle: John, 94
Tomer: Jno., 110; John, 4,
23, 42, 43, 56, 60, 67, 70,
84, 108, 119
Tompson: Stephens, 14,
16, 64
Toomer: John, 96, 108
Trotter: Wm., 146
Tunley: William, 7, 25,
47, 50, 90; Willm., 5, 29,
34, 64, 65, 75, 86; Wm.,
1, 2, 8, 15, 28, 29, 31, 34,
51, 57, 61, 65, 68, 72, 79,
84, 85, 88, 90, 93, 100,
103, 107, 160
Tunly: Wm., 4, 111, 117,
133, 141, 143, 144, 151,
153, 156, 157, 158, 160,
165, 166, 169, 171
Turner: John, 6, 11, 161;
Richd., 139; Thomas, 8
Tyler: Francis, 176;
Henry, 6, 10, 28, 48, 71,

www.ingramcontent.com/pod-product-compliance
Lightning Source LLC
Chambersburg PA
CBHW071122280326

41935CB00010B/1087